HIGH-EXPECTATION CURRICULA

HIGH-EXPECTATION CURRICULA

Helping All Students Succeed with Powerful Learning

EDITED BY
Curt Dudley-Marling
Sarah Michaels

Foreword by Allan Luke

Teachers College, Columbia University
New York and London

Published by Teachers College Press, 1234 Amsterdam Avenue, New York, NY 10027

Library of Congress Cataloging-in-Publication Data

High-expectation curricula : helping all students engage in powerful learning / edited by Curt Dudley-Marling, Sarah Michaels ; foreword by Allan Luke.
   p. cm.
Includes index.
ISBN 978-0-8077-5366-8 (pbk. : alk. paper) — ISBN 978-0-8077-5367-5 (hardcover : alk. paper)
   1. Children with social disabilities—Education—United States. 2. Children of minorities—Education—United States. 3. Educational equalization—United States. 4. Education—Curricula—United States. I. Dudley-Marling, Curt. II. Michaels, Sarah.
LC4091.H54 2012
371.93--dc23   2012032028

ISBN 978-0-8077-5366-8 (paperback)
ISBN 978-0-8077-5367-5 (hardcover)

Printed on acid-free paper
Manufactured in the United States of America

19   18   17   16   15   14   13   12   8   7   6   5   4   3   2   1

Contents

Foreword

Curt Dudley-Marling and Sarah Michaels have brought together an outstanding collection of studies of classroom talk, pedagogy, and curriculum. It features work by some of this generation's leading researchers on classroom talk. But it also provides an accessible entry into a century-long conversation about what works in the education of those students whose socioeconomic and cultural backgrounds have led to educational marginalization, lower achievement, and, in some instances, systematically engineered failure.

High-Expectation Curricula arrived on my desk at an important time. We are undertaking an evaluation and overview of a major federal policy and leadership intervention for Aboriginal and Torres Strait Islander school reform in Australia (Luke et al., 2011). Allow me to explain how the analyses in this book have become a powerful tool for understanding the challenges and the limits of reform.

I concur with the views of leading Aboriginal school reformer Chris Sarra (2011) that low expectations are part of a toxic cocktail of cultural stereotypes, structural racism, ignorance of students' cultural and linguistic community resources, and systemic practices such as streaming and tracking in schools that deters the achievement of Indigenous youth. Several generations of teachers and teacher educators are quite familiar with the axiom of the "self-fulfilling prophecy" (Sharp & Green, 1975): that student performance and achievement tend to rise or fall according to teacher expectations—those overtly stated in face-to-face talk; those structurally embedded in grouping, streaming, and tracking; and those subtly conveyed in the way that teachers deliberately and subliminally shape the enacted curriculum.

There are several common strategies in policy and practice that attempt to address the problem of low expectations. On the one hand, the response from mainstream neoliberal policy is to reverse what is perceived and referred to as the "dumbing-down" of expectations by identifying and mandating standards, realizing these through the teaching of the "basics" and enforcing this through standardized testing, teacher and school ranking, scripted and packaged curricula, teacher merit pay, and other accountability measures. On the other hand, the response from critical teacher educators has been to directly attack the proliferation of deficit thinking. This is undertaken variously though the development and implementation of antiracist programs, consciousness-raising approaches in preservice teacher education, and a stronger foundational and curricular focus on minority and low-socioeconomic-status students' cultural and linguistic resources that are typically ignored or unrecognized in schools.

Yet in and of themselves, neither of these approaches is sufficient for setting the conditions for *all* children to learn. Recall that the prototypical study of how heightened teacher expectations can generate improved student achievement was titled "Pygmalion *in the Classroom*" [emphasis added] (Rosenthal & Jacobson, 1968/2003). In our current study of schooling for Aboriginal and Torres Strait Islander students, we have found that antiracist interventions can successfully counter stereotypes and generate increased dialogue among Australian teachers about race, difference, and their own cultural standpoints. This in turn can yield more focused engagement with Aboriginal community knowledge, practice, and resources. But even where teachers and principals deliberately discard discourses of deficit—even where they begin to speak a staffroom language of "high expectations"— the conversion of this intention into effective classroom pedagogy too often simply gets lost in translation. This is the hardest translation of all for any of us who work in schools: the turning of normative discourses of social justice into face-to-face material social relations. It requires the remaking of our own ideals and political commitments into knowledge practices that have material impacts on students' lives, aspirations, and pathways.

High-Expectation Curricula, then, is about the enactment of high-expectation curricula in everyday practice. The chapters here document specific classroom strategies across the curriculum that make a difference in the learning of those students from low-socioeconomic-status backgrounds and cultural and linguistic minority communities. The common thread running through these studies is the centrality of scaffolded classroom talk and interaction as the principal media and means for heightening expectations. In sociocultural terms, this entails continually upping the ante of intellectual demand, teaching in advance of development, and generating substantive engagement with curriculum knowledge and technical discourses as ways of reading and remaking the social and scientific lifeworlds around us. In this volume, you'll encounter examples from science and mathematics education, language and literacy education, and the teaching of the arts and social sciences, within both traditional print and emergent digital contexts.

We have come through a decade where governments have pulled a number of policy levers in the attempt to close the gap in achievement, only to find that the focus on standards, testing, basic skills, and accountability has generated mixed results at best and, at worst, "collateral damage" for the students and communities it aimed to help (Nichols & Berliner, 2007). This is ironic, when the compass of much of the school reform research points us to the central role of sustained conversation and meaningful classroom dialogue around substantive ideas and tasks as the key to sustained learning for the most at-risk students (Hattie, 2008; Ladwig, 2007; Newmann & Associates, 1996). If there is indeed a classroom universal, it is not the basics or standards but simply, as Cazden, John, and Hymes (1972) showed us 4 decades ago, the construction of knowledge through classroom discourse.

High-Expectation Curricula provides teachers, teacher educators, and researchers with an accessible map of the territory, with practical directions for making a difference through everyday classroom talk and curriculum practice. The art of effective teaching and curriculum requires precisely this—maps and models for professional reflection and action (Dewey, 1906). Far better this, as we emerge from a policy era where the step-by-step, unthinking script or curriculum package became the de facto curriculum for those students and communities hankering for substantive knowledge of the world.

—Allan Luke, Brisbane, Australia

REFERENCES

Cazden, C., John, V., & Hymes, D. (Eds). (1972). *Functions of language in the classroom.* New York: Teachers College Press.

Dewey, J. (1906). *The child and the curriculum.* Chicago: University of Chicago Press.

Hattie, J. (2008). *Visible learning.* London: Routledge.

Ladwig, J. (2007). Modelling pedagogy in Australian school reform. *Pedagogies: An International Journal, 2*(2), 57–76.

Luke, A., Cazden, C., Coopes, R., Klenowski, V., Ladwig, J., Lester, J., . . . Woods, A. (2011). *A formative evaluation of the Stronger Smarter Learning Communities Project* (2011 report). Canberra, Australia: Department of Education, Employment and Workplace Relations. Retrieved from http://eprints.qut.edu.au/47539/

Newmann, F. M., & Associates. (1996). *Authentic achievement.* San Francisco: Jossey-Bass.

Nichols, S., & Berliner, D. (2007). *Collateral damage.* Cambridge, MA: Harvard Education Press.

Rosenthal R., & Jacobson, L. (2003) *Pygmalion in the classroom.* New York: Holt, Rinehart and Winston. (Original work published 1968)

Sarra, C. (2011). *Strong and smart: Towards a pedagogy for emancipation.* New York: Routledge.

Sharp, R., & Green, A. (1975). *Education and social control.* London: Routledge and Kegan Paul.

Acknowledgments

We wish to thank all the scholars who generously contributed to this text. We invited these scholars to share their work because we have long admired their contributions to countering destructive deficit discourses by offering alternative, high-expectation curriula. We believe that their work has made a difference and it is our hope that bringing them all together in this volume will help shift the discourse from *fixing* students to *challenging* them—by building on the knowledge, language, and experience all students bring with them to school each day.

Introduction

Curt Dudley-Marling
Sarah Michaels

The publication of *A Nation at Risk* by the National Commission on Excellence in Education in 1983 unleashed a torrent of criticism of American education that has only intensified over the years. Although *A Nation at Risk* was intended as a general indictment of K–12 education, the focus of concern about American schooling has shifted over the last 25 years. Various critiques (e.g., Berliner & Biddle, 1995; McQuillan, 1998), data from the National Assessment of Educational Progress (NAEP), and findings from international comparisons of students in math, reading, and science indicate that many students are well served by current structures of schooling. Recent NAEP data, for example, indicate that approximately one-third of 4th- and 8th-grade American schoolchildren performed at proficient or advanced levels in reading and math (NAEP, 2011). U.S. schoolchildren attending schools that serve few or no children living in poverty also do well in international comparisons like PIRLS and PISA (Nichols & Berliner, 2007). White students also perform well in math, reading, and science compared to students in other countries (Nichols & Berliner, 2007). Black and Hispanic students, however, do not, on average, fare as well in comparison to either their White counterparts in this country or students in other countries. Additionally, poor students do less well in school compared to more affluent students (NAEP, 2011). It is worth emphasizing, however, that these statistics refer to averages for various groups. Certainly, many Black and Hispanic students do very well on PIRLS, PISA, the NAEP, and other assessments. Similarly, many White students, including some affluent White students, do poorly on these assessments.

The relatively poor academic performance of Black and Hispanic students and economically disadvantaged students points to what most observers agree is the real crisis in American education: an "achievement gap" that favors White students compared to their Black and Hispanic peers and relatively more affluent students compared to students living in poverty. Recent NAEP (2011) data, for example, indicate significant disparities in reading, math, and science between White (non-Hispanic) students and Black and Hispanic students. Poor students also score poorly on NAEP assessments compared to the rest of the student population, regardless of ethnicity or race. The No Child Left Behind Act (NCLB) of 2001 established the elimination of the achievement gap as a national priority. Progress toward this goal has been modest at best, however. For example, although the gap in reading achievement between White and Black students has narrowed slightly since 1992, the average reading scores for Black students in 8th grade still lag 27 points behind their White classmates, down from a 30-point gap in 1992. The difference between White and Hispanic students in 8th grade is now 25 points, down from 26 points in 1992. Similarly, the gap between poor 8th-grade students (defined as those eligible for free lunch) and students not living in poverty has decreased only slightly since 2003[1] (NAEP, 2011). These disparities persist despite enormous federal resources that have been provided to improve reading achievement in underperforming schools. At the current rate of improvement, it will take another 135 years for the average NAEP reading performance of Black students to pull even with that of White students. Using the same logic, it will take 375 years for the average reading performance of Hispanic students to catch up to that of their White classmates.

The situation in math and science is even more discouraging. Among 8th-graders, the discrepancy in NAEP math scores between White and Black students and White and Hispanic students actually increased between 1990 and 2005, while the achievement gap between Blacks and Whites and Whites and Hispanics in science is relatively unchanged. The achievement gap has also grown between 8th-grade low-income students and their peers in science, although there is a slight reduction in the disparity between poor students and their fellow students in NAEP math scores (NAEP, 2011).

High school completion rates, another widely used measure of school success, show similar trends. According to U.S. government statistics for the year 2000, 16- through 24-year-old Black students were nearly twice as likely to drop out of high school as White students (6.9% vs. 13.1%), and Hispanic students were approximately four times more likely to drop out of school compared to their White peers (6.9% vs. 27.8%). Low-income students dropped out of school at a rate four times greater than high-income students (2.5% vs. 10.4%) (Balfanz & Legters, 2006). Since the government data do not include students who leave school before 10th grade, the disparities between these groups may actually be even worse than these statistics suggest.

College attendance figures complete this dismal picture of educational achievement for many Black and Hispanic students living in poverty. College attendance rates within the Black and Hispanic population are substantially lower than college attendance rates for Whites. Thirty-seven percent of Whites, compared to 26% of Blacks and 15% of Hispanics in the United States attend 4-year colleges (Forster, 2006). Not surprisingly, poor students from all groups are much less likely to obtain a college degree than students from more affluent families. A U.S. Department of Education study that followed 8th-graders for 12 years indicated that only 29% of high-achieving students of low socioeconomic status (SES) obtained a bachelor's degree, compared to 74% of high-achievement students from high-SES families. Indeed, the lowest-scoring students from high-SES families were as likely to complete college as the most talented students from low-SES families (Fox, Connolly, & Snyder, 2005).

Overall, these data support the obvious conclusion: Schools fail a disproportionate number of Black and Hispanic students and students living in poverty (often these are the same students), exacerbating the effects of poverty and discrimination that already limit the life chances of these students. The important question is, why should this be the case? Through the lens of the deficit thinking that dominates many current versions of educational reform, the problem resides in the language and culture of students and their families (Dudley-Marling, 2007; Valencia, 1997). From this perspective, the background knowledge, language, and experiences of some students—specifically, poor students and students of color—is insufficient for success in school. An alternative perspective implicates the structures of schooling in high levels of academic failure among poor and minority students. From this point of view, disproportionate failure among poor and minority students is linked to inequities in the experience of schooling. Jonathon Kozol (e.g., 1992, 2005) and Jeannie Oakes (e.g., 1985/2005, 2008), for example, have written extensively about how inadequate resources and circumscribed, low-level curricula diminish the educational prospects of many poor, urban students.

We begin by critically examining the deficit perspective that has dominated thinking about high levels of educational failure among poor and minority students. We then consider an alternative, social constructivist perspective to explain disproportionate academic failure among Black, Hispanic, and poor students. Finally, we provide a brief overview of this volume illustrating the possibilities of challenging, high-expectation curricula with students who have experienced high levels of academic failure.

DEFICIT PERSPECTIVES

In the 1960s, President Lyndon Johnson declared a "War on Poverty," relying on programs like Head Start to help the poor lift themselves out of poverty. The pedagogical practices that emerged during this period were firmly rooted in a discourse of *cultural deprivation* (Ladson-Billings, 1999) that explains "disproportionate academic problems among low status students as largely being due to pathologies or deficits in their sociocultural background" (Valencia, 1986, p. 3). From the perspective of cultural deprivation theory, the lives of poor children, their families, and the communities in which they live are *deficient* in opportunities for acquiring "the knowledge and ability which are consistently held to be valuable in school" (Bereiter & Engelmann, 1966, p. 24). Bereiter and Englemann (1966), for example, claimed that poor, Black children lacked the ability to use language "to explain, to describe, to instruct, to inquire, to hypothesize, to analyze, to compare, to deduce, and to test . . . the uses [of language] that are necessary for academic success" (p. 31). A particularly pernicious version of cultural deprivation theory explains persistent social and economic inequities in terms of genetic differences (e.g., Herrnstein & Murray, 1994). From this social Darwinist perspective, programs designed to lift the poor out of poverty are doomed to failure since poor children and their families lack the necessary cultural, linguistic, and cognitive resources to succeed.

Over the years, cultural deprivation theory appeared to wane in the face of severe criticism that this stance pathologized the language and culture of parents and children from nondominant groups (e.g., Labov, 1972; Ladson-Billings, 1999). However, the cultural deprivation explanation for persistent educational failure among students living in poverty, particularly poor Black and Hispanic children, reemerged in the age of "at-risk" students—what Ayers (1993) has called "cultural deprivation recycled for the 1990s" (p. 29). Betty Hart and Todd Risley (1995), for example, beginning with their observation that the War on Poverty had failed to eliminate intergenerational poverty, undertook a study that examined the language and culture of the poor to explain the persistence of poverty in American society. Based on their longitudinal study of language practices in the homes of poor, working-class, and middle- and upper-class (professional) families, Hart and Risley concluded that poor children are deficient in language, particularly vocabulary development, and that the responsibility for this situation rests with parents who fail to provide their children the quality and quantity of language experiences common in homes of more affluent families. According to Hart and Risley (1995), "by age 3 the children in professional families would have heard more than 30 million words, the children in working-class families 20 million, and the children in welfare families 10 million" (p. 132). Compared to the welfare families, the professional parents not only exposed their children to more words, they displayed more words of all kinds to their children, "more multi-clause sentences, more past and future verb tenses, more declaratives, and more questions of all kinds" (pp. 123–124).

In this view, children's linguistic and academic deficits are traceable to deficiencies in parenting. Despite numerous critiques of the deficit stance that underpins Hart and Risley's research (see Valencia, 1997, for a collection of critiques of deficit thinking as well as Dudley-Marling, 2007; Dudley-Marling & Lucas, 2009), their research has been enormously influential. The report of the National Council on Teacher Quality (NCTQ) (Walsh, Glaser, & Wilcox, 2006), for example, describes the Hart and Risley study as "groundbreaking work . . . essential reading in any course dealing with early literacy skills" (p. 38). The Hart and Risley study has been cited in Congressional hearings and in numerous articles in the popular press, usually in support of early intervention programs targeting poor children and their families (e.g., Tough, 2006). A search of the *Social Science Citation Index* revealed close to 600 references to the Hart and Risley study in scholarly journals, nearly half of these in the past 5 years (Dudley-Marling & Lucas, 2009).

The popularity of Ruby Payne's emphasis on the "culture of poverty" (Payne, 2005) further illustrates the "return of the deficit" (Dudley-Marling, 2007). Payne has created an immensely popular professional development program based on her claims about a "culture of poverty" that underpins the generally low academic performance of poor children. Payne portrays the lives of the poor as deficient in the cognitive, linguistic, emotional, and spiritual resources needed to escape poverty and move into the middle class. Payne's claims about people living in poverty have been severely criticized for pathologizing the language and culture of people living in poverty (see Gorski, 2008, for a summary of critiques of Payne's work). Furthermore, Payne's claims about the language and culture of the poor, based largely on Oscar Lewis's discredited work on a "culture of poverty" (Foley, 1997), have been found to be without any research base (Bomer, Dworin, May, & Semingson, 2008). Yet, despite severe critiques of her work, Payne has become one of the most influential figures in U.S. education (Gorski, 2008). Her self-published book *A Framework for Understanding Poverty* (Payne, 2005), for example, has sold over a million copies, and Payne and her organization are in high demand for keynote speeches, seminars, and professional development workshops (Keller, 2006).

In the context of No Child Left Behind, deficit thinking has reemerged as a powerful explanation for disproportionately high levels of school failure among students living in poverty (Dudley-Marling, 2007; Kozol, 2005). Deficit-based family literacy initiatives,[2] for example, seek to *fix* families from nondominant groups by getting them to adopt literacy practices associated with middle-class families (Taylor, 1997). Similarly, full-day kindergarten and expanded preschool programs for children living in poverty are often premised on the need to provide poor children with stimulating learning environments (DeCicca, 2007; Jacobson, 2006) based on the implicit—and sometimes explicit—assumption that the home environments of poor children are not stimulating (i.e., they are *deficient*) and external intervention is needed to prepare these children for school.

Deficit thinking holds poor children and their families responsible for educational and vocational failures, a classic form of blaming the victim (Valencia, 1997). Valencia concludes, however, that deficit thinking is "unduly simplistic, lacks empirical verification, is more ideological than scientific, grounded in classism and racism, and offers counterproductive educational prescriptions for school success" (p. 2). No child profits from a perspective that portrays her, her family, or her community as deprived or deficient, but it isn't a deficit stance per se that's problematic as much as what comes from this stance. The position here is that a deficit gaze that pathologizes individuals, families, and communities is often instantiated in pedagogical practices and dispositions that are primarily responsible for disproportionate levels of failure among poor and minority populations.

SOCIAL CONSTRUCTIVIST PERSPECTIVES

"What is it about school," James Gee (2004) asks, "that manages to transform children who are good at learning . . . regardless of their economic and cultural differences, into children who are not good at learning, if they are poor or members of certain minority groups?" (p. 10). We would argue that the problem lies not in children's heads, their families, their language, or their culture, but with uninspired, tedious, basic-skills curricula that dominate instruction for low-achieving children. Valencia (1997) concludes:

> The historical emphasis upon capacity for learning has been to perceive school learning as primarily dependent upon the presumed ability of the student, rather than upon the quality of the learning environment. However, there appears to be a growing recognition that school failure and student achievement are socially determined. (p. 8)

In her seminal study of curricular practices in schools populated by students from working-class, middle-class, and affluent, professional-class families, Jean Anyon (1980) found that children from different socioeconomic groups experienced qualitatively different forms of schooling that affected their educational and vocational aspirations. The curricular experiences of students attending working-class schools, for example, emphasized mechanical, rote behavior "involving very little decision making or choice. . . . Teachers rarely explain why the work is being assigned, how it might connect to other assignments, or what the idea is that lies behind the procedure or gives it coherence and perhaps meaning or significance" (Anyon, 1980, p. 73). This "pedagogy of poverty" (Haberman, 1991) contrasts sharply with the practices Anyon found in schools serving the affluent, professional class, where students experienced a curriculum in which schoolwork was carried out creatively and independently and they were "continually asked to express and apply ideas and concepts." Schoolwork in such schools emphasized "individual thought and expressiveness, expansion and illustration of ideas, and choice of appropriate method and material" (p. 79).

More recent research on curricular tracking largely mirrors the results of Anyon's research. Watanabe (2008), for example, reported that, compared to students in lower academic tracks, students in "academically gifted tracks" spent less time on explicit test preparation, which meant they had more time to engage in other curricula that teachers deemed important; received more opportunities to practice a wider range of reading and writing skills and, therefore, overall did more reading and writing; engaged in more challenging instruction and assignments; and received more written and immediate feedback on essay assignments. Additionally, students in academically gifted classes had more opportunities to write in different genres for authentic audiences beyond the five-paragraph essay and had more opportunities to complete assignments out of class, freeing up time in class for more challenging and interesting work. Watanabe's findings are consistent with a substantial body of research documenting the predominance of qualitatively inferior curricula in "lower" academic tracks (e.g., Allington, 2000; McDermott, 1976; Oakes, 1985/2005; Smith, 1998), places overpopulated by poor students and students of color.

Snow, Burns, and Griffin (1998) observed that "children living in high-poverty areas tend to fall further behind, regardless of their initial . . . skill level" (p. 98). The controlling, directive *pedagogy of poverty* that dominates in lower academic tracks and underperforming schools creates high levels of academic failure by severely constraining students' opportunities to engage with the challenging, thoughtful curricula common in higher performing schools and classrooms (Dudley-Marling & Paugh, 2005; Haberman, 1991). Ultimately, the corrosive effects of "low-expectation" curricula have undermined substantial efforts to reform education for children attending underperforming, underresourced schools (Haberman, 1991).

Ray Rist (1970) observed that there is a greater tragedy than being labeled a poor learner: being treated like a poor learner. Put differently, the problem isn't so much the deficit gaze that pathologizes some children and their families as much as what results from this stance. The typical treatment of students in lower academic tracks or ability groups—because of what they are taught and what they are not taught (Harklau, 1994)—virtually ensures that these students will struggle academically regardless of their learning needs when they enter school. What struggling learners need most is to be afforded the same opportunities and quality of instruction as that afforded to more academically able students (Allington, 1983, 2000; Oakes, 1985/2005; Rhodes & Dudley-Marling, 1996; Rist, 1970). However, more evidence is needed on the effects of *high-expectation curricula* on students for whom school has been a struggle.

OVERVIEW OF THIS BOOK

We began this book inspired by the challenge posed by McDermott, Goldman, and Varenne (2006) that "to counteract the cultural inclination to focus on what is wrong with individual children, we must seek data showing children more skilled than schools have categories or time to notice, describe, diagnose, record, and remediate" (p. 15). We have taken up the challenge by assembling a collection of chapters from educators and educational researchers who have endeavored to bring high-expectation curricula to settings typically characterized by instruction in low-level skills and tedious pedagogy. In Part I the chapters present a broad framework for creating high-expectation curricula. Part II provides a number of powerful illustrations of high-expectation literacy curricula in urban classrooms. Part III presents illustrative examples of rich math and science curricula. In Part IV contributors provide examples of high-expectation curricula for second language learners, students with disabilities, and struggling readers.

Taken together, the chapters in this volume present powerful illustrations of how high-expectation curricula can engage students and promote high levels of learning. These chapters offer an indictment of the deficit-driven (low-level, basic skills) curricula that dominate in underachieving schools and classrooms. As the chapters of this book make very clear, given the right sort of opportunities, all children will confirm our belief that they are competent thinkers, speakers, readers, and writers. Put another way, under the right circumstances, ordinary people (students and teachers alike) are capable of extraordinary things. And we should be suspicious of any evidence to the contrary.

NOTES

1. The first-year reading data are available for students from low-income families.
2. To be fair, not all family literacy initiatives are deficit based.

REFERENCES

Allington, R. L. (1983). The reading instruction provided readers of differing abilities. *The Elementary School Journal, 83*(5), 548–559.

Allington, R. L. (2000). *What really matters for struggling readers: Designing research-based programs*. New York: Longman.

Anyon, J. (1980). Social class and the hidden curriculum of work. *Journal of Education, 162*(1), 67–92.

Ayers, W. (1993). *To teach: The journey of a teacher*. New York: Teachers College Press.

Balfanz, R., & Legters, N. (2006). The graduation rate crisis we know and what can be done about it. *Education Week*. Retrieved from http://web.jhu.edu/CSOS/graduation-gap/edweek/Crisis_Commentary.pdf

Bereiter, C., & Engelmann, S. (1966). *Teaching disadvantaged children in the preschool*. Englewood Cliffs, NJ: Prentice-Hall.

Berliner, D. C., & Biddle, B. J. (1995). *The manufactured crisis: Myths, fraud, and the attack on America's public schools*. Reading, MA: Addison-Wesley.

Bomer, R., Dworin, J., May, L., & Semingson, P. (2008). Miseducating teachers about the poor: A critical analysis of Ruby Payne's claims about poverty. *Teachers College Record, 110*, 2497–2531.

DeCicca, P. (2007, February). Does full-day kindergarten matter? Evidence from the first two years of schooling. *Economics of Education Review, 26*(1), 67–82.

Dudley-Marling, C. (2007). Return of the deficit. *Journal of Educational Controversy, 2*(1). Retrieved from http://www.wce.wwu.edu/Resources/CEP/eJournal/v002n001/Index.shtml

Dudley-Marling, C., & Lucas, K. (2009). Pathologizing the language and culture of poor children.*Language Arts, 86*, 362–370.

Dudley-Marling, C., & Paugh, P. (2005). The rich get richer, the poor get Direct Instruction. In B. Altwerger (Ed.), *Reading for profit* (pp. 156–171). Portsmouth, NH: Heinemann.

Foley, D. E. (1997). Deficit thinking models based on culture: The anthropological protest. In R. R. Valencia (Ed.), *The evolution of deficit thinking* (pp. 113–131). London: Falmer Press.

Forster, G. (2006, March 10). The embarrassing good news on college. *Chronicle of Higher Education*. Retrieved from http://chronicle.com/free/v52/i27/27b05001.htm

Fox, M. A., Connolly, B. A., & Snyder, T. D. (2005). *Youth indicators 2005: Trends in the well-being of American youth*. Washington, DC: National Center for Education Statistics. Retrieved from http://nces.ed.gov/pubsearch/pubsinfo.asp?pubid=2005050

Gee, J. P. (2004). *Situated language and learning: A critique of traditional schooling.* New York: Routledge.

Gorski, P. (2008). Peddling poverty for profit: A synthesis of criticisms of Ruby Payne's framework. *Equity and Excellence in Education, 41*(1), 130–148.

Haberman, M. (1991). The pedagogy of poverty versus good teaching. *Phi Delta Kappan, 73,* 290–294.

Harklau, L. (1994). Tracking and linguistic minority students: Consequences of ability grouping for second language learners. *Linguistics and Education, 6,* 217–244.

Hart, B., & Risley, T. R. (1995). *Meaningful differences in the everyday experiences of young American children.* Baltimore, MD: Paul H. Brookes.

Herrnstein, R. J., & Murray, C. (1994). *The bell curve: Intelligence and class structure in American life.* New York: Free Press.

Jacobson, L. (2006, February 22). Kindergarten comparison. *Education Week, 25*(24), 16.

Keller, B. (2006). Payne's pursuits. *Education Week, 25*(34), 30–32.

Kozol, J. (1992). *Savage inequalities: Children in America's schools.* New York: Harper-Collins.

Kozol, J. (2005). *The shame of the nation: The restoration of apartheid schooling in America.* New York: Crown.

Labov, W. (1972). *The language of the inner city.* Philadelphia, PA: University of Pennsylvania Press.

Ladson-Billings, G. (1999). Preparing teachers for diverse student populations: A critical race theory perspective. In A. Iran-Nejad & P. D. Pearson (Eds.), *Review of research in education* (vol. 24, pp. 211–247). Washington, DC: American Educational Research Association.

McDermott, R. (1976). *Kids make sense: An ethnographic account of the interactional management of success and failure in one first-grade classroom* (Unpublished doctoral dissertation). Stanford University, Stanford, CA.

McDermott, R., Goldman, S., & Varenne, H. (2006). The cultural work of learning disabilities, *Educational Researcher, 35*(6), 12–17.

McQuillan, J. (1998). *The literacy crisis: False claims and real solutions.* Portsmouth, NH: Heinemann.

National Assessment of Educational Progress (NAEP). (2011). *The nation's report card.* Washington, DC: National Center for Educational Statistics. retrieved from http://nces.ed.gov/nationsreportcard

National Commission on Excellence in Education. (1983). *A nation at risk: the imperative for educational reform.* Washington, DC: Author.

Nichols, S. L., & Berliner, D. C. (2007). *Collateral damage: How high-stakes testing corrupts America's schools.* Cambridge, MA: Harvard Educational Publishing Group.

Oakes, J. (2005). *Keeping track: How schools structure inequality* (2nd ed.). New Haven, CT: Yale University Press. (Original work published 1985)

Oakes, J. (2008). Keeping track: Structuring equality and inequality in an era of accountability. *Teachers College Record, 110,* 700–712.

Payne, R. K. (2005). *A framework for understanding poverty (4th ed.)*. Highlands, TX: Aha! Process.

Rhodes, L. K., & Dudley-Marling, C. (1996). *Readers and writers with a difference* (2nd ed.). Portsmouth, NH: Heinemann.

Rist, R. C. (1970). Student social class and teacher expectations: The self-fulfilling prophecy in ghetto education. *Harvard Educational Review, 40*, 72–73.

Smith, F. (1998). *The book of learning and forgetting*. New York: Teachers College Press.

Snow, C. E., Burns, M. S., & Griffin, P. (1998). *Preventing reading difficulties in young children*. Washington, DC: National Research Council.

Taylor, D. (1997). *Many families, many literacies: An international declaration of principles*. Portsmouth, NH: Heinemann.

Tough, P. (2006, November 26). What it takes to make a student. *New York Times Magazine*, p. 44.

Valencia, R. R. (1986). *Chicano school failure and success: Research and policy agendas for the 1990s*. New York: Falmer.

Valencia, R. R. (1997*). The evolution of deficit thinking: Educational thought and practice*. New York: RoutledgeFalmer.

Walsh, K., Glaser, D., & Wilcox, D. D. (2006). *What education schools aren't teaching about reading and what elementary teachers aren't learning*. Washington, DC: National Council on Teacher Quality.

Watanabe, M. (2008). Tracking in the era of high stakes state accountability reform: Case studies of classroom instruction in North Carolina. *Teachers College Record, 110* (3), 489–534. Retrieved from http://222.tccrecord.org (ID Number: 14612).

SCHOOLWIDE REFORM

Part I takes a broad perspective on what it means to develop educational programs (schools, courses of study, curricula, or classroom instructional practices) that do not assume a deficit perspective. In Chapter 1, Hugh Mehan discusses detracking as a means of giving all students access to the kind of rich, engaging curricula common in affluent, high-achieving schools. In Chapter 2, Eric DeMeulenaere offers an overview of a curriculum based on trust that he argues is fundamental to students' success with challenging curricula.

These chapters examine high-expectation programs and practices through different lenses and at different levels (Chapter 1 emphasizes schoolwide restructuring, while Chapter 2 explores the design features of a single course of study). Taken together, they offer a principled and well-theorized approach to rethinking what's possible with previously underperforming students and provide evidence of demonstrated success.

Detracking

Re-Forming Schools to Provide Students with Equitable Access to College and Career

Hugh Mehan

The conventional way in which high schools are organized holds instructional time constant and varies the curriculum offered to students. These organizational arrangements often produce *tracking*, in which some students are placed in high-track classes in which they receive abstract and symbolic instruction in courses that are intended to propel them toward college. Other students are placed in fewer and less demanding low-track or vocational education (voc-ed) courses, in which students receive instruction that aims them toward the world of work after high school.

In this chapter, I discuss a strategy to unite the high-expectation academic demands of college prep courses with the hands-on experiences of voc-ed courses. After examining the conventional ways of grouping students and providing a critique of tracking practices, I then explore detracking—an alternative to tracking—and use the Preuss School, located on the UC San Diego campus, as an example of a successful application of this strategy. The Preuss School demonstrates that detracking goes beyond technical or structural changes, involving a cultural change in teachers' beliefs, attitudes, and values; changes in the curriculum; and the organization of instruction. This shift has the potential to provide all students with access to a full range of postsecondary options, including access to college.

CONVENTIONAL WAYS OF GROUPING STUDENTS

Historically, educators in the United States have responded to differences among individuals and groups by separating students and exposing them to different curricula through the practice of tracking. Often an informal arrangement in elementary school, tracking becomes institutionalized in middle schools and high schools. Since the 1920s, most high schools have offered a tracked curriculum—sequences of academic classes that range from slow-paced remedial courses to rigorous academic ones. Tracking starts as early as elementary school. Students who are perceived to have similar skills are placed in small working groups, often called ability groups, for the purposes of instruction. Students who have less measured ability are placed in low-ability groups; students with greater amounts of measured ability are placed into high-ability groups. The curriculum for low-ability groups is reduced in scope, content, and pace relative to high-ability groups. For instance, students placed in academic tracks, with the expectation that they will attend college, typically receive instruction that is text based and demands written and verbal displays of knowledge. Other students are placed in less demanding low-track or voc-ed courses, in which students receive instruction that aims them toward the world of work after high school. Instruction and assessments in college prep classes are often verbal, while instruction in voc-ed courses is often hands-on, allowing students to demonstrate the knowledge they acquired in many modalities, including exhibitions.

Tracking was justified at the height of industrialization because it supported an emerging belief in the United States and Great Britain that a crucial function of schools was to prepare students for jobs. Industrial leaders who adopted a factory model of production divided labor into jobs that required different kinds of skills. As a result, workers with different kinds of knowledge were needed to fill those different kinds of jobs. The school was to serve as a rational sorting device as well as providing training, matching students' talents to the demands of the workplace (Turner, 1960). Thus rigorous academic classes would prepare students heading for jobs that required college degrees, whereas voc-ed programs would prepare students for less skilled jobs or for technical training after high school.

Tracking students for different working lives was thought to be fair because students were thought to possess different intellectual abilities, motivations, and aspirations that could be matched to jobs that require different skills and talents. Thus a tracked curriculum with its ability-grouped classes was viewed as both functional and democratic. Tracking was functional because it matched students to the appropriate slots in the workplace. Tracking was democratic because schools presumably sorted students based on their talent, effort, and hard work, thereby providing students with the education that best met their abilities (Turner, 1960).

CRITIQUES OF TRACKING

Research and public commentary have shown that the schools' practice of tracking does not fulfill either of its promises. It neither provides students with equal educational opportunities nor serves the needs of employers for a well-educated, albeit compliant, workforce. More seriously, the distribution of students to high-, middle-, and low-ability groups or academic and voc-ed tracks seems to be related to ethnicity and socioeconomic status. Children from low-income or one-parent households, or from families with an unemployed worker, or from linguistic and ethnic minority groups are more likely to be assigned to low-ability groups or tracks. Furthermore, ethnic and linguistic minority students are consistently underrepresented in programs for the "gifted and talented" (Oakes, 2005).

Similarly, schools serving predominantly poor and minority students offer fewer advanced and more remedial courses in academic subjects than schools serving more affluent and majority students. Even in comprehensive high schools that bring students from different backgrounds together under one roof, researchers have found a strong relationship between socioeconomic background, ethnicity, and educational opportunity. The relationships are both simple and direct. The greater the percentage of minorities, the larger the low-track program; the poorer the students, the less rigorous the college prep program. Moreover, as college aspirations increase, the college track itself is increasingly subdivided into multiple tracks—with the most advantaged students typically found in tracks consisting of Advanced Placement classes and honors sections of college preparatory classes (Oakes, 2005).

Researchers also report *differential treatment* of students once they have been placed in different tracks (Cicourel & Mehan, 1983; Varenne & McDermott, 1998). In elementary school classrooms, different ability groups are taught by the same teacher, but students in different groups do not receive the same instruction. Low-ability groups are taught less frequently and are subjected to more control by the teacher. High-ability groups progress farther in the curriculum over the course of a school year, and this advantage accumulates over time. As a result, students with a sustained membership in high-ability groups are likely to have covered considerably more material by the end of elementary school. Differential treatment of students in different tracks continues in secondary schools: Low-track classes consistently offer less exposure to more demanding topics, whereas high-track classes typically include more complex material. Lower-track students take fewer math and science courses, and these courses are usually less demanding. In comparison, students in the academic track take three to five times as many advanced courses in math and science and more honors and advanced courses generally (Haycock, 2006).

In addition to differential access to curriculum and instruction, students in different tracks get different kinds of teachers. Many schools and school districts allow teachers to choose their teaching assignments based on seniority, whereas other schools and districts rotate the teaching of low- and high-ability classes among teachers. In either case, it is not uncommon for class assignments to be used as a reward for teachers judged to be more powerful or successful and as a sanction against teachers judged to be weaker or undeserving. Many teachers covet high-track classes because they find that students in these classes more willing to participate in academic work and that they pose fewer disciplinary problems. Whether schools assign teachers or teachers choose their assignments, students in low-income and minority neighborhoods are more likely to get less experienced teachers than students in more affluent neighborhoods.

Teachers of low-track classes at the secondary level in math and science are consistently less experienced, are less likely to be certified in math or science, hold fewer degrees in these subjects, have less training in the use of computers, and are less likely to think of themselves as master teachers (Haycock, 2006). A vicious cycle for low tracks is the result. Repeated assignment to the bottom of the school's status hierarchy may demoralize teachers, reducing their competency, which in turn may give students who have the greatest need for the best teachers the least qualified—and least motivated—teachers.

Perhaps the most severe criticism of tracking is that it takes on a caste-like character. Once students are placed into low-ability groups, they are seldom promoted to high-ability groups. Students placed in low-ability groups in elementary school are more likely to be placed in general and vocational tracks in high school, whereas students placed in high-ability groups in elementary school are more likely to be placed in college prep tracks in high school. Placement in vocational and nonacademic classes can trap ethnic and linguistic minority students despite their achievements in school. Tracking has distorted Horace Mann's vision for the "common school," an institution that was intended to educate students from all sectors of society—rich and poor students, children of new immigrants and children of established families.

Tracking practices have also distorted John Dewey's (1900, 1902/1956) progressive approach to pedagogy, which is often invoked to support working with and learning from workplace tools. It is true that Dewey suggested the use of tools like the printing press and the weaving loom and recommended that students till the earth as gardeners. These vocational-related experiences were not intended for low-achieving students; they were carefully designed as springboards for all children to jump into central intellectual quests of literacy and problem solving. Dewey insisted that *all* students be instructed with techniques that enable students to manipulate their environment, make real-world connections, and communicate the results of their investigations in multiple modalities.

Unfortunately, Dewey's universalist ideas were never institutionalized. Instead, educational reformers—ironically, often invoking Dewey—relegated hands-on, real-world education as a terminal experience for students who were not believed to have the capacity for symbolic thought. Reformers reserved text- and literacy-based education for students aimed for college. In the late 19th century, vocational schools with agricultural and mechanical programs provided a practical reason for Irish immigrant children and rural students to attend public school (Rosenstock & Steinberg, 1995). The Smith-Hughes Act of 1917, which began the federal support for vocational education, cemented the distinction between liberal arts and vocational education. Voc ed became a separate, second-class system under separate control. Dewey saw the segregated vocational education favored by business as a "form of class education which would make the schools a more efficient agency for the reproduction of an undemocratic society" (quoted in Rosenstock & Steinberg, 1995, p. 44). In short, tracking practices have deemed vocational education to be more appropriate for low-achieving students—students not expected to be successful in an academic track or proceed to college.

In a word, then, tracking is undemocratic and dysfunctional. Although originally justified because schools presumably sorted students on the basis of achievement, not ascription, tracking has carried a racial, ethnic, and social-class bias from its inception. It has also not accomplished its job of matching the talents of students with the demands of the workplace. Starting with the critique of American schools contained in *A Nation at Risk* (National Commission on Education and the Economy [NCEE], 1983), a steady stream of employers, policy makers, national opinion leaders, and educators have expressed dissatisfaction with students' knowledge, skills, and attitudes:

> The primary mission of our public educational system is to give every student the opportunity to live a meaningful and productive life, which includes earning a wage sufficient to support a small family. All students need to develop the knowledge and skills that will give them real options after high school. No student's choices should be limited by a system than can sometimes appear to have different goals for different groups. Educating some students to a lesser standard than others narrows their options to jobs that in today's economy, no longer pay well enough to support a family of four. (ACT, 2006, p. 2)

This commission that produced *A Nation at Risk* asserts that changes in the nature of work— from manufacturing and industrial to service and skilled technology—contribute to dissatisfaction with the present tracking system. Skilled technology jobs require workers to think their way through unfamiliar problems, use sophisticated computers and other technologies, and interpret, compare, and analyze all manner of printed information, including graphs, charts, and tables (ACT, 2006). The demands of these jobs require educators to teach problem-solving skills and the ability to interpret complex information. Literacy and math are skills necessary to acquire the knowledge to be a problem solver in any field. Hence, whether students are planning on entering the workforce or college immediately after high school, they need to be educated to a comparable level of readiness in reading and mathematics. Anything less will not provide graduates the foundation needed to learn additional skills as their jobs change or as they change jobs (Murnane & Levy, 2004).

DETRACKING AS AN ALTERNATIVE

Recognizing that tracked schools are both inequitable and ineffective, educators have been exploring alternatives to tracking practices since the 1980s. This chapter focuses on an effort of the Preuss School at the University of California, San Diego (UCSD), to redefine and restructure the academic curriculum, pedagogy, and course structures of high schools. The educators at the Preuss School have established high instructional standards and present rigorous curricula to all students, while simultaneously varying the supports available to enable all students to meet high academic standards. Often called detracking (Alvarez & Mehan, 2006; Burris, Wiley, Welner, & Murphy, 2008; Hallinan, 2004; Oakes, Wells, Jones, & Datnow, 1997; Rubin, 2006), this strategy offers a rigorous academic curriculum to all students, accompanied by an extensive system of academic and social supports, or scaffolds.

Detracking at the Preuss School

The Preuss School is a single-track, college preparatory public charter school on the UCSD campus serving students from low-income backgrounds whose parents or guardians have not graduated from a 4-year college or university. Developed in the aftermath of the elimination of affirmative action admissions policies in the University of California (Rosen & Mehan, 2003), the school prepares students from underrepresented minority backgrounds to enroll in competitive colleges and universities and enter careers well prepared.

Through a lottery, the school selects low-income 6th-grade students with high potential but underdeveloped skills. "Low income" is defined as a family income that is no more than twice the federal level required to be eligible for a free and reduced-priced lunch. In the 2010–2011 school year, 17.2% of the students enrolled in the school were Asian, 65.6% were Hispanic, 3.7% were White, and 9.6% were African American; 100% were Title 1 students and 5.8% were English Learners (htpp://Preuss.ucsd.edu).

The evidence indicates that the Preuss School has achieved a measure of success. The school has accumulated an impressive list of accolades, most notably inclusion in the "Top Transformative High School in 2011" (*Newsweek*, June 19, 2011) and the 2010 "National Blue Ribbon School"award, given to 25 schools in California for superior academic performance in serving economically disadvantaged students. Other awards the school has garnered are the "Best High School in California Serving Low Income Youth" (*Business Week*, January 2009), the "8th Best High School in the United States" (*U.S. News & World Report*, December 4, 2008), and a "U.S. Top Twenty High Schools" award for the 4th straight year—the only California school to be so honored (*Newsweek*, June 2010).

An average of 84% of the students in the first graduating classes (2004–2009) have enrolled in 4-year colleges (Bohren & McClure, 2011). Preuss also achieved one of the highest Academic Performance Index (API) scores among San Diego County high schools in 2009, 2010, and 2011. This achievement is significant because in each year Preuss outpaced high schools with a much lower percentage of Title 1 (i.e., low-income) students.

Enough students applied to the school in 1999 and 2000 that those students who applied but were not accepted formed a comparison group for the graduating classes of 2005 and 2006. Using admittedly incomplete information available from the National Student Clearinghouse, Strick (2009) reports that a minimum of 74.2% and a maximum of 93.4% of students in the Preuss graduating class of 2005 enrolled in 4-year colleges, while a minimum of 40% and a maximum of 55% of students in the comparison group enrolled in 4-year colleges after graduating from high school. A minimum of 75% and a maximum of 87.5% of Preuss students graduating in 2006 enrolled in 4-year colleges, while a minimum of 34.4% and a maximum of 59.4% in the comparison group enrolled in 4-year colleges after graduating from high school. This record compares favorably to the national average of 40% college enrollment among low-income students (Advisory Council, 2010).

A College-Going School Culture

The educators at the Preuss School seek to establish a "college-going school culture" (Oakes, 2003). A college-going culture develops when "teachers, administrators, and students expect students to have all the experiences they need for high achievement and college preparation. . . . Students believe that college is for *them* and is not reserved for the exceptional few who triumph over adversity to rise above all others" (Oakes, 2003, p. 2, emphasis added). Elements of a college-going culture include a shared purpose shown through rituals, traditions, values, symbols, artifacts, and relationships.

Some of the symbols that focus Preuss students on college are the school's dress code, the location of the school, and the daily presence of UCSD students as tutors. Preuss students wear uniforms to school, which are explicitly intended to symbolize their participation in a college preparatory school. The presence of the school on the university's campus is intended to orient students to many dimensions of college life. Preuss students take courses at the university and serve as interns in academic departments on campus, which gives them access to professors and students, thereby increasing their knowledge of the college-going experience and connecting them to valuable social networks.

UCSD students serve as tutors at the school. In addition to assisting Preuss students with their academic work—which is their explicit purpose—they also serve as role models for the students they tutor. Preuss graduates who return to campus for alumni days also provide insight into the college-going experience. The middle school was built next to the high school to help foster a college-going culture. This introduces students to the idea of preparing for college early and enables younger students to learn some aspects of the "hidden curriculum" from older students. The ecology of Preuss classrooms reinforces college going. Tutoring spaces are built into each classroom. "How to Get to College" posters, which include the University of California entrance requirements, adorn classroom walls—information intended to reinforce the expectation that Preuss students are college-bound.

The application process itself introduces students to Preuss's college-going culture. The application form resembles a college application, which is intended to invite students to think about college from the start. Students are asked to describe their reasons for wanting to attend the school, discuss their commitment to the rigorous courses they will encounter, and express their interest in attending college. While enrolled at Preuss, students explore different types of colleges and learn about requirements, costs, and potential sources of support. They tour college campuses and interact with college tutors on a daily basis. The college application process, including writing college essays, is a regular part of the students' daily life. All of these activities are intended to bolster the expectation that Preuss students will attend college.

Rigorous Academic Curriculum

Students enrolled in higher-level courses perform better overall than those in lower-level courses. Haycock (1997) reports that students who take fewer than four vocational education credits in high school score higher on the National Assessment of Educational Progress (NAEP) reading tests, whereas students who take eight or more vocational credits score much lower on those same tests. White, Black, and Latino students who take pre-calculus or calculus courses score on average 40 points higher on NAEP mathematics tests than students who take only pre-algebra or general math courses (Haycock, 1997). Students who take 4 years of English and 3 or more years of math and science score, on average, 151 points above those who do not (College Board, 2010). These results illuminate the traditional divide between college prep and voc-ed courses, with college prep classes making more academic demands than voc-ed courses and voc-ed courses emphasizing hands-on learning. The detracking strategy at Preuss exposes students to the hands-on, career-training, real-world work experience *and* an academic curriculum.

The Preuss School unites the best features of college prep courses with the best features of vocational education. Preuss classes emphasize project-based learning and a portfolio of assessments. The school's curriculum fulfills or exceeds the University of California (UC) and California State University (CSU) entry requirements. The college prep curriculum symbolizes the high expectations that the school has for each student and emphasizes the college-going culture of learning being instantiated at the school.

Designed to prepare students for the types of evaluations they will encounter in college and the workplace, the evaluation practices adopted by the Preuss School can also be traced through the Coalition of Essential Schools (Sizer, 1992) to Dewey (1900, 1902/1956). In addition to taking the required regimen of state-mandated standardized tests and UC/CSU-mandated college entrance exams, Preuss students are expected to exhibit their work annually in the form of a written and oral presentation to a panel of judges—ideally composed of a Preuss faculty member, a UCSD faculty member, and a parent or community member. A portfolio of measures—test scores, coursework, grades, exhibitions—is intended to give a more comprehensive view of students' academic progress than high-stakes tests alone afford (Baker et al., 2010).

My informal assessment of this practice, gathered as a judge, suggests that it develops students' confidence in speaking with adults. This skill empowers students in the classroom and the workplace because it reflects ease and familiarity with the dominant culture's norms, manners, and ways of speaking. Together, these skills promote students' social and cultural capital, and, in turn, opportunities to learn and advance through the educational and economic systems (Lareau, 2011).

Intensive Academic and Social Supports

Preuss students are not typical of the students who routinely apply to college from private or affluent public schools. Some of the students speak English as a second language. Some have not been successful in elementary or middle school, and none of the students' parents have graduated from college or, in some cases, even high school. Recognizing that the students who enroll at Preuss are differentially prepared, the educators at the school have instituted a variety of academic and social supports, or scaffolds, to help students meet the challenges of the rigorous curriculum required for entering 4-year colleges and universities. The most notable structural change is the extension of the school year by 18 days, which gives students more opportunities to meet the school's academic demands.

Students in need of additional help receive tutoring from UCSD students and are invited to participate in an additional structural innovation—tutoring sessions during "Saturday Academies." In this way, the Preuss School has reversed the conventional time–curriculum relationship. The school has established high instructional standards and presents a rigorous curriculum to *all* students, at the same time varying the academic and social supports to enable all students to meet those high academic standards. The better the students' academic performance, the fewer scaffolds are needed; the greater the students' academic needs, the more academic and social supports are activated.

Cultural features enhance these structural features. Students have an advisory teacher who serves as advocate and counselor for the same group from grades 6–12. Modeled after the successful AVID program (Mehan, Villanueva, Hubbard, & Lintz, 1996), the advisory class is a regular feature in the students' schedule, thereby emphasizing its importance. This class enables students and teachers to develop trusting relationships (Noddings, 2003) and provides a means of closely monitoring student progress (Meier, 1995; Sizer, 1992). Research on the college preparation practices of well-to-do students and elite schools (Cookson & Persell, 1985; Lareau, 2011; McDonough, 1997) shows that parents and counselors invest considerable energy in developing students' portfolios and connecting them to college admissions officers. Because the parents of Preuss School students have not graduated from college, they often lack the cultural and social capital needed to make these connections. Advisory teachers and the school's college prep counselor assume these responsibilities on behalf of the students, encouraging them to take requisite admissions tests, secure fee waivers, obtain letters of recommendation, and apply to colleges.

CONCLUSION

The conventional educational practice of tracking neither provides students with equal educational opportunities nor serves the needs of employers for a well-educated workforce. Students from low-income and ethnic or linguistic minority backgrounds are disproportionately represented in low-track classes and vocational education and seldom receive the educational resources that are equivalent to students who are placed in high-track classes. They often suffer the stigmatizing consequences of negative labeling. They are not prepared well for careers or college.

Whether they are planning to enter college or the workplace after graduation, high school students need to be educated to a high level in reading comprehension, computation, writing, problem solving, and reasoning (ACT, 2006; Murnane & Levy, 2004). High school graduates need this high level of preparation if they are to succeed in college courses without remediation or to enter workforce training programs ready to learn job-specific skills. This line of thinking concludes that preparing students for college and preparing students for careers are more similar than they are different. Further, the educational practice of differentiating the curriculum such that one group of students is placed on a college prep track and another group of students is placed on a traditional voc-ed track is neither productive nor democratic. The increasing demands of the workplace and the long-standing need for well-prepared citizens to sustain the fragile democratic system reinforce the need to dismantle the present tracking system.

I have described detracking as one model for preparing students for college and careers when they complete high school. Uniting the high academic expectations of college prep courses with the hands-on experiences of vocational education courses fulfills Dewey's dream of making quality education a universal good for all students (Burris et al., 2008), which, in turn, will do a better job of preparing *all* students to be able to make informed choices about life after high school.

REFERENCES

ACT. (2006). *Ready for college and ready for work: Same or different?* Iowa City: Author.
Advisory Council on Students' Financial Aid. (2010). *The rising cost of inequality.* Washington, DC: Author.

Alvarez, D., &. Mehan, H. (2006). Whole school detracking: A strategy for equity and excellence. *Theory into Practice, 45*(1), 82–89.

Baker, E. L., Barton, P. E., Darling-Hammond, L., Haertel, E., Ladd, H. F., Linn, R. L., Ravitch, D., Rothstein, R., Shavelson, R. J., & Shepard, L. A. (2010). *Problems with the use of student test scores to evaluate teachers.* Washington, DC: Economic Policy Institute.

Bohren, A., & McClure, L. (2011). *The Preuss School UCSD: School characteristics and students' achievement.* La Jolla: University of California at San Diego CREATE.

Burris, C. C., Wiley, E., Welner, K., & Murphy, J. (2008). Accountability, rigor, and detracking: Achievement effects of embracing a challenging curriculum as a universal good for all students. *Teachers College Record, 110*(3), 571–607.

Cicourel, A. V., & Mehan, H. (1983). Universal development, stratifying practices and status attainment. *Research in Social Stratification and Mobility, 4,* 3–27.

College Board. (2010). *College-bound seniors results underscore importance of academic rigor. New York: The College Board* (press release). New York: Author.

Cookson, P. W., Jr., & Persell, C. H. (1985). *Preparing for power: America's elite boarding schools.* New York: Basic Books.

Dewey, J. (1956). *The child and the curriculum/The school and society.* Chicago: University of Chicago Press. (Original works published 1902 and 1900, respectively)

Hallinan, M. T. (2004). *The detracking movement.* Stanford, CA: The Hoover Institution.

Haycock, K. (1997). *Closing the achievement gap.* Washington, DC: The Education Trust.

Haycock, K. (2006). *Improving achievement and closing gaps between groups.* Washington, DC: The Education Trust.

Lareau, A. (2011). *Unequal childhoods: Class, race and family life.* 2nd ed., with an update a decade later. Berkeley: University of California Press.

McDonough, P. (1997). *Choosing colleges: How social class and schools structure opportunity.* Albany: State University of New York Press.

Mehan, H., Villanueva, I., Hubbard, L., & Lintz, A. (1996). *Constructing school success: The consequences of untracking low achieving students.* Cambridge, UK: Cambridge University Press.

Meier, D. (1995). *The Power of their ideas: Lessons for America from a small school in Harlem.* Boston: Beacon Press.

Murnane, R. J., & Levy, F. (2004). *Teaching the new basic skills: Principles for educating children to thrive in a changing economy.* New York: The Free Press.

National Commission on Education and the Economy (NCEE). (1983). *A nation at risk.* Washington, DC: Author.

Noddings, N. (2003). *Caring: A feminine approach to ethics and moral education* (2nd ed.). Berkeley: University of California Press.

Oakes, J. (2003). *Critical conditions for equity and diversity in college access: Informing policy and monitoring results.* Los Angeles: University of California ACCORD.

Oakes, J. (2005). *Keeping track: How schools structure inequality* (2nd ed.). New Haven, CT: Yale University Press.

Oakes, J., Wells, A., Jones, M., & Datnow, A. (1997). Detracking: The social construction of ability, cultural politics, and resistance to reform. *Teachers College Record 98*(3), 482–510.

Rosen, L., & Mehan, H. (2003). Reconstructing equality on new political ground: The politics of representation in the charter school debate at the University of California, San Diego. *American Educational Research Journal, 40*(3), 655–682.

Rosenstock, L., & Steinberg, A. (1995). Beyond the shop: Reinventing vocational education. In M. W. Apple & J. A. Beane (Eds.), *Democractic schools*. (pp. 41–57). Alexandria, VA: ASCD.

Rubin, B. (Ed.). (2006). Detracking and heterogeneous grouping. Special Issue. *Theory into Practice, 45*(1).

Sizer, T. R. (1992). *Horace's school: Redesigning the American high school*. New York: Houghton Mifflin.

Strick, B. (2009). *College enrollment and persistence of Preuss and comparison students in the classes of 2005 and 2006*. La Jolla: University of California at San Diego CREATE.

Turner, R. H. (1960). Sponsored and contest mobility and the school system. *American Sociological Review, 25*, 855–867.

Varenne, H., & McDermott, R. P. (1998). *Successful failure: The schools that America builds*. Boulder, CO: Westview Press.

CHAPTER 2

Toward a Pedagogy of Trust

Eric DeMeulenaere

There is a large body of research documenting how and why poor urban students of color distrust schools. Studies have addressed the lack of multicultural curricula (Banks, 1986; Dei, Mazzuca, McIsaac, & Zine, 1997; McCarthy, 1990); cultural mismatches between home and school (Delpit, 1995; Heath, 1983; Irvine, 1990; Kochman, 1981); educators' lack of concern for Black and Latino students (Stevenson & Ellsworth, 1993); and the prevalence of White teachers teaching students of color (Sleeter & McLaren, 1995) as factors underlying students' mistrust of schooling. Tied to this is the threat of stereotyping (Steele & Aronson, 1995). Jeannie Oakes (1985) has shown how stereotypes predominantly place Blacks and Latinos and poor children into lower-tracked classes. Others have poignantly elucidated the structural effects of unequal funding in urban and predominantly Black and Latino neighborhoods (Anyon, 2005; Kozol, 1992, 2005; Maeroff, 1994). Still others have argued that low-income Black and Latino students don't accept the meritocratic assumption embedded in schooling (Mickelson, 1990) and therefore develop an oppositional identity toward school (Fordham, 1988; Ogbu, 1994).

Regardless of the theoretical framing, there is clear legitimacy in urban students' distrust of and resistance to schooling. However, too often, as Herb Kohl (1994) warns, "conscious, willed refusal of schooling for political or cultural reasons is not acknowledged as an appropriate response to oppressive education" (p. 30). Instead schools label these resisters as deviant and isolate or extract them from a school system that demands rigid conformity. Effective urban teachers "respect the truth behind this massive rejection of schooling by students from poor and oppressed communities" (p. 30). An awareness of this distrust should prevent all teachers from assuming trust from their students. But how do teachers with a critical awareness of their status within an oppressive educational system begin to *earn* the trust of their students? This question is particularly daunting for teachers from communities of privilege who are striving to become critically conscious and culturally relevant educators across the boundaries of race and class.

Several authors have provided insightful portrayals of effective urban teaching. These authors have offered powerful models of culturally relevant teaching (Delpit, 1995; Hemmings, 1994; Ladson-Billings, 1994, 1995; Lee, 1998; Sleeter & McLaren, 1995) or critical pedagogy (Duncan-Andrade & Morrell, 2008; Freire, 1993; hooks, 1994) that are both practical and inspirational. However, their focus on effective pedagogical practices leads them to highlight the moments of teaching in which trust has been established already. They do not attend explicitly to how teachers establish trust.

The purpose of this chapter is to clearly elucidate the process for achieving the trust requisite for establishing the high expectations and powerful learning described eloquently elsewhere, including the other chapters in this volume. As an outgrowth of a critical teacher inquiry project, I teamed with two Worcester teachers who work in one of the lowest achieving schools in Massachusetts to design and coteach a course for 27 high school seniors. Here, I examine the role that a pedagogy of trust played in students' improved academic performance. This examination includes the importance of trust between students and teachers from very different social backgrounds and among students from different social cliques. This chapter explores the process of creating a classroom culture based on trust, which, in turn, creates the conditions for students to achieve high levels of learning. This analysis outlines a framework for a pedagogy of trust that can be used to develop more effective urban educators, as these individuals work with youth in schools marked by extensive distrust.

This research relied on critically reflective action research (Carr & Kemmis, 1986; Carson, 1990) to develop the case of the class of 27 students. It reflected the commitment of all three teachers to effect change in the material and social reality of the youth with whom we worked, while simultaneously working to reflect on and learn from our actions. This methodology is grounded in an epistemological stance rooted in critical theory and committed to using knowledge to affect social change (Collins, 1991; Habermas, 1972).

Two university faculty and seven undergraduate students engaged with two high school teachers and 27 high school students from the school to collect and analyze data. The data were collected during a year-long high school senior class entitled Roots and Routes (R&R). The data include the following:

- Videotaping of every class
- Student work samples

- Students' attendance records and transcripts (9th–12th grades)
- College acceptance letters
- Focal student interviews
- Focal student-created videos on their lives
- Teacher journaling
- Field notes of several class sessions
- Videos of student presentations to broader audiences
- Digital dialogues with students (through e-mail, digital chat spaces, and text messaging) related to research questions

These data were coded and reexamined continually.

The demographics of this class reflected the school as a whole. All of the students in the class except one qualified for federal Pell grants for low-income students. Racially, of the 27 students, 4 were Black, 12 Latino, 3 Vietnamese, 6 White (which included 3 Albanian immigrants), and 2 identified as mixed race (one Latino/White, another Vietnamese/White). In terms of their home environment, we had 12 students who lived in two-parent homes, 11 students from single-parent homes, and 4 students who lived in foster care or independent from parental guardians. Academically, the class was representative of the school as a whole, in which 49% of students failed to reach proficiency in English language arts tests and 78% failed to meet proficiency in math tests. The participants also included the teachers of the high school course, who, like 90% of the school's teaching force, were from White and middle-class backgrounds.

BUILDING TRUST IN AN URBAN CLASSROOM

There are six components of the initial framework for a pedagogy of trust:

1. The use of community rituals
2. The development of powerful shared experiences
3. Risk taking on the part of the teachers
4. The addressing of conflict
5. The teachers' alignment with students
6. The grounding of the course's curriculum in students' realities

The level of trust in the R&R classroom was an important part of the marked improvement our students achieved. Several students explained how the level of trust established in R&R encouraged them to cross boundaries into new social worlds and embrace their potential as learners. One student eloquently wrote about the creation of a sense of community as a result of this developed trust: "When I first came into this class I only talked to my group of friends. But . . . I feel like this class kind of brought a sense of unity within the Class [of '09]. It's like a place where we can all be ourselves and be accepted for that." R&R fostered a level of trust between students that allowed them to cross entrenched social boundaries and learn from one another.

Students also felt empowered to cross the boundary that constructs teachers as adversaries. Students recognized the risks that teachers of R&R took daily, making themselves vulnerable, inviting critique, and making mistakes as they endeavored to improve their practice. One student succinctly captured this sentiment, writing, "The R&R teachers take that risk. They trust us and I think that's what helped us get stronger throughout this time."

This trusting relationship with teachers led to students striving and working extra hard to not betray the established trust. One student explained, "It was this force of editing my paper a fifth time and writing an extra two paragraphs on an analysis because I didn't want to disappoint my teachers." Another student wrote, "Having someone putting so much faith in you transforms you. Having teachers who say they are proud—I don't want to let them down."

Across race and class, teachers of R&R established trusting relationships with students that resulted in improved academic achievement. As White teachers of urban students of color, we realized that neither an explicit critical pedagogy nor years of experience were enough to dismantle entrenched levels of distrust rooted in institutionalized racial and socioeconomic differences. Despite the social divides, we developed trust-filled relationships that both teachers and students recognized as surpassing any level of trust they had encountered previously. It was this pedagogy of trust that ultimately made room for a deeply honest learning of challenging curriculum in R&R.

The following section unpacks the pedagogical practices that promoted a trust-filled space in R&R. I present six components of an initial framework for a pedagogy of trust.

Use of Community Rituals

In R&R, the instructors purposefully cultivated and nurtured rituals that affirmed and built a collective community. Traditional school rituals, such as using bells to monitor time and placing desks in rows to facilitate surveillance, discipline the body and minds of students in ways similar to methods used in prisons, factories, hospitals, and the military (Foucault, 1995). To foster a community built on collaboration and trust, we inserted new rituals into our classroom to disrupt the traditional rituals that maintain control and docility in schools.

On the first day of class, we began with a darkened room. In the rear of the room the words "Why are we here?" were projected onto a screen. A side wall displayed a series of slides with life aspirations flashing in bold letters: "Write a Novel," "Hike the Appalachian Trail," "Be a Mom," "Live off the grid," and so on. We waited several minutes after the bell rang in darkness before one instructor walked to the middle of students seated in a circle to present a staged reading of his own personal memoir.

This ritualistic beginning of the first class created a different space than is typical in most high school classrooms. The darkness, delay, and dramatic reading conveyed the space of a theater more than one of a factory, prison, or school. It carved a space that interrupted the normal "first day of class" rituals.

Another ritual we developed was to regularly gather around a make-shift altar to share personally about ourselves. For example, after constructing personal artist books that held a personally designed symbol and a list of individual lifetime goals, we gathered around the altar to ritually share and showcase our artist books. The class offered appreciation for the sharing, and each artist placed his or her book on the altar. The altar became a sacred space in the room where class members (as well as students from other classes) would go to look at the items placed upon it. We returned to it from time to time (such as when we shared photos of lost loved ones during a Day of the Dead ritual). These rituals evoked a space and community associated with sacredness and emotion, rather than the traditional (and often alienating) intellectual space of school. They created a space for students and teachers to develop trust by connecting more deeply with each other's humanity.

These examples capture a pedagogical move that served to promote a classroom culture built on trust. When we shared symbols of our identities or shared the pain of lost loved ones, we built trust that enabled us to take the risk of sharing our work with each other. These rituals served to disrupt the common rituals of school affiliated with distrust and, in their place, create separate, sacred spaces where we could honestly connect with each other as full human beings and begin the process of establishing trust.

Powerful Shared Experiences

At the end of the first week of school, we took the students on an outdoor challenge designed to encourage them to rely on each other. At 11:30 A.M. on the first Friday, we climbed into two large vans and headed to Mt. Wachusett. We divided the students into three groups. Each group was dropped off at a different unknown place at the base of the small mountain with a map, an opened 5-gallon bottle of water, an egg, a balloon, and a small bag of ice. They were told that they needed to get their entire group to the top of the mountain before the ice completely melted without breaking the egg, losing the balloon, or spilling any of the water on the ground. The students dived into the task, devising creative ways to cover the water bottles and carry them. All three groups became disoriented at some point, but they all eventually found their way to the mountaintop, sharing a collective sense of accomplishment.

As designed, the mountain climb became a metaphor for collaboration and the relentless struggle to reach life goals. It also served as a powerful experience that fostered a sense of community and was recounted in various forms by teachers and students throughout the year. Several wrote about the experience in their college applications. One student wrote, "From the top of the mountain, I saw the city I grew up in with a new perspective and began to see myself and the people I grew up with in a new light."

This field trip was only one of many powerful shared experiences we had throughout the year. Another, for example, was a high ropes course challenge. At the ropes course, we literally held each other's lives in our hands. Shaky legs and nervous voices unmasked our fears and vulnerability but also brought encouragement from classmates—not unlike the vulnerability and encouragement that occurred later, when we shared our personal writings.

In addition to these types of experiences outside of school, we also shared experiences in class. For example, we made masks that represented how we thought the world saw us and how we viewed ourselves. We shared our masks in special artist talks. We regularly constructed and shared art together and engaged in large simulation activities, which allowed individuals to share more about themselves to the whole class. These shared experiences became spaces for building a trust-filled community.

Whether in class or outside of class, these shared experiences diverged from the typical school day, making them memorable for their difference. Often, they were also memorable because they involved overcoming a struggle and experiencing the thrill of accomplishing a difficult task together. Thus they worked to build a collective identity for the class based on trust, which enabled us to raise the academic expectations for everyone.

Risk Taking by Teachers

As teachers, we took the initial steps to create a trusting community by trusting the students first. We started by sharing stories about life-defining moments in our personal lives. On the first day of school, one instructor shared a memoir about his father, who walked out on the family after his mother suffered a debilitating stroke. Another spoke about the murder of one of his students. Later, at the altar, each instructor shared her or his own life goals. We reflected on our teaching publicly, opening ourselves to critique and making ourselves vulnerable in class before calling on students to do the same.

One powerful symbolic moment of this trust occurred when we made our plaster masks (see Figure 2.1). This task required us to trust others to build our mask on our face while we sat still as they covered our eyes, mouth, and entire face with wet plaster. Students carefully applied and smoothed across my face the cool plaster strips, comforting my sense of claustrophobia with words of assurance. I had to trust my students to take care of my mask and me while it was being made.

Shawn Ginwright (2010) implores adults who work with urban youth to become vulnerable truth tellers who "cry, become angry, and share painful experiences" with the youth (p. 86). In so doing, he argues, they create a space of vulnerability and trust for youth to navigate their own pain and struggles. The trust we established in R&R among students and between students and teachers developed, in part, because we as teachers initiated this trust by sharing our struggles and making ourselves vulnerable.

Embracing Conflict

Trust, we recognized, is difficult to build and easy to lose. In our experience as teachers of R&R, we found that how we responded to conflicts that arose in class affected our ability to maintain trust.

Figure 2.1. Student Masks Representing How the World Perceives Them

On the day we climbed Mt. Wachusett, one of the teachers pulled me aside to share that a handful of students had used a permanent marker to write their names on a stone outcrop. We believed this tagging in a public space could not be ignored. But we also knew that an intense "zero tolerance" punishment of the culprits could undermine the trust we had begun to build.

To address this first conflict in our community, we decided to discuss it as a community—students included. Before returning to school, we gathered everyone and explained what had happened. We asked everyone to think about this incident over the weekend but not to talk about it with anyone—not even others in the class—until we could address the situation on Monday.

On Monday we formed a classroom circle. I shared why I was upset with the tagging. The youth who had done it explained their actions. The students involved were prepared to go to the principal and take full responsibility and suffer whatever consequences. Through discussion as a class, though, we decided we wanted to resolve the situation ourselves. We decided that a teacher would drive the students back to the site and they would buy the cleaning supplies and restore the outcrop. That Wednesday, three teachers and several students, including some who did not tag their names, drove back to the mountaintop and spent the entire afternoon cleaning the granite outcrop.

The trust was developed by avoiding the most typical responses to school conflicts. We didn't involve the traditional school disciplinary apparatus that is based on an individualized, pathologized, punitive, and often racist framework, but we nonetheless took the incident seriously and developed consequences. As a result of the class discussion, other uninvolved students stepped up to embrace the consequences. This was powerful for building trust because everyone—and even the classroom culture itself—was implicated. The issues were confronted collaboratively, and the final, morally reasonable resolution was determined by working together.

This was the earliest conflict, but others occurred throughout the year. We had several class meetings to debrief and resolve conflicts. Sometimes they were caused by inappropriate comments, arguments, or people not doing what they said they would do. Sometimes we put a lot of effort into resolving what might be considered a smaller issue. We didn't always have a whole-class meeting, but we always tried to embrace the conflicts that arose as learning and trust-building opportunities. Our determination, as teachers, to confront conflict seriously and authentically played an important role in fostering trust. Establishing such trust also built a classroom culture that minimized conflict and promoted its de-escalation when it did emerge. This meant that although we spent a lot of time early in the year addressing conflicts, this was time well spent. We believe that the culture of trust we developed as a result of this early work afforded us more time in the end to focus on powerful learning because we had minimized future conflicts.

Teachers Aligning with Students

Our pedagogy of trust sought to explicitly dismantle the (justifiable) distrust of school that our students held. To earn their trust and build trusting relationships among students, we allied ourselves with students whenever possible. Small acts, like providing a student a ride home or helping a student study for a math test, were acts of solidarity. Listening to social problems and offering help in small ways were important acts, reflecting empathy toward their reality.

In other ways, too, we stood in solidarity with students. When one student had to go to court, we, his teachers, wrote letters on his behalf. I also took him and his mother to the courthouse and spoke on his behalf to the judge. When students were suspended from school for actions taken outside of our classroom, we helped them stay on-task, keeping them out of trouble and getting them caught up in their work. Efforts to break the cycle of distrust pervasive in urban schools required us to step out of the traditional teacher roles. When the school or criminal justice system acted against our students, we supported them. Students and their families recognized these acts of solidarity and came to view us not as part of the school system but as their allies. This built trust.

Curriculum Grounded in Student Realities

A visit to the courtroom proved relevant to our curriculum on power in society. Much of our students' lived realities were tapped as instructive. We designed the curriculum to connect students' personal marginalization with a critical consciousness about larger structures of oppression. Employing a Freirean (1993) pedagogy, we developed our students' critical consciousness and sense of agency, beginning with their lived realities. We read powerful memoirs of marginalized youth as we worked with our students to develop their own personal memoirs. These memoirs were starting points that we used to develop an array of artwork, reflective writings, discussions, and college statements. We displayed the artwork in a professional exhibition and published the memoirs.

As they confronted the pain of gang violence, death of family members, and domestic violence in their memoirs, we read bell hooks's (1990) call to embrace the margins not only as spaces of pain but also as places of radical insight. Through pictures and writings and research projects, we examined their reality as students in school, living in a low-income neighborhood with personal knowledge of factories, prisons, and the postindustrial economy. We then analyzed these realities through an in-depth reading of Foucault (1995). This led into a study of Gramsci's (1971) idea of cultural hegemony and the need for our students to become organic intellectuals engaged in counterhegemonic work.

We purposely designed the course so that students could develop canonical knowledge about authors and writings often studied in under-graduate and graduate courses but rarely read in secondary schools. We read nonfiction by Jimmy Santiago Baca, Alice Walker, bell hooks, Lawrence Kohlberg, Antonio Gramsci, Michel Foucault, Toni Morrison, Audre Lorde, and William Golding, in addition to a wide array of narrative writings. We did so using a Freirean methodology that connected the analysis to the students' own lived experiences. We used these acclaimed authors to help students develop their critical analysis of their own lives, but we also wanted to equip them with a cultural capital valued in academia, since we knew that they might be underprepared for college in many other ways.

THE COURSE'S IMPACT

The R&R course was a senior seminar built on a Freirean pedagogy de-signed to engage students in a critical analysis of and action in their world. It also encouraged students to think deeply about their own life trajecto-ries. Students read and analyzed texts, wrote memoirs and college essays, developed and presented professional art exhibitions, and presented at various academic conferences throughout the year. This work, grounded in a pedagogy of trust, resulted in significant improvements in traditional measures of student academic performance. Twenty-six out of the 27 stu-dents increased their overall GPAs. The average GPA of all 27 students increased from 2.76 to 3.39 in the year of the study. Furthermore, 8 students made gains of over 1 entire grade point.

This senior seminar targeted increased college application and matric-ulation rates for students. In contrast with the low historical matriculation rate at the school (under 20%), 82% of students enrolled in R&R entered college the year after they graduated (see Figure 2.2). Importantly, the di-versity of colleges and universities at which students were accepted in-creased over prior years. Several students were accepted at highly ranked schools like Boston University, Middlebury College, Worcester Polytech-nic Institute, Northeastern, Holy Cross, and Clark University.

Analysis of qualitative data revealed that students experienced the course as transformative, affecting their sense of self and their relationships to schooling and learning. In addition, students indicated that their involve-ment in the course went beyond learning the course content; the course also

Figure 2.2. Increases in College Matriculation

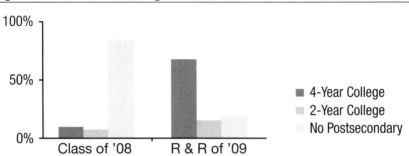

changed *how* they learned new content. One young woman stated that the R&R class "showed me that there is a different way of writing and there is a different way of looking and analyzing things." Another student indicated that the course taught students how to "think and analyze on our own, to feel fear but not be afraid to overcome it, and to strive even if we may fail but never give in." Yet another student, who had been low-performing throughout his schooling prior to this course, stated, "[This class] showed me what life is about and . . . helped me become a better student." These comments are representative of similar comments made by other students throughout the year and reflect the fact that R&R impacted student performance not only within the course but also in other classes. Students changed their academic identities and trajectories as a result of this course.

In a school system designed around standardized state frameworks and based on abstract knowledge disconnected from the lived realities of urban youth, a curriculum that affirms and builds on the culture and knowledge base of urban youth is transformative. Situating our students as the "organic intellectuals" that people in the university needed to learn from (rather than learn about) not only empowered our students but also built trust, as students came to see that their teachers were not only impressed by their work but also learned from it. Our students produced high-quality work in the form of narrative writings, conference presentations, research reports, and artwork, receiving praise from a diverse array of members of academia and the community.

CONCLUSION

In *Black Youth Rising,* Shawn Ginwright (2010) offers a framework for promoting radical healing for oppressed youth. His framework recognizes that in addition to empowering urban youth as social change agents through critical pedagogy and activism, we must address the pain and distrust created by racism and other forms of oppression. In his analysis, he asserts that our urban youth live surrounded by social toxins. This social toxicity interferes with our ability to engage youth in powerful community work. The toxicity must be acknowledged and healing must occur if any authentic community youth work is to begin. This healing work must remain a central component of work with youth, both in and out of schools.

The social toxins in our urban schools are prevalent and foster distrust. Effective urban educators must acknowledge and confront this distrust, this "massive rejection of schooling by students from poor and oppressed communities" (Kohl, 1994, p. 30). Such teachers must work carefully to build a healthy, trust-filled community.

Developing such a pedagogy of trust is even more challenging, yet more necessary, when teachers seek to build trust across the divides of race and class. Despite the challenge, a pedagogy of trust can foster a classroom community that bridges social differences and enables students to take risks and achieve incredible academic and social successes. Indeed, we assert that without the development of a trust-filled community, powerful learning is difficult to accomplish. Because of the pedagogical moves employed in the R&R class, a strong community of trust enabled powerful learning to occur.

The R&R students attended this daily, 48-minute course only during their senior year. While it is unusual to have a course with three teachers, the impact this course had on students' academic performances and trajectories beyond the confines of R&R was remarkable. This highlights the potential impact that one course can have. We often wonder what we could have achieved with these students if we had started to work with them in 9th grade or if we had had a team of like-minded teachers working collaboratively across multiple classes to implement a pedagogy of trust.

This chapter both serves as a call for urban teachers to confront the distrust prevalent in urban schools and offers an initial outline for a pedagogy of trust. While the importance of establishing trust as an educator may be rather intuitive, the process of how to do it is less apparent. Through analyzing the pedagogical moves from a class in which a high level of trust was established and strong indicators of academic and social growth were evident, we offer this preliminary framework for a pedagogy of trust.

REFERENCES

Anyon, J. (2005). *Radical possibilities: Public policy, urban education, and a new social movement*. New York: Routledge.

Banks, J. (1986). Multicultural education: Development, paradigms, and goals. In J. Banks & J. Lynch (Eds.), *Multicultural education in western societies* (pp. 1–29). London: Holt.

Carr, W., & Kemmis, S. (1986). *Becoming critical: Education, knowledge and action research*. Geelong, Victoria, Australia: Daekin University Press.

Carson, T. (1990). What kind of knowing is critical action research? *Theory into Practice, 29*(3), 167–173.

Collins, P. H. (1991). *Black feminist thought: Knowledge, consciousness, and the politics of empowerment* (vol. 2). New York: Routledge.

Dei, G. J. S., Mazzuca, J., McIsaac, E., & Zine, J. (1997). *Reconstructing "drop-out": A critical ethnography of the dynamics of Black students' disengagement from school.* Toronto, Ontario, Canada: University of Toronto Press.

Delpit, L. D. (1995). *Other people's children: Cultural conflict in the classroom.* New York: New Press.

Duncan-Andrade, J. M. R., & Morrell, E. (2008). *The art of critical pedagogy: Possibilities for moving from theory to practice in urban schools.* New York: Peter Lang.

Fordham, S. (1988). Racelessness as a factor in Black students' school success: Pragmatic strategy or Pyrrhic victory? *Harvard Educational Review, 58*(1), 54–84.

Foucault, M. (1995). *Discipline and punish: The birth of the prison* (2nd ed.). New York: Vintage Books.

Freire, P. (1993). *Pedagogy of the oppressed* (new rev. 20th anniversary ed.). New York: Continuum.

Ginwright, S. A. (2010). *Black youth rising: Activism & radical healing in urban America.* New York: Teachers College Press.

Gramsci, A. (1971). *Selections from the prison notebooks* (Q. Hoare & G. N. Smith, Trans.). New York: International Publishers.

Habermas, J. (1972). *Knowledge and human interests* (J. Shapiro, Trans.). Boston: Beacon Press.

Heath, S. B. (1983) *Ways with words: Language, life and work in communities and classrooms.* New York: Cambridge University Press.

Hemmings, A. (1994). *Culturally responsive teaching: When and how high school teachers should cross cultural boundaries to reach students.* Paper presented at the American Educational Research Association Conference, New Orleans, LA, April 4-8. (ERIC Document Reproduction Service No. ED 376242)

hooks, b. (1990). *Yearning: Race, gender, and cultural politics.* Boston: South End Press.

hooks, b. (1994). *Teaching to transgress: Education as the practice of freedom.* New York: Routledge.

Irvine, J. J. (1990). *Black students and school failure.* Westport, CT: Greenwood Press.

Kochman, T. (1981). *Black and White styles in conflict.* Chicago, IL: University of Chicago Press.

Kohl, H. R. (1994). *"I won't learn from you" and other thoughts on creative maladjustment.* New York: The New Press.

Kozol, J. (1992). *Savage inequalities: Children in America's schools.* New York: HarperCollins.

Kozol, J. (2005). *The shame of the nation: The restoration of apartheid schooling in America.* New York: Crown.

Ladson-Billings, G. (1994). *The dreamkeepers: Successful teachers of African American children*. San Francisco: Jossey-Bass.

Ladson-Billings, G. (1995). Toward a theory of culturally relevant pedagogy. *American Educational Research Journal, 32(3)*, 465–491.

Lee, C. D. (1998). Culturally responsive pedagogy and performance-based assessment. *Journal of Negro Education, 67*(3), 269–279.

Maeroff, G. I. (1994). Withered hopes, stillborn dreams: The dismal panorama of urban schools. In E. J. Nussel & J. Kretovics (Eds.), *Transforming urban education: Problems & possibilities for equality of educational opportunity* (pp. 32–42). Boston: Allyn and Bacon.

McCarthy, C. (1990). *Race and curriculum: Social inequality and the theories and politics of difference in contemporary research on schooling*. Bristol, PA: Falmer.

Mickelson, R. A. (1990). The attitude-achievement paradox among Black adolescents. *Sociology of Education, 63*(1), 44–61.

Oakes, J. (1985). *Keeping track: How schools structure inequality*. New Haven, CT: Yale University Press.

Ogbu, J. U. (1994). From cultural differences to differences in cultural frame of reference. In P. M. Greenfield & R. R. Cocking (Eds.), *Cross-cultural roots of minority child development* (pp. 365–392). Hillsdale, NJ: Lawrence Erlbaum.

Sleeter, C. E., & McLaren, P. L. (1995). *Multicultural education, critical pedagogy, and the politics of difference*. Albany: State University of New York Press.

Steele, C. M., & Aronson, J. (1995). Stereotype threat and the intellectual test performance of African Americans. *Journal of Personality and Social Psychology, 69*(5), 797–811.

Stevenson, R., & Ellsworth, J. (1993). Dropouts and the silencing of critical voices. In L. Weis & M. Fine (Eds.), *Beyond silenced voices* (pp. 259–271). Albany: State University of New York Press.

LITERACY CURRICULA IN URBAN CLASSROOMS

Part II provides illustrations of high-expectation literacy programs, curricula, or practices as they play out in urban classrooms. The examples span the grade levels, from 1st-graders, to middle grade students, to high school seniors. Each chapter provides examples of the intellectual practices students engage in, with evidence of how scaffolded support for talk and interrogation of text support robust learning.

In Chapter 3, Marty Rutherford introduces "Poetry Inside Out," where students from diverse cultural and linguistic backgrounds learn to translate masterworks of poetry from a variety of languages into English. Students dig into the richness and complexity of language and experience the challenge of making words do what you want them to.

In Chapter 4 Debra Goodman argues that the Dewey Center for Urban Education is a school that uses a learner-centered, inquiry-based whole language curriculum to validate and build on the linguistic and cultural know-how that kids bring to school. The chapter highlights the literacy events and experiences of two 2nd-graders: Lauren, a typical reader and writer, and Marco, a less proficient one. Whole language is presented as a "dual curriculum" that facilitates meaning-making processes and content-focused learning.

In Chapter 5, Janette Klingner, Alison Boardman, and Subini Annamma describe a program known as Collaborative Strategic Reading (CSR), designed to support heterogeneously grouped students in the middle grades to read and discuss challenging texts. The program builds in high expectations for students in the classroom norms, routines, and discussion practices that take place. High expectations for teachers are also evident, woven into the fabric of the professional learning that takes place in support of CSR in the classroom.

In Chapter 6, Sophie Haroutunian-Gordon demonstrates the practice of interpretive discussion with a group of underprepared high school seniors (the same group of students that DeMeulenaere discusses in his chapter on the Roots and Routes course of study). Students in low-socioeconomic-status school environments are often presumed to be incapable of the skills and habits of mind necessary to take part in high-level interpretive discussion. She highlights a skill-building exercise—the line-by-line analysis of a text—by offering a case study of a group of students who read and discussed Toni Morrison's Nobel Lecture with her. Haroutunian-Gordon illustrates how the students learned to both cultivate questions as readers and work toward resolving these questions through discussion.

In Chapter 7, Curt Dudley-Marling and Sarah Michaels describe what happened when a low-performing school in the South Bronx adopted a high-expectation literacy curriculum, "The Junior Great Books." After 6 months, standardized test scores rose dramatically in both English and math. These gains were sustained over the following years, after the grant funding expired. This chapter focuses on the "shared inquiry" discussions that took place throughout the school by looking closely at an example in a 4th-grade classroom. Their analysis suggests that students were guided in a complex social practice that enabled them to explicate their ideas, build arguments with evidence, and apply their thinking to that of their peers.

In each of these chapters—illustrating different programs, in different parts of the country, and at different grade levels—we see students grappling with the complexity of language as they interrogate, produce, or translate rich and meaningful texts. Students—positioned as thinkers, writers, interpreters, and poets—are invited to use their minds in a pleasurably athletic way in robust intellectual practices.

CHAPTER 3

Poetry Inside Out

A High-Expectation, Cross-Cultural Literacy Program

Marty Rutherford

Original Poem:	Collaborative Student Translation:
El Nido by Alfredo Espino	**The Nest**
Es porque un pajarito de la montaña ha hecho,	It is because a tiny bird from the moutain has made,
en el hueco de un árbol su nido matinal,	in the hollow of a tree its morning nest,
que el árbol amanece con música en el pecho,	that the tree wakes up with music in his chest,
como que si tuviera corazón musical . . .	as if it had a musical heart . . .
Si el dulce pajarito por entre el hueco asoma,	If the sweet bird peeks through the hole
para beber rocío, para beber aroma,	to drink the dew, to drink the aroma,
el árbol de la sierra me da la sensación	the tree from the mountain gives me the sensation,
de que se le ha salido, cantando, el corazón . . .	that its heart has come out singing . . .

Davina: In line three of "El Nido" we think the translation should say
that the tree wakes up with music in its chest because a bird
put a nest in the hole in the tree. When the bird sings, the tree
sounds musical. Translating the line that way makes sense
because it goes with the overall meaning of the poem, which is
that music is part of nature and nature is part of music.

Danny: We agree that the line should be that the tree wakes with music
in its chest. We chose this translation because it connects with
the lines before. This translation flows with the poem because
part of the poem talks about the connection between the tree
and the bird. The meaning of the poem is to teach us that the
bird is part of the tree. This translation makes sense because part
of the poem talks about a musical morning—so the tree and the

bird woke up feeling musical. *Chest* also rhymes with a word in
the other line so it should be translated that way in English.

Sydneé: When 34 people read the same thing, they each come up with
different ideas. Their minds picture different things because
they understand the words differently. The thing that happens
is that each mind works in its own way, so we see things
differently and then our mind makes its own connections.

Something remarkable is happening here. In the preceding example, a
class of middle school students, speaking six different languages, from the
lowest-performing public school in one of the lowest performing districts
in the country, spent over an hour and a half translating Mexican poet
Alfredo Espino's "El Nido" from Spanish to English and then defended
their translations.

In brief, here is a summary of the process. First, the students translated the poem. To do this, they learned a translation protocol developed
at the Center for the Art of Translation called Translations Circles. More
will be said about this later, but for now it is enough to know that students work in groups of four to translate the poem. Each student works
with his or her own poem page and a translation worksheet. The poem
page is designed as a scaffold for the translation process. Each poem
page has the poem, a brief biography of the poet, a glossary that includes
each word of the poem in its original language, a definition in English,
and two or more English synonyms for the word. Using the Translation
Circle protocol, each group works through a translation of the poem.
Once this process is complete, students share, discuss, and defend their
translations by explaining the sometimes subtle, and not so subtle, nuances for their choices.

Such intense student participation in this activity raises certain questions, especially in a book focused on high-expectation curricula: What is
so compelling about this curriculum that it captures students' attention
at this level, for this length of time? What is it about their experience that
prompts such a deep and intricate analysis? How were they drawn into a
discussion that involved this level of detail and explanation?

The students participating in this discussion are midway through a
program called Poetry Inside Out (PIO). PIO was established in 2000 as
part of the Center for the Art of Translation. Since then, over 5,000 linguistically diverse students from throughout the San Francisco Bay Area
have participated in Poetry Inside Out's in-school workshops, learning to
translate extraordinary poems from their original language into English.
Newly translated work creates fertile ground for the students to craft their
own poems. Through participation in PIO, students deepen their awareness of language, discovering for themselves that the purpose of reading is

to build knowledge, gain insights, explore possibilities, and broaden one's perspective. They learn that writing is a tool for exploring ideas—lived and learned—and communicating with others.

Two essential components form the basis of this dynamic curriculum. Students learn the craft of literary translation and how to write poetry, creating a synergy that allows them access to experiences that build strong literacy skills. The act of translating is a transformative process focused on the written word, which leads to a deeper understanding of the form and function of language (Rabassa, 1989). Of all genres, poetry is the most complicated (Felstiner, 1980), and its translation generates the closest possible relationship with text (Grossman, 2010), in part because attention to syntax, grammar, vocabulary, rhythm, nuances, and colloquialisms of both source and target language is vital. The back-and-forth from one language to another, between the whole and the parts, allows the translator to build a new version of the text.

Just as every word on a page has a relationship to every other word, phrase, paragraph, and to the entire piece, the whole text transacts with the sociocultural context in which it is composed and translated (Rabassa, 1989; Valdés, 2003; Weissbort, 2006). The act of translating builds awareness that meaning is found not in individual words but in the unraveling of the context within which the piece is written and read (Bakhtin, 1981). It is the translator's work to find meaning in the details that surround the word (Grossman, 2010). As a 4th-grade PIO student explained, "When I translate a poem, I look for what the author is trying to tell us, but you have to figure it out. You need to look at all the words and what they mean. It's like a riddle."

By teaching students to translate, we bring them into the closest possible contact and study with master poets. This is not a new invention. Literature studies in universities worldwide and increasingly in the United Sates insist that students translate great works in order to more fully comprehend the author's intent and to learn the craft of writing. The nature of the work enables the translator to delve between and into the lines of a poem in a way that does not happen when just reading a poem. The act of translation allows the translator to inhabit the world of the poet for a time. Upon this deep understanding—the relationship between translator and the work one is translating—Poetry Inside Out was created.

UNPACKING POETRY INSIDE OUT

The premise of PIO is straightforward. We believe that by exposing kids to great poets from all parts of the planet—for example, from the Diné nation, the Quechua peoples, China, Russia, Africa, Latin America, North

America, and so on—their worlds get bigger. And while we could give them many of these same poems in English, it is richer and more satisfying to encounter this work in its original form. There is something magical about unraveling great works of art from another language, another culture, to find meaning.

Poetry Inside Out is framed by five essential principles. The first is that our students see inspiration as a resource. PIO students are inspired by reading and translating great poems in their first language, written by luminaries that include their classmates and teachers. The second is to understand imagination as a tool. Participation in PIO fosters the use of the imagination—including helping students to imagine themselves as poets and translators; imagining the worlds where the poets who created the poems lived; imagining how what they know and understand makes translation possible, and more. The third principle is to make practice a habit. Becoming an expert at anything, including translating and writing poetry, requires practice. The fourth is to realize performance as a goal. The end goal of performance provides students the opportunity to understand that their work has consequence. It is important and necessary. How they ultimately publish their work varies; the final text can be transformed into performance, a community resource—the possibilities are endless. What matters most is that the students know the value of their work. The final principle is that language is an essential tool.

Language is perhaps the most useful tool we have for understanding, interpreting, translating, responding to, and making sense out of our worlds (Bruner, 1986; Cazden, 2001; Gee, 2007). Success in school, in business, in life depends on how well we understand the form, function, and use of language. Every context, including school, has a certain kind of vocabulary that allows or inhibits access depending on how well we know and understand the language of that situation or institution. Learning to translate a poem—which is essentially impossible—allows students to engage in a kind of gymnastics with words. In order to find the right translation, it is necessary to stretch, expand, and sometimes contort the meaning of one word to find the meaning of the poem. My understanding of this powerful idea was enhanced by an encounter with Sydneé, a student from the conversation that opens this chapter, who came running up to me when I entered that classroom:

> "Marty," she said in a disgusted tone, "you told me when we were translating poems to consider the context. You said that the context meant the words in the poem, surrounding the poem. But that is just not true—context is much bigger. To understand the context of a poem, I have to know something about the poet—was it a man or

a woman? Who were they as people? Were they happy when they wrote the poem, miserable, scared? Marty, there is so much more to context than the words on the page."

When we listen carefully, students will tell us all we need to know. They know that a mundane, content-free curriculum does not serve their needs. To learn what they need in order to build complex understandings about how language functions, to build their own theories about things like context, to understand what it means to communicate, and more, our students need rich, generative material.

THE PIO WORKSHOP STRUCTURE

Poetry Inside Out workshops consist of 16 lessons presented in three *cycles*. During the first cycle, the focus is on learning rudimentary translation skills; during the second cycle, the focus is on poetics; during the third cycle, students revise and publish their own work. Workshops usually occur two to three times a week for one hour. Typically we work within the regular school day, but the PIO program could be done after school.

Although the basic PIO structure is unchanging, each workshop is modified to fit the particular needs of the context where it is implemented. The composition of the class, the age, linguistic makeup, community resources, cultural considerations—and more—all inspire modifications, including the choice of poems, poets, countries, and languages. Figure 3.1 summarizes the basic flow of the three cycles.

In order to more completely understand how a Poetry Inside Out workshop functions, it is important to be acquainted with our most essential instructional tool, the *poem page*. Every poem and poet is introduced to students via a poem page. At the end of each workshop, students produce their own poem pages and student-made poem pages are collected into a class book.

All poem pages contain the same elements. Each page includes the poem, the title, the country of origin, and the date of the poet's birth and death (if applicable). When possible, a picture of the poet is included. A small biography of the featured poet allows our young translators to know something about the author and to explain the context, as Sydneé would tell us. Each poem page contains a translator's glossary that is a helpful key to accessing the poem. The translator's glossary includes a definition of the word and, when possible, synonyms in English. Figure 3.2 shows the poem page that formed the basis of the discussion described earlier.

Figure 3.1. Basic Poetry Inside Out Workshop Structure

Cycle	Content	Objective
Cycle 1 Class sessions 1–6	The emphasis in the first six classes is on learning basic translation skills.	Students learn: About the craft of literary translation Tools for the close reading of a text One reads in order to understand Meaning is found in context
Cycle 2 Class sessions 7–12	The emphasis turns to creating original poems. Students still work with poems and translation but now do so in order to create their own poems. A variety of different poetic forms and qualities are introduced.	Students learn: About writing poetry inspired by translating a poem Poems come in many forms and serve many functions About writing poems
Cycle 3 Class sessions 13–16	The emphasis is on students building their own poem pages, which are compiled into a class book. Each poem page is composed of an original poem, a glossary, a small biography, and a picture of the author.	Students learn: The value of making their work public How to make a poem page The form and function of a glossary Revision, editing, and formatting

Cycle 1

The emphasis in the first six or so classes is on learning basic translation skills, using poems that become increasingly complex to translate. Teachers and students engage in the work of creating a literary translation by considering the context, lines, words, cadences, and structure of the poem. While many of the students in this classroom, and many who have participated in PIO, are bilingual, they come to understand that literary translation is very different from the kind of interpretation work they do outside of school. As 6th-grade student Luis explains:

Translating a conversation is different. I might have to translate a meeting for my parents and my teacher. My parents want to know

Figure 3.2. Alfredo Espino Poem Page

ALFREDO ESPINO
EL SALVADOR (1900–1946)
Language: Spanish

El Nido

Es porque un pajarito de la montaña ha hecho,
en el hueco de un árbol su nido matinal,
que el árbol amanece con música en el pecho,
como que si tuviera corazón musical . . .

Si el dulce pajarito por entre el hueco asoma,
para beber rocío, para beber aroma,
el árbol de la sierra me da la sensación
de que se le ha salido, cantando, el corazón . . .

Alfredo Espino is one of the most beloved poets of El Salvador. He is best known for his most beautiful poems about nature. His sister Hortensia explained to those that were interested that Alfredo's love of nature was his muse. When they were children their father would take them for long walks in the country. They ran and played in nature, enjoying everything immensely. For Alfredo these were times of great inspiration. After such adventures he would produce marvelous poems.

Translator's Glossary

Amanece (Amanecer): (v.) Daybreak, awake, beginning; **wake up, dawn, appearing**
Árbol: (n.) Large, perennial, woody plant; **tree**
Asoma (Asomar): (v.) Push something out; **pokes out**
Beber: (v.) Swallow liquid; **drink, imbibe, swallow, sip**
Cantando (Cantar): (v.) Melodic songs; **singing**
Corazon: (n.) Basis of emotional life; **heart, spirit**
De: (prep.) Connecting words, often nouns; **of, from, by**
Da (dar): (v.) Pass something to someone; **give, provide**
Dulce: (adj.) Pleasing to the senses; **sweet, fresh, gentle**
Entre: (prep.) Inside place; **within, in, contained by**
Ha hecho (Hacer): (v.) Present perfect tense signifies an action in the past; **has made, made**
Hueco: (n.) A concave place in a solid body or surface; **hollow, hole, nook, burrow**
Le: (pron.) Unspecified person; **you, him, it, her**
Matinal: (n.) From sunrise to noon; **morning**
Nido: (n.) Place birds lay eggs & shelter young; **nest**
Pajarito: (n.) Two-legged winged animal; little bird
Para: (conj.) Aim or objective; **in order to, so as to**
Pecho: (n.) front part of body; **chest, breast**
Porque: (conj.) For reason that; **because, for**
Rocío: (n.) Water droplets on cool outdoor surfaces; **dew**
Salido—se ha salido (Salir): (v.) Reflexive verb, past action, go away from; **has gone, left**
Si: (conj.) Modifying statement; **if, whether**
Tuviera (Tener): (v.) Imperfect subjunctive tense of verb to have; **he, she, or it had**

why the teacher wants to see them, and I have to speak for my teacher about why she thinks I did something wrong. Sometimes I do not understand what the teacher is saying and I get confused—so my parents get confused . . . that's hard. . . . But you have to find the words right then . . . in that moment.

When you translate a poem, it is different. There is time. The words you use every day could be in a poem—but in a poem, one word can have many meanings . . . but in an everyday conversation you look for the straight meaning. When you are looking at a poem, you have lots of words and many choices. When you are translating for a person, you have to have the right meaning for the right moment. I may not think a poem means the same thing that you think it means—and that is okay.

When students translate, the process is so layered that they build the necessary skills to move the text from the source language to a new language. Students experience poems as having different characteristics and qualities. A poet communicates many concepts, including feelings, emotions, opinions, and perspectives. Language can be subtle, bold, aggressive, full of slang, or very elegant. PIO students learn to consider each word and phrase on its own and within the context of the piece.

One way we help students learn to do literary translation is through a protocol we call the *Translation Circles* (see Figure 3.3). Translation Circles is a metacognitive strategy that seeks to make the process of translation transparent so that students understand their own learning. We use basic, well-known translation techniques during translation circles. However, the main ingredient of this activity is for students to engage in deep conversation about translating the poem.

Translation circles are organized in the following way: A translation circle activity lasts from 30 to 45 minutes. Students begin by working in pairs, first reading the poem a number of times as they look for meaning in the sound of the words, searching for cognates and using a translator's glossary provided on every poem page and a dictionary if they choose. During this phase of the translation process, students are constructing

Figure 3.3. Translation Circle Worksheet: David Huerta—*Formas y Colores*

Poem	Phrase-by-Phrase	Make-it-Flow
Escucha una palabra con atencion cualquier palabra. Es puro sonido pero algo quiere decir:		

a phrase-by-phrase' translation. Once the students complete phrase-by-phrase translations, they form groups of four and create a "make-it-flow" version of their translation. An important design feature of this activity is to have the stages of the translation side by side so the translator can constantly refer to the initial and revised versions of the poem. At this stage, it is important to complete the entire phrase-by-phrase version before making the text flow because the translator needs to grasp the whole meaning before editing her work.

Once students enter the make-it-flow phase of the work, they talk and argue about what could be an accurate representation of the poem in English. The grammatical and syntactical elements are usually straightforward. The most interesting debates happen around the defense of word choice. Although each student may have his own particular translation, the group is expected to present a version to the class with an explanation about their reasons for settling on a particular translation. The conversation presented at the beginning of the chapter was an excerpt from a whole-class discussion in which students were defending their group's translation. Upon completion of the translation process, students write their own poems.

The example in Figure 3.4 demonstrates how Danny, the focal student, took what he experienced during a translation circle and then created his own poem. In this example, Danny is working with the poem "Formas y Colores" by David Huerta. Only part of the poem is shown.

Figure 3.4. Translation Circle of Huerta Poem

David Huerta's Poem	Phrase-by-Phrase	Make-it-Flow
Formas y Colores	Forms and Colors	Forms and Colors
Escucha una palabra con atención,	Listen one word with focus	Listen to a word with attention
cualquier palabra.	Whichever word	Any word
Es puro sonido	Is pure sound	It is pure sound
pero algo quiere decir:	But something it wants to say:	It has something to say:
Naranja, una fruta;	Orange, a fruit	Orange, a fruit
avión, máquina que vuela;	Plane, machine that flies	Airplane, a flying machine
Clodomiro, nombre de una persona;	Clodomiro, name of a person	Clodomiro, a name
Azucena, flor blanca.	Lily, white flower	Azucena, white flower
Ahora vuelve a escucharlas	Now return to listen to them	Now come back and listen again
y encuéntrales formas y colores:	And encounter the forms and colors:	And find the forms and colors:

Many factors came together in order for Danny to complete this work. First, his own knowledge about the Spanish language contributed to his ability to translate this poem. Second, Danny made use of the collective expertise of the group, including both the English and the Spanish speakers. When translating a poem, knowledge of the target language—in this case, English—is as important as knowledge of the original language. Expertise in English enhances the make-it-flow version in terms of sensitivity to syntax, grammar, and the nuances of vocabulary. Finally, Danny and the other students in his translation circle used the translator's glossary.

As is the case with all PIO poem pages, the translator's glossary has various suggestions for words when possible. To understand this point, look at Danny's translation of the word *cualquier*. In the phrase-by-phrase translation, Danny and his partner chose to translate *cualquier* as *whichever*. In the glossary, three possibilities for that word were presented—*whichever, whatever, any*. Once his group reconvened and read and reread the phrase-by-phrase translations, Danny changed his translation of *cualquier* from *whichever* to *any*, deciding that this was a better fit.

Close examination of Danny's translation of the poem reveals that each line has a small but important change—*listen to one word with focus* becomes *listen to a word with attention*. Later in the translation, *Now return to listen to them* becomes *Now come back and listen again*. Because this is poetry, the acute attention to seemingly small details makes a world of difference.

The translator, Danny, is working with David Huerta to bring this work to a wider audience. Through this work, Danny is acquiring important literacy skills. He is learning the value of a close read, a reading of text that demands that the reader read and read again. Danny is learning to read for meaning, for sound, for the lyrical qualities of the piece, in search of correct grammar and syntax and so much more. In the process, he's building vocabulary and securing his right to inhabit the world of translators.

Cycle 2

Cycle 2 emphasizes learning the craft of writing poetry, including lessons about basic poetic elements, such as line and stanza, repetition, refrain, and so on. We work with poetic forms—couplets, quatrains, ballads, odes, haikus, sonnets, and others—and with various forms of figurative language. Teachers choose what kind of poetry they want to focus on based on the interest of their students, points they want to cover, functions of language they want to highlight, or other considerations. Great poems are used as inspirational tools.

Using selected poems as models, students enter into an apprenticeship with master poets. The close encounters that flow from the translation process allow the apprentice (the student) to understand more about how master poets structure their poems, choose one word over another, and infuse a poem with meaning and feeling. PIO students often begin by replicating parts of the model and then moving further and further away from the model to creating their own work. In the example in Figure 3.5 Danny created his own poem by building on the work of David Huerta.

The rhythm and cadence of this poem clearly have their roots in the Huerta poem. For example, Huerta begins with *listen to the word with*

Figure 3.5. Danny's Poem Page

DANNY RYAN MARTINEZ (1998–)
BERKELEY, CA

Words

Listen to each word.
Every word.
Listen for the meaning.
Different meanings.
What is the difference?
Do you hear it?
Words flow
through your mind
like a river.
You choose the way.
You choose the end.
It goes to your mind
It goes to your heart.

I am an X-Box 360 gamer. I enjoy listening to music, cooking, on computer (surfing web), and spending time with my family and friends. I also love playing video games like "Call of Duty," "Left 4 Dead," and things like that. I recently started to skateboard every now and then. Those are my hobbies. I see great artists write about their neighborhoods. This is important for me. I hope to go to college, make a family, and get a job I enjoy.

Translator's Glossary

Choose: (Verb) Decide among a range of options, to make a decision: **elegir, escoger**
Listen: (Verb) Make a conscious effort to hear, pay attention: **eschuchar**
End: Extrimity of object, limit, final part, goal: **fin, al final, por fin, finalizar**
Heart: Blood-pumping organ, basis of emotional life, compassion: **corazón**
Meaning: What something signifies, what somebody wants to express: **significación, intención**
Mind: Seat of thought, way of thinking, state of thought or feeling: **mente, espíritu, opinión**
Word: Meaningful unit of language sounds, brief utterance: **palabra, noticia, dicho**

attention. Danny begins with *listen to each word.* The rest of the poem echoes the Huerta poem but is clearly a creation of this young poet.

Cycle 3

In cycle 3, participants apply what they have learned to create something of consequence. They publish their poems by making their own poem pages. In so doing, they learn the value of selecting the best of their work and the art of revising. In creating their own poem pages, students also make self-portraits, which teaches them that while we are all the same, we are also different—just like a poem. Finally, PIO participants make their own translator's glossaries. Through this process, a new level of understanding emerges about how words and definitions of words function as road maps to understanding.

CONCLUSION

Jerome Bruner (1960) famously said, "Any subject can be taught effectively in some intellectually honest form to any child at any stage of development" (p. 33). To accomplish this, we must first change our thinking and see all young people as intellectually capable. The students represented in this classroom were from the lowest performing school in a district that is infamous for its low academic performance. With ease, they participated and excelled in a program that could easily have been a college course. Why did they succeed? Because we expected that they would succeed and we gave them the tools for success.

Second, we must embrace diversity as an asset. It is diversity that makes us strong (Capra, 1996; Dyson, 1999). School districts across the nation are populated with students who come from homes speaking over 100 different languages. Each language brings its own history, culture, and traditions. Programs like Poetry Inside Out tap into this resource in authentic ways. We know that our traditions, home wisdom, and cultures allow us make sense of the worlds we live in—including school. We make use of what Moll, Amanti, Neff, and González (1992) call "funds of knowledge" through the implementation of curricula that intentionally connect home and school in such a way that everyone benefits. Parents and community members have authentic roles in the classroom. They become essential bridges between home and school, between their cultures and what is being studied. Pedagogy and culture meet in powerful ways to facilitate learning (Gutiérrez, Zepeda, & Castro, 2010).

Third, we need to accept that language is the medium of education and act accordingly (Bruner, 1986; Cazden, 2001). Through participation

in Poetry Inside Out, students come to understand how language functions and, in doing so, they learn how to manipulate language for their
own purposes—to read for understanding and to write to communicate a
myriad of things.

Understanding of context extends beyond what is written on the page.
It is not enough to know the words on the page and move them from one
language to another. To translate poems, you need to know something
about the poets: Who are they? How old are they? Where do they come
from? Why did they write this? The process of translating poetry makes
everything more complex and thereby demands deep thinking about even
the most basic word choices. To comprehend text, students must utilize
clues from the text that come from multiple readings, engage their own
common sense, and take advantage of their personal histories and culture
(Moll et al., 1992). PIO students find that in order for a text to make sense,
"you have to figure it out," because comprehension is both active and con-
structive (Snow, Griffin, & Burns, 2005).

Poetry Inside Out rests on a set of theory-grounded and practice-
elaborated principles that support the notion that literacy is achieved
through active manipulation of parts of language and meanings. Poetry is an
exemplary genre for learning about constructing and displaying meaning.
Engaging in literary translation that leads to the creation of original poetry
powerfully activates and makes use of a myriad of language abilities. PIO
students learn that words are more than sequences of letters and that examining words in context is essential to understanding what a writer is saying.
They speculate about the ways languages differ, especially when dealing
with the challenge of building meaning when words in one language do not
simply map onto words in another. As a 4th-grade PIO student articulated:

> Translation made me use words that I knew but did not say, . . .
> made me think of other words with other people with different
> languages, . . . made me use words that I didn't even know.
> Translation helped me learn how to say what I want to say, . . . how
> to choose my words, and say what I mean for the people who read
> my poems to understand.

There is something profoundly wonderful about translating poetry.
It is impossible, and because it is impossible, it is possible. In a school climate where kids are universally taught that there *is* such a thing as a right
answer, a *yes* or a *no*, it is marvelous and liberating to encounter a course
of study that says, "There are many right answers; just be very clear about
why you are choosing what you are choosing." That is gold, giving kids
the awareness that a well-reasoned answer is more "true" than a so-called
right answer. This is a life skill that serves us all.

Kids are smart. When you give them something important and honest to do, they will engage their brains. When young people see the value of the task, they rise to the occasion. The work simply needs to have consequence—that is, to be an important, necessary, and provocative contribution to the world.

REFERENCES

Bakhtin, M. (1981). The dialogic imagination. In M. Holquist (Ed.), *The dialogic imagination: Four essays by M. Bakhtin* (pp. 259–422). Austin: University of Texas Press.

Bruner, J. (1960). *The process of education*. Cambridge, MA: Harvard University Press.

Bruner, J. (1986) *Actual minds, possible worlds*. Cambridge, MA: Harvard University Press.

Capra, F. (1996). *The web of life: A new scientific understanding of living systems*. New York: Anchor Books.

Cazden, C. (2001). *Classroom discourse: The language of teaching and learning* (2nd ed.). Portsmouth, NH: Heinemann.

Dyson, A. H. (1999). Transforming transfer: Unruly children, contrary texts, and the persistence of the pedagogical order. *Review of Research in Education, 24,* 141–171.

Felstiner, J. (1980). *Translating Neruda: The way to Machu Pichu*. Stanford, CA: Stanford University Press.

Gee, J. (2007). *What video games have to teach us about learning and literacy* (2nd ed.). New York: Palgrave Macmillan Press.

Grossman, E. (2010). *Why translation matters*. New Haven, CT: Yale University Press.

Gutiérrez, K. D., Zepeda, M., & Castro, D. C. (2010). Advancing early literacy learning for all children: Implications of the NELP report for dual-language learners. *Educational Researcher, 39,* 334–339.

Moll, L., Amanti, C., Neff, D., & González, N. (1992). Funds of knowledge for teaching: Using a qualitative approach to connect homes and classrooms. *Theory into Practice, 21,* 132–141.

Rabassa, G. (1989). No two snowflakes are alike: Translation as metaphor. In J. Biguenet & R. Shulte (Eds.), *The craft of translation* (pp. 1–12). Chicago: The University of Chicago Press.

Snow, C., Griffin, P., & Burns, M. S. (Eds.). (2005). *Knowledge to support the teaching of reading*. San Francisco, CA: Jossey-Bass.

Valdés, G. (2003). *Expanding definitions of giftedness: The case of young interpreters from immigrant communities*. Mahwah, NJ: Lawrence Erlbaum.

Weissbort, D. (2006). Postface. In D. Weissbort & A. Eysteinsson (Eds.), *Translation: Theory and practice: A historical reader* (pp. 609–616). Oxford, UK: Oxford University Press.

CHAPTER 4

Becoming Literate in an Inner-City, Whole Language School

Debra Goodman

Views of inner-city children and classrooms as "failing" are pervasive and unquestioned in public debates about education. Educational policies such as No Child Left Behind (NCLB) and Race to the Top increasingly place the blame for social inequity on public education and teacher performance. Underlying these national policies are definitions of literacy as a finite set of skills that can be measured and assigned a number. Challenging these prevalent assumptions about the failure of public education, meta-analyses of test scores and other achievement data have shown consistent and significant gains in literacy in the United States in the past century (Berliner & Biddle, 1996; Kaestle, 1991; Nichols & Berliner, 2007), although there are continued gaps in achievement scores and other indicators of academic success linked to race and social class.

My experiences working with knowledgeable teachers within a collaborative teaching and learning community provide a contrast to public images of rampant illiteracy among inner-city populations. The Dewey Center for Urban Education emerged at a time (late 1980s to mid-1990s) when pedagogical innovations and local school empowerment were encouraged by district policy and state restructuring grants. The Dewey Center was a public school-of-choice with a whole language philosophy. The population, of mixed socioeconomic status (SES), was predominately African American, including neighborhood families living in subsidized housing and citywide families who elected to send children to the school.

Within this school, *whole language* was a learner-centered, inquiry-based "theory-in-practice" (Edelsky, Altwerger, & Flores, 1991) with the premise that language learning is supported in meaningful, purposeful learning experiences that build on the linguistic and cultural repertoire

children bring to school. Naming the school after John Dewey emphasized that whole language was theoretically grounded in a long tradition
of progressive education, addressing concerns about experimental programs in impoverished communities. Dewey wrote, "What the best and
wisest parent wants for his own child, that must the community want for
all of its children. Any other ideal for our schools is narrow and unlovely;
acted upon it destroys our democracy" (Dewey, 1900/1956, p. 7). The
goal of the school leadership team was to create a holistic, democratic
public community school for all children (see Goodman, 2007a).

This chapter focuses on the literacy experiences of Lauren and Marco, both students in Susan Austin's 2nd-grade classroom. Both children
have attended the Dewey Center since kindergarten, working with exemplary whole language teachers. Lauren is a fairly typical reader and
writer in this class, while Marco is one of the less proficient readers and
writers. The students were observed throughout the school day in order to document the complexity of their literacy experiences. Data were
collected through ethnographic observations, recordings, work samples,
and debriefing interviews.

PARTICIPATION IN CLASSROOM LITERACY EVENTS

Observing Lauren and Marco's *participation* in multilayered *literacy events*
sheds light on learning experiences from the learner's perspective. I used
Edelsky's (2006) definition of *literary events* as social activities involving
a *written text used as a text* where the child is a *participant*. Documenting
children's *participation* in literacy events moves beyond reading and writing proficiencies to include literacy development across social roles (e.g.,
reader, writer, listener, speaker, observer) and meaning making across modalities (e.g., language, art, music, movement). Within these observable
literacy events, Marco and Lauren experience and come to know the social
literacy practices used in this classroom and the larger community. Table
4.1 summarizes Marco's and Lauren's *literacy activities* (social practices) as
they participated in the 69 *literacy events* occurring on the 2 sample days
selected for this study.

As a participant observer for 3 years, I knew Marco and Lauren were
immersed in a richly literate classroom community. I was still surprised by
the breadth and depth of literacy events in their daily classroom lives. On
one day in March, Marco participates directly in 30 literacy events involving
27 texts. A week later, Lauren participates in 37 events involving 29 texts.
At this rate, over the 180-day school year, it is likely that Lauren and Marco
experienced well over 4,000 texts within more than 5,000 literacy events.
As participants in these events, Marco and Lauren are learning to read and

Table 4.1. Literacy Activities Within Literacy Events

Literacy Activity	Occurrences*	
Reading or writing literature	29/69 events	43%
Reading or listening to a book or poem	(18/69 events)	26%
Writing or observing classmate writing a literature text	(6/69 events)	9%
Preparing (materials, composing) to read or write literature	(5/69 events)	7%
Reading and writing in pursuit of other social activity	(25/69 events)	36%
Recording or reporting information	(17/69 events)	25%
Planning, organizing, or regulating activities and behavior	(8/69 events)	11%
Talking about a text†	(13/69 events)	19%
Doing a school "exercise"	(8/69 events)	11%
Writing (or pasting) answers on math worksheet	3	
Participating in guided lesson with a math sheet	3	
Circling, labeling, or coloring targeted responses (phonics)	2	

*Percentages provide a *sense* of patterns and frequency; identification of specific events is not exact, and six events cross categories.
†Talk occurs in most events. Here the *primary activity* is to *discuss* a text rather than read or write.

write. At the same time, they are developing understandings of cultural literacy practices—how people use literacy within particular social activities.

In a program called Books to Go, children take turns reading to the class after rehearsing at home with their families. On this day, Marco and his classmates sit on an area rug listening to Amber (a fellow classmate) read the nonfiction book *Snakes* (Demuth, 1993). Amber reads:

> "There are over 2,400 different kinds of snakes in the world." Children gasp and mime amazement. Amber continues, "Snakes slither and slide on their belly." Marco places his hands in front of him, forming a snake's head. He makes a slithering motion with his upper body. When Amber shows the picture, Marco looks at it closely and makes a comment to Jackie. Amber reads, "The giant of all snakes is the anaconda."

As he listens to Amber, Marco is actively engaged in meaning making involving art as well as oral and written language. Using the motion of the snake, Marco expresses his parallel text construction. Although *Snakes* is an informational text, Marco's body language suggests the lived-through aesthetic experience Rosenblatt (1978) describes as "evoking a poem" (p. 48). Informal conversations during the read-aloud explored conceptual information.

> Amber reads, "Snakes shed their skin two or three times a year."
> Marco looks at the picture and says, "He changing." He looks at
> Susan, "Miss Austin, why he changing?" Ms. Austin says, "Cause
> he's growing. He doesn't fit his skin anymore."

Participating as a listener, Marco gains access to complex language and concepts with a text he could not read independently. When we talked about the anaconda later, Marco said, "It's longer than a school bus," recalling the metaphoric language of the book. As he listens, Marco observes multiple demonstrations of meaning making and learning processes. When Alyssa hears how often snakes shed their skin, she says, "If a snake were 7 years old, it would shed its skin 20 times." Ms. Austin asks, "How did you figure that out?" and Alyssa responds, "I just counted by threes." This vignette exemplifies the learner-centered nature of this classroom. Children and teacher explore a text together that is connected with a thematic inquiry into the rain forest.

In Ms. Austin's classroom, work times were typically organized in workshops where children—guided by a menu of assignments and invitations—were able to select materials and topics, organize time and space, and work collaboratively with other learners. On this morning, Lauren has completed her math assignment and is considering what to do next when her friend Alyssa stops by:

> Alyssa plays with Lauren's hair twists, pulling them down and
> watching them spring back. Lauren asks, "Do you know what Alyssa
> means? My mama got a *name book.*" Alyssa says, "I don't know what
> it means, but I know what Lauren means." When Lauren challenges
> her, Alyssa says, "It means soft and gentle and meddlesome and
> [unclear]." Lauren says, "No, it doesn't!" She tells Alyssa what her
> name means. Alyssa repeats Lauren's definition and laughs. Lauren
> says, "Yeah, I got a *name book.* So you're a liar."

In this playful conversation, Lauren uses a text as a reference to prove that she is right and Alyssa is "a liar." Although not typical school texts, *name books* appeared to be familiar to both girls. The girls understood that names have symbolic meanings, and Alyssa's invented definition uses adjectives to characterize her friend. This "unofficial" literacy event (Dyson,

1997) brings the children's repertoire of family literacy practices into the classroom. Lauren and Marco both demonstrate meaning making and symbolic thinking within a classroom community that offers rich, meaningful learning experiences.

BECOMING READERS AND WRITERS

The class has just finished a read-aloud requiring "a lot of listening energy," so Susan and the students negotiate a "quiet reading and writing time" as a break before book club presentations.

> Lauren and Katherine settle on pillows at the front of the room with nine books scattered between them. Lauren begins reading *Dragon's Fat Cat* (Pilkey, 1992), an illustrated chapter book. Ms. Austin says, "Hurry and get what you [need]. Everybody has to find a spot quickly." Katherine glances up, but Lauren continues reading. Katherine leans over to listen to Lauren before opening her own book. Nearby, Sharonda is reading *If a Tree Could Talk* (Williams, 1994b). Sharonda asks, "Does this say *when*?" Lauren goes over to assist Sharonda.

During this brief observation, Lauren and her friends demonstrate agency in selecting books, organizing their learning space, and participating in *sustained reading*. All three girls are engaged with books before "Quiet Reading and Writing" officially begins. Lauren's focused attention and oral miscues (e.g., "stinky" for "smelly") indicate that she is constructing meaning. When Sharonda comes across unfamiliar text, she seeks out Lauren's expertise. Lauren and Kristen select short chapter books, while Sharonda reads predictable song and poetry books. Although books and readers are not "leveled" in this classroom, each girl selects appropriate materials and reads with confidence and proficiency. While Lauren is reading with her friends, Marco is listening to Jackie talk about her writing:

> Jackie says they are using "book names" instead of real names. When I ask why, she says, "It was kinda simple. We didn't want our real names to be in the book. In biography books we want our names to be in them." Marco shows me a handmade book with the title "Pictionary" on the cover. "I'm making a dictionary," he says.

The children's talk indicates their understandings about the nature of texts and genre. In this active learning community, all children appear to be readers and writers, and children and teacher share their expertise.

Marco's pattern of observing demonstrations of readers and writers around him continues during the Silent Writing workshop.

Marco and David sit side by side working on their "autobiographies," drawing pictures and occasionally sharing their work. Jackie shows me an illustration in a book she is writing about dinosaurs. Looking across the table, Marco gasps and rolls his eyes back, miming fear. I say to Jackie, "You're into dinosaurs now, huh?" Marco says, "Yep. They got . . . they go'n make a big book." Jackie shows me *Digging Up Dinosaurs* by Aliki (1988). Turning the pages, she talks about paleontology. Marco claps his hands, applauding Jackie's talk. Marco tells David, "They been working on that book about 20 days." Marco looks up from his drawing as Jackie talks about how fossils are found. When Jackie shows a picture of dinosaur teeth, Marco gasps. Jackie says, "They have sharp teeth." "Rats have sharp teeth," Marco comments.

During this writing workshop, Marco draws, orally composes, and writes a sentence in his autobiography. But he also enjoys rich opportunities to listen in and observe *demonstrations* of what it means to be a writer. Impressed with Jackie's talk, he applauds and makes connections with his own experiences. His side comments show his awareness of his classmates' writing.

During Silent Writing a week later, Lauren takes out her handmade picture book, *My Best Friend's Little Baby Sister*. She has been writing this book for several weeks, pulling it out whenever she has time to write. Lauren reads the last page aloud to me:

> "When we had got into the car, we saw my best friend and her mother and her baby sister. We had to drop them off because her mother had got off early. And I haven't finished this part."
>
> I ask what she's planning next. Lauren says, "I'm going to write about when they had got into the house and they had called my mother."
>
> "So you already know what's coming next?"
>
> "Mhm," Lauren continues. "And they gonna have a sleepover party."
>
> "And then what's gonna happen?"
>
> "Then I think . . ." Lauren begins to smile. "And their mother went on a trip. And the baby had stayed at home with them. And she was a bad baby."

Even before she starts writing, Lauren is thinking about her story and composing upcoming events. Her smile as she discusses the "bad baby" indicates she is enjoying the creative process and is entertained by her own humor.

Ms. Austin begins counting backwards, signaling the start of Silent Writing. Lauren writes, "Wen tey gat in thr heme they het call my mommy." Ms. Austin says, "Zero. Everyone should be writing now." Lauren is lying across the table, totally engrossed in her story. She says, *"and ask can her daughter spend the night"* and writes,"and ask can her dar sem aen neyt." She reads over her page and says, "My mother said . . ." She writes, "My mommy sed yes." As she writes, she says the words again slowly, "My . . . mommy . . . said . . . yes." Lauren looks over the page and draws a picture under the written text. She shows me her picture and says, "This the telephone cord."

Lauren takes a while to get down to work. However, she works steadily throughout the writing time. The writing is not always smooth. She stops to think, looks in on her friends' work, and shares her progress. The workshop provides Lauren with time, materials, and choices that allow her to develop her own writing process. I asked Lauren if she remembered *thinking about the words she wants to use when she is writing:*

> When I went, "I couldn't believe my eyes," I put her mouth open like that. Lauren opens her mouth wide, miming surprise, while pointing at a picture. I ask if she sees a picture in her mind while she is writing and she agrees, "Mhm."

Later Lauren adds:

> "When I said that I was getting up really early in the morning . . . *[She shows me the page.]* This is her mother's purse. And I didn't have room . . . to draw the picture and have them when they kissed their mother in the kitchen."
>   I ask, "What did you want to do with the picture?"
>   Lauren explained, "I wanted their mother to be in the kitchen cooking their lunch."
>   "So you just showed her leaving with her purse."
>   "Mhm," Lauren agreed, "and their lunch boxes."

Lauren's description of how she uses images and words to compose her story illustrates a distinction between the "author's text" in her mind and the picture book developing on the pages. Lauren pictures the mother in the kitchen preparing lunch when the girls come in and kiss their mother good-bye. Lauren represents this composition with an illustration, consisting of a purse and two lunch boxes, along with the written text, "We had to get up really early. Mama had to pack our lunch so when we eat at school." When she writes a piece called *My Friend's Little Baby Sister,* she includes many elements of a well-constructed narrative. Lauren's opening focuses immediately on the story plot. ("I saw my friend and couldn't believe my eyes.") She develops characters through dialogue and action and includes suspense in anticipating the moment of finally meeting the new baby. She introduces "complicating action" (Labov, 1972) when the children are left alone with the baby. She writes with realism and humor. Lauren's experiences as a reader influence her author's voice and the literary quality of her work. When asked what she liked about 2nd grade, Lauren said, "I love Miss Austin's books." When Lauren was a 1st-grader, I asked her about the sister that pops up in so many of her stories, and she informed me that she didn't have a sister. "That's fiction," she said. Lauren is constructing written language conventions as she writes. Her use of complex sentence structures with multiple clauses indicates her intuitive understandings of syntax. Invented spellings allow Lauren to express her ideas using creative wordings, and through writing she constructs understandings of spelling patterns.

My analysis of Marco's and Lauren's activities as participants in literacy events (see Table 4.2) shows both children engaged in meaning making across a range of collaborative literacy experiences. This parity in participation is possible because of the supportive learning community and *extended* opportunities to engage in meaningful literacy experiences in whole-class, small-group, and workshop settings.

Within this learning community, Marco often seeks support from other learners and makes use of resources such as listening, illustrations, movement, and dialogue for meaning making. During a book club meeting, Marco read excerpts from *What's in My Pocket?* (Williams, 1994a) and used the predictable pattern to write his own contributions to the group project. When I asked how Marco *first learned* to read this text, he described a shared reading

Table 4.2. Marco's and Lauren's Activities Related to Reading and Writing Literature

What Marco Does on Marco's Day	What Lauren Does on Lauren's Day
Official Class Activities	
Listens to books read aloud	Listens to books read aloud
Listens to choral reading	Choral reading/book club presentation
Illustrates autobiography	Illustrates fiction book
Starts to write autobiography page	Writes three pages of fiction book
Makes symbolic outline for writing	Selects books to read
Reads book excerpts while writing	Reads book to self during silent reading
Unofficial Activities	
Listens to Jackie talk about her writing (and reading)	Reads her own book to Amber
	Assists Sharonda, Kristen with unfamiliar texts

with the other children in his book club. As Smith (1988) describes, when we invite learners to "join the literacy club," more experienced members assist novice readers as they gain expertise. Lauren needed no special invitation or motivation. All she needed was an opportunity to read and write and learn. At one time I might have considered Lauren an independent learner, but I have come to see that the social milieu of reading and writing within a community creates a space for learners like Lauren to thrive.

In the following section, I explore the pedagogical practices and conditions of learning that Susan Austin developed to promote engagement and scaffold literacy development.

A CLASSROOM PEDAGOGY AND CURRICULUM THAT SUPPORTS LITERACY LEARNING

In the examples above, both Marco and Lauren approach learning with confidence and agency—what Cambourne (1995) describes as "engagement." According to Cambourne, engagement occurs when learners (1) find the task "doable," (2) see relevance to their daily lives, and (3) "feel safe to make mistakes without reprisal" (p. 186). In the following sections, I consider learning experiences in this classroom that promoted engagement and scaffolded literacy development.

Organizing for Learning

In this classroom, time and space was organized to promote meaning making and learning. Over 75% of Marco's day was devoted to class meetings and workshops where children engaged directly in learning experiences (Goodman, 2007b). While 25% of class time involved transitions (cleanup or setup), more than half of transitional time was available for work projects. In the example above, by the time Quiet Reading and Writing officially starts, Lauren is busy reading and Sharonda is on her third book. Within the workshop structure, students select topics, texts, and materials, maximizing opportunities for reading and writing and minimizing interruptions.

During Marco's day, little class time was devoted to procedural instructions (8 minutes) or disciplinary interruptions (3 minutes). In the workshop, the teacher has time to work with students individually and in small groups. During Silent Writing, Ms. Austin spoke with Marco about his autobiography project, and Marco had extended opportunities to engage with his teacher during a small-group math lesson. The only time I observed Marco waiting was after book club cleanup, when he sat for a few moments crooning a popular tune into the recorder microphone.

Meaningful, Purposeful Experiences

Marco and Lauren were *immersed* in authentic and purposeful learning experiences with extended and varied *demonstrations* of meaning making, essential conditions in families of young children learning to talk (Cambourne, 1995). Ninety percent of the documented literacy events Marco and Lauren experienced involved *meaningful* literacy events relevant in children's daily lives (see Table 4.1). Marco and Lauren were immersed in children's literature (nonfiction trade books, magazines, and song and poetry books); in events involving science investigations, literary discussions, and responses; and in enjoyment or self-expression. In these 2 days, literature experiences included choral reading, reading with a friend, reading independently, reading excerpts as a reference for writing, writing illustrated books, shared writing for book club, selecting or browsing texts, and outlining written work.

Literacy events involving "instrumental texts" such as labels, charts, and lists were also pervasive, as teacher and children used reading and writing for planning class activities, navigating learning experiences, recordkeeping, and so on. At the beginning of a math workshop, Ms. Austin explains the math choices as she lists them on the board.

> Children signal to each other, silently planning out their activities. Marco gestures to Jonathan. Ms. Austin says, "Okay, let me read the names of the kids who are going to stay with me. . . . If I don't call your name, you know you can make choices."

As Ms. Austin *writes a list* and later *reads names,* the children attend closely. Children easily negotiate "math choices" because these are familiar literacy practices (listing, labeling, recording, etc.) in children's families and social worlds outside of school. Literacy practices such as "finding your writing folder" are so deeply imbedded in the overall learning experience that reading and writing become transparent. However, Ms. Austin was highly aware of the significance of these literacy practices for the children's literacy development. Charts, poems, signs, and children's work hung on the walls, chalkboard, windows, and wires across the room. These are not pretty bulletin board displays, but texts that represent and inform daily experiences. Guidelines for "peacekeepers" (for example, "Be Kind") establish expectations for behavior, a calendar records dates and weather, the "missing persons graph" tracks absences, and so on. Meaningful, purposeful experiences build on home literacy repertoires and engage children in reading and writing with a focus on conceptual learning.

Dual Curriculum

Ken Goodman (1986) describes whole language as a "dual curriculum" where children learn meaning-making *processes* within *content-focused* learning experiences. As they engage with content, children articulate, share, and expand understandings of concepts and texts.

> Amber reads, "It grabs it with its needle sharp teeth, then it . . ."
> "Swallows it," Marco whispers loudly as Amber pauses. Ms. Austin says, "Marco has a prediction. Say it out loud, Marco."
> "Swallows it," Marco says. Amber continues to read, ". . . sinks its fangs into the mouse."

When Amber finished reading the page, Susan explained that Marco's *prediction* made sense with what came before it, but not with what came after. As an experienced "kidwatcher" (Owocki & Goodman, 2002), Susan picked up Marco's whispered comment and highlighted his thinking for the class, providing an impromptu *reading strategy lesson.* She used the term *prediction* to *make explicit* the effective meaning-making strategy that Marco used intuitively.

This example illustrates underlying patterns of the dual curriculum in this classroom. The students are listening to a nonfiction book and exploring concepts related to a classroom inquiry. Reading and writing (as well as math and other thought systems) are *tools for learning* rather than school subjects. To make a finer point, children's literature is not being used to teach reading. Instead, engaging with literature and concepts compels children to read, write, talk, listen, view, draw, and think.

As children engage with concepts and texts, they are socially constructing understandings of how reading and writing works. In the "math choices" example above, Susan demonstrated the process of making a list and also demonstrated how members of this community use lists to organize their work. In orchestrating this language-learning experience, Susan took familiar family literacy practices and extended them to school literacy. She attended closely to underlying meaning-making processes and documented linguistic understandings. Through skillful kidwatching, children's *implicit* language and thinking processes and strategies were made *explicit* and available to all learners.

In contrast with the current trend of leveling readers as well as texts, Marco particularly benefited from engaging with the readers and writers around him. During a debriefing interview, Marco articulated a meaning-focused view of the reading process and confidently described meaning-making strategies that went beyond his current abilities as a reader (Goodman, 2005). When I returned to visit Marco in 4th grade, the classroom was organized in straight rows and Marco was isolated near the teacher's desk. His reading proficiency had improved, but he approached reading with little confidence or excitement.

These connections between home and school literacy are difficult when school literacy events are *exercises* (Edelsky, 2006) meant primarily for instruction. Although rare in this classroom, a few "exercise" experiences occurred in preparation for a standardized test. The nature of these experiences is revealed by the children's talk. When Lauren glues the last square down on a math worksheet, she announces, "Got it. I got all of them right." When Marco completes a phonics exercise involving circling long-*o* words, he shows his paper to David and says, "I did all those." The focus of these learning experiences is *accuracy* and *completion*. By contrast, after Lauren finishes her math worksheet, she pulls out her handmade book and offers to read it to Amber, saying, "Let me read this book to you." Here Lauren indicates she is writing a meaningful text worthy of sharing with her friend.

CONCLUSION

In this classroom, children's home language and linguistic and cultural repertoires are valued and made visible. Lauren's home language, including features of African American Language, is a resource for writing complex texts and elaborate stories. Children's inventions and approximations are celebrated in much the same way that we celebrate children's early language development as they are learning to talk. When Susan highlights Marco's prediction, she advocates for reading as a meaning-construction process but also advocates for Marco (a less proficient student) as a meaning maker.

Brian Street (1995) writes that "reading and writing are located within the real social and linguistic practices that give them meaning" (p. 3). Language learning occurs as children participate in learning experiences as scientists, historians, geographers, artists, and so on. In the examples above, collaborative learning experiences, mixed-ability groupings, and opportunities to talk and reflect highlight children's abilities, prior experiences, cultural knowledge, and expertise. Observing children in "real social and linguistic practices" makes visible knowledge and expertise that is often overlooked in "failing schools" when development is evaluated by test scores and statistical data.

Lauren's and Marco's learning experiences in Susan Austin's classroom grew out of 6 years of curriculum development within a professional learning community of teachers and families. This school change process was supported by a district focus on empowered schools and a small state restructuring grant ($300,000 over 3 years). As national and state policies shifted away from locally empowered schools, this urban district abandoned community-led innovation and returned to a skills-based reading program, promoted by its publisher as "proven to be especially effective with students who come from disadvantaged backgrounds, have limited proficiency in English, or have special needs. Lesson plans are highly structured." Although produced by the same publishing conglomerate, literature-based programs are reserved for "districts where students begin formal schooling with basic skills acquired at home or in academic preschools" (Shannon, 2007, p. 179).

In the current climate of national core standards and devastating teacher accountability measures, these close observations of how whole language learning experiences support learning and scaffold literacy development might almost appear irrelevant. However, I continue to advocate for rich opportunities for all children rather than special programs for "disadvantaged" children. If our goal is to address inequity, it's critical that we continue to work to create spaces for teachers, children, and families to negotiate meaningful learning experiences in the classroom—particularly in urban districts.

According to Cambourne (1995), parents assume their children will learn to talk, and "expectations" for language learning at home are universal. However, parents and teachers may not have these same unquestioned expectations as children are learning to read and write. In the examples above, all children are expected to be learners. At an authors' celebration at the end of the year, Mrs. Green (mother of Lauren's friend Kristen) shared her experiences with this classroom community. She said, "My daughter has been in whole language from the beginning. . . . It's a joy to be around a child who has a whole language experience. Because learning for them is a joy. It's an adventure, and they're always coming up with something new. It's never the drudgery of 'I have to do this, we have to do this.' It's the excitement of what I can learn—how this applies to my life."

REFERENCES

Aliki. (1988). *Digging up dinosaurs*. New York: Harper & Row.

Berliner, D., & Biddle, B. (1996). *Manufactured crisis: Myths, fraud and attack on America's public schools*. Boston: Addison-Wesley.

Cambourne, B. (1995). Toward an educationally relevant theory of literacy learning: Twenty years of inquiry. *The Reading Teacher, 49*(3), 182–190.

Demuth, P. (1993). *Snakes*. New York: Grosset & Dunlap.

Dewey, J. (1956). *The child and the curriculum/The school and society*. Chicago: University of Chicago Press. (Original work published 1900)

Dyson, A. H. (1997). *Writing superheroes: Contemporary childhood, popular culture and classroom literacy*. New York: Teachers College Press.

Edelsky, C. (2006). *With literacy and justice for all: Rethinking the social in language and education*. Mahwah, NJ: Erlbaum.

Edelsky, C., Altwerger, B., & Flores, B. (1991). *Whole language: What's the difference*. Portsmouth, NH: Heinemann.

Goodman, D. (2005) Why Marco can read: Becoming literate in a classroom community. *Language Arts, 86*(6), 431–440.

Goodman, D. (2007a). The whole language movement in Detroit—A teacher's story: Part two. In M. Taylor (Ed.), *Whole language teaching, whole-hearted practice: Looking back, looking forward* (pp. 45–53). New York: Peter Lang.

Goodman, D. (2007b). Creating social spaces for learning in a whole language classroom. *Talking Points, 18*(2), 5–10.

Goodman, K. (1986). *What's whole in whole language*. Portsmouth, NH: Heinemann.

Kaestle, C. F. (1991). *Literacy in the United States*. New Haven, CT: Yale University Press.

Labov, W. (1972). *Language in the inner city: Studies in Black English vernacular*. Philadelphia, PA: University of Pennsylvania Press.

Nichols, S., & Berliner, D. (2007). *Collateral damage: How high-stakes testing corrupts American schools*. Cambridge, MA: Harvard Educational Press.

Owocki, G., & Goodman, Y. (2002). *Kidwatching: Documenting children's literacy development*. Portsmouth, NH: Heinemann.

Pilkey, D. (1992). *Dragon's fat cat*. New York: Orchard.

Rosenblatt, L. (1978). *The reader, the text, the poem: The transactional theory of the literary work*. Carbondale: Southern Illinois University Press.

Shannon, P. (2007). *Reading against democracy: The broken promises of reading instruction*. Portsmouth, NH: Heinemann.

Smith, F. (1988). *Joining the literacy club: Further essays into education*. Portsmouth, NH: Heinemann.

Street, B. V. (1995). *Social literacies: Critical approaches to literacy in development, ethnography, and education*. London and New York: Longman.

Williams, R. L. (1994a). *What's in my pocket?* Cypress, CA: Creative Teacher Press.

Williams, R. L. (1994b). *If a tree could talk*. Cypress, CA: Creative Teacher Press.

CHAPTER 5

Promoting High Expectations with Collaborative Strategic Reading

Janette Klingner
Alison Boardman
Subini Annamma

In this chapter, we focus on how teachers promote students' reading comprehension, content learning, and higher level thinking through Collaborative Strategic Reading (CSR). CSR is a high-expectation, evidence-based practice found to be effective in diverse, heterogeneous classrooms in grades 3 through 8 (Klingner, Vaughn, & Boardman, 2007). Over the last 2 years, we have taught middle school reading and language arts teachers to use CSR (Vaughn et al., 2011). Our goals in this chapter are to briefly describe CSR and provide numerous examples from our recent research of what reading comprehension instruction looks like in culturally, linguistically, and socioeconomically diverse middle school classrooms in which the teachers are implementing CSR and promoting a high-expectation curriculum for all students. Our examples include students' discussions and teachers' feedback to students, and we address how teachers set up classrooms to facilitate students' active participation in CSR lessons. But first, let us describe what it means for teachers to have high expectations.

HIGH-EXPECTATION TEACHERS

Teachers who have high expectations do not let "just okay" be good enough. If one approach does not seem to be effective, they try something else and keep trying until they succeed. Failure is not an option. In other words, they have high expectations not only for their students, but also for themselves, and a strong sense of efficacy (Fuller, Wood, Rapoport, &

Dornbusch, 1982). Teachers who have high expectations are in tune with their students and aware of what they understand and when they need more support. They base instructional decisions on assessment information. They design activities so that all students are involved and all activities support students' self-regulation (Bohn, Roehrig, & Pressley, 2004; Rubie-Davies, 2007).

Teachers also communicate expectations to students through interactions that occur with the whole class, within small groups, and with individuals. This high-expectations talk falls into categories such as emphasizing effective teaching (e.g., providing information, strategy instruction, summarizing), providing timely, targeted feedback, avoiding sending negative messages regarding student ability, conveying a can-do attitude (Blair, Rupley, & Nichols, 2007), asking questions, communicating procedures, managing the learning environment, and encouraging students to engage in high-level thinking about what they are learning. Teachers can be high- or low-expectation teachers (or somewhere in between), depending in part on the nature of these interactions (e.g., Bohn et al., 2004; Rubie-Davies, 2007; Topping & Ferguson, 2005).

COLLABORATIVE STRATEGIC READING

CSR facilitates reading comprehension for students of various achievement levels, struggling readers, students with learning disabilities (LD), and English Language Learners (ELLs) in diverse general education classrooms as well as in resource rooms (Klingner, Vaughn, Dimino, Schumm, & Bryant, 2001). CSR was originally adapted from reciprocal teaching (Palincsar & Brown, 1984) by adding strategies designed to make it more appropriate for English Language Learners and content learning, and by incorporating many features associated with effective instruction (e.g., collaborative group work, interactive dialogue, procedural strategies). CSR addresses four prevailing educational challenges: how can teachers promote the following:

1. Students' reading comprehension, particularly of discipline-specific expository text
2. Text-based content learning of ELLs, students with LD, and struggling readers
3. Students' engagement in high-level academic discussions
4. ELLs' language acquisition through academic discourse with peers

CSR helps students develop metacognitive awareness and learn specific strategies associated with enhanced reading comprehension, including the following:

- Brainstorming (i.e., connecting with prior knowledge), predicting, and setting a purpose for reading (*preview*)
- Monitoring understanding and taking steps to figure out unknown words or confusing ideas (*click and clunk*)
- Determining the main idea of a section of text (*get the gist*)
- Generating teacher-like questions and reviewing key ideas in the text (*wrap up*)

The teacher instructs students on how to implement the strategies using modeling, think-alouds, and guided practice.

Once students have developed some proficiency in using the strategies, they learn how to use them while working together in small cooperative groups of about four students. In these groups, each student plays an important role (e.g., leader, clunk expert, gist expert, and question expert). Cue cards help students learn their roles and provide the support needed for students of varying achievement levels to be successful. Students take turns reading the day's text aloud. They record their brainstorms, predictions, clunks (i.e., words or ideas they do not understand), gists (i.e., main idea statements), questions, and review statements in individual CSR learning logs. Jotting down their ideas before discussing them provides students with the "wait time" needed to formulate their thoughts, thus increasing participation and the quality of students' conversations. Students focus on learning the content covered in the reading and helping their peers learn it as well. CSR emphasizes the effective application of comprehension strategies as well as meaningful discussions about text content (see Klingner et al., 2007).

CSR provides students with multiple opportunities to engage in higher level critical thinking—an important aspect of promoting high expectations for students. Peer discourse can serve a catalytic function, stimulating cognitive development as students share their ideas with one another and engage in mutual problem solving (Cazden, 1988; Piaget, 1950). With CSR, we encourage an active exchange of ideas, with multiple contributions by students.

CSR small-group discussions may be particularly beneficial for ELLs, students with LD, and struggling readers who tend to be marginalized during whole-class discussions. Moreover, ELLs and students with LD typically receive fewer chances to engage in higher level discussions than do their peers (August & Shanahan, 2006, regarding ELLs; Ellis, 2002, regarding students with LD). Yet ELLs and students with LD should be provided with more, rather than less, frequent opportunities to engage in higher level thinking. Ellis (2002) refers to this as "watering up the curriculum." This is one of the principles of Sheltered English Instruction for ELLs (Echevarria, Vogt, & Short, 2004).

Examples of Students' Discourse in CSR Groups

The following examples of "student talk" exemplify high expectations by demonstrating students using critical thinking as they state their positions and defend their ideas. In the first excerpt, students are in an 8th-grade language arts class in a diverse, semi-urban school with about half of the students receiving free or reduced-price lunches.

Example 1. In this first example, the students are trying to agree on the main idea of a section of text about Frederick Douglass. Student 1 offers a gist:

Student 1: Frederick Douglass married a White woman and died from a stroke, after . . .

Student 2: *[interrupting]* You've gotta put something about . . . [how] over the whole entire passage he stayed a strong abolitionist.

Student 3: *[supporting student 2]* Marrying a White person, or being with somebody White, it wasn't the main idea.

Student 1: Yeah, but he . . .

Student 2: It's a key point, but it's not the main idea!

Teacher: Why are we yelling at each other? You guys are sitting right next to each other.

Student 4: It's a heated controversy!

Teacher: So, well, let's see . . . You guys all agree who Frederick Douglass is. We have three people saying the most important thing is he married a White woman and that race lines can be crossed, right? However, we have two of you saying that the most important thing of this section is how he remained true to his cause even after the war, because he knew the fight was not over.

Student 4: *[pause]* We need to mix 'em together.

Student 3: Okay, well, like, we've already said that he's an abolitionist . . . in like the last two gists. And now in this one, what is important, like, it *is* important that he married a White woman.

Student 2: But it's very key that he stayed an abolitionist after the Civil War. He could have just been like, "Oh, my job's done!"

Student 4: Here's the milk. Here's the cereal. Put the milk and cereal together.

Student 1: Yep, see . . .

Student 3: Douglass tried bridging the racial gap after the Civil War . . . Is that good?

Later, during a whole-class wrap, the teacher asked the group to explain how they came up with their gist statement.

Student 1: Okay, so half of our group had an idea that the main idea of this passage was that Douglass helped kind of bridge the White and Black gap, and like put it together. And then the other half of our group thought . . . that the main important idea of the passage was that Douglass still stayed an abolitionist and stayed true to his cause after the Civil War.

Teacher: So, guys, those two things are huge, because they made great points. And, yeah, I could say one is better than the other. I could have said that, but then [student 1] defended her stance by saying, look, that was unheard of back then, you don't do that. So it's huge, it might even be symbolic of what he did his whole life. [Student 2] said, "no, no, no." That's just a nice little happy ending; however, he stayed true to his cause, even after they won. Which is most important? [Student 4], what did we decide we had to do?

Student 4: Mix them together, put the milk [*laughing*] with the cereal.

Teacher: Put the milk in the cereal [*laughing*]. That's right, baby! Yeah! So, and they did that, and what did you guys come up with?

Student 2: Okay, we came up with, "Douglass continued to bridge the racial gap after the Civil War."

Example 2. The next example is from a different language arts class, this time with 7th-graders in an urban school in which more than 90% of the students are Latino, almost all receive free or reduced-price lunches, and many are English Language Learners. Students are on the last CSR strategy—Review—and are stating what they think the most important idea in the passage is. The passage is about how the polar icecap is melting.

Student 4: [*reading from cue card*] Write one or two of the most important ideas from this passage.

Student 3: I put the temperatures are increasing so the perennial ice is melting and that perennial ice is that really thick, thick ice . . .

Student 4: I kind of said the same thing as her, that the perennial ice is melting and that's like really important because the ice has been frozen for many, many years.

Student 3: And that it's, like, really thick ice and it shouldn't be melting.

Student 4: Which explains that it is really hitting high temperatures.

Student 1: I put that the temperatures are higher than their usual, which has brought lots of damage like the annual ice, which is like not normal because that's the ice that has been there, too.

Student 4: Are you finished, [student name]?

Student 2 (a student with LD):   I put that the temperatures are increasing and are causing the thick ice to melt.

Student 4: And so it is a very important thing that the article said.

Student 1: Because there would be a lot of damage to us, too.

Student 4: Uh-huh, and also, for me, it's really big, too, because if that just happened in a year, can you imagine what would happen in another year and 3 years, it would all be gone.

Student 1: It's like, an unusual cold has raised hopes, so maybe they will recover it, but maybe not.

Student 4: [overlapping] It's like a 50/50 chance.

Student 1: Maybe it will start to break again and maybe . . .

Student 4: [overlapping] Maybe it will not.

Student 1: Like 75%, maybe, 'cause this was 2008, so, 65, and we're 2009.

Student 3: We don't know what has happened already.

Student 1: We don't know that we're causing this.

Toward the end of this discussion, the teacher approached the group and sat and listened. It is notable that she did not speak and that the students did not interrupt their conversation upon her arrival. The students understood that this was their discussion. They appeared engrossed in providing evidence for why they believed their ideas were important.

THE TEACHER'S ROLE IN PROMOTING HIGH EXPECTATIONS DURING GROUP WORK

While a body of literature is emerging related to the qualities and characteristics of effective and high-expectation teachers (e.g., Berliner, 2004; Bohn et al., 2004; Rubie-Davies, 2007), less is known about how to develop these characteristics in existing teachers. In our work with CSR, we promote both high expectations through the CSR instructional model and professional development and classroom support focused on the effective implementation of CSR. We provide teachers with instructional tools that foster high-expectation teaching. In fact, we have observed teachers who promote high expectations during CSR instruction but do not foster the same quality of thinking and learning when they are not teaching CSR. We follow with examples of the ways teachers communicate high expectations to students during CSR instruction through the use of the CSR routine, the nature of their feedback, and emphasis on high expectations during coaching.

Providing Specific Feedback

A critical component of the teacher's role is the type of feedback that is provided to students. Effective feedback is specific, communicates where students are in their learning, and sets goals for where they need to go (Hattie & Timperley, 2007). In the following example, a 7th-grade language arts teacher sits with a group for a mere 30 seconds before speaking, but in that time she reads students' gists written in their learning logs, listens to the discussion, and decides what type of feedback is needed.

Teacher: Let's go back to your gist—that last section. So, if we look at that last section. What is it talking about?
[Students and teacher discuss the content of the section.]
Teacher: Into clothes, right? So, instead of ending up in the landfill, instead of ending up in the trash, we can use those to make clothes. So, your gist should reflect that.
Student 3: Okay.
Teacher: Do you need to say what the byproducts are in your gist?
Student 2: No.
Teacher: No, you can just use the word, *byproducts,* from the article, right? So, do you have that in your gist? Who has that in their gist?
Student 3: I have the names.
Teacher: You have the names of the byproducts in yours. Let me hear your gist.
Student 3: Many scientists are studying agricultural so they can make clothes out of corn husks, chicken feathers, and rice straw.
Teacher: Is that ten?
Student 3: No *[smiling].*
Teacher: Is it a lot more than ten?
Student 3: Yeah.
Teacher: So, you could replace all that end part with what?
Student 3: Byproducts.
Teacher: Byproducts, right? Good. *[She turns to another student.]* What was yours?

Student 2:   Farm waste clothes are not in stores yet but you can buy
             other organic clothes.
Teacher: That works because you talked about the farm waste and
             you talked about the fact that there are some types that are
             available.

The conversation continues, with the teacher providing specific feedback on each student's gist statement. The students know what to do next and begin work immediately when the teacher moves on. When this specific and informative feedback is complete, students have reworked their gists slightly to include the most important information. A review of student work following this lesson indicated that all students in this group had appropriate gist statements for this section.

Providing Just Enough Feedback

Through the CSR routine, the teacher is able to quickly understand where students are in their learning, what they need help with, and where and how to provide them with just the right amount of support. In this excerpted conversation from a 7th- and 8th-grade reading intervention class, the teacher is present in the group throughout the discussion but spends most of her time listening to students and, in fact, says very little. Yet she enters with important corrections, clarifications, and redirections that support students in coming to the meaning of the unknown word, *consciously*.

Student 1:   Does anyone have any other clunks?
Student 2:   *Consciously*.
Student 1:   Does anyone know what that means?
Student 3:   *Consciously*? I have to see where that word is.
Student 2:   It's . . .
Student 1:   *[overlapping]* It's like *conscious*.
Student 3:   *[reading]* "I quickly became convinced that I was in the
             presence of a consciously crafted work to illustrate . . .". So,
             consciously is like, when it says crafted work of literature. I'm
             thinking of something like, sort of *marks* that work.
Student 1:   To pause, I think.
Teacher: It's what?
Student 1:   To pause.
Teacher: Okay. What are your strategies? What are you trying to . . .
             what other strategies are you going to use?
Student 1:   Reread the sentences before and after the clunk.
Teacher: Okay. You've done that.
Student 2:   Look for a root word, prefix, or suffix to *[inaudible]*.

Student 4: *Consciously.*
Student 3: If you take out the *con*, that will make it . . .
Student 2: *[overlapping] Conscious* is a root word. It's a root word.
Teacher: Okay. What about *conscious*? What does that mean?
Student 3: *Conscience.* It's like . . .
Teacher: Not *conscience. Conscious.*

The students now focus on the word part *conscious*, engaging in several exchanges to narrow their definition.

Student 3: *Conscious* means awake.
Student 2: Yeah.
Teacher: There you go.
Student 1: So then *consciously* is . . .
Student 4: Awake.
Student 2: Yeah.
Student 3: *[rereads]* "A consciously crafted work of literature."
Teacher: Okay. You're really, really close.
Student 4: Popular?
Teacher: Hmm . . .
Student 4: Like real?
Student 2: So, living, conscious. Yeah, living.
Student 3: Thinking about.
Teacher: Thinking about. Exactly. Thoughtful. Absolutely. You got there. Good job.

Of note is the teacher's choice to provide a final summarized definition once students have come to some consensus and exhausted their resources. The teacher uses her final comment to guide students to an accurate definition and to conclude this discussion so they can move on.

Supporting Teachers to Provide Effective Feedback

We have many examples of teachers providing students with excellent feedback that supports content understanding and strategy use. Still, some teachers initially struggle to provide effective feedback to students working in small groups. It is common for teachers to rely on vague and overly generalized check-ins. Yet comments such as "How are you doing?" or "Nice work" rarely lead to productive interactions. Still other teachers quickly take over student conversations, appropriating students' ownership of their discussions. In our support to teachers, we provide specific strategies to maximize the quality of interactions with students. Teachers are entering a conversation that is in progress; just as students are taught to take turns and not to interrupt, teachers model this same skill with their own entrée into the group. Thus the first step is for teachers to listen and read. As you saw in the examples above, the teacher takes a quick account of where students are in CSR to determine the type and amount of feedback that is needed or whether feedback is needed at all.

Through the use of audio and video recordings, we discuss and provide opportunities for teachers to practice together ways to provide feedback that is likely to encourage high-level thinking and learning. An activity that teachers have reported as very helpful is one in which they work together to brainstorm feedback options using classroom vignettes. We provide both model examples as well as nonexamples in these group coaching sessions. In the following activity, teachers first listened to an audio recording of teacher feedback that was *not* effective:

Student 1: *Biodiversity* mean preserving on and on. Diversity of a certain subject?

Teacher: You can also break it down and look at the prefix of the word. What is *bio-*?

Student 1: Living.

Teacher: Okay. Living. And *diverse*. If something is diverse it's made of many different things. So what is biodiversity?

Student 1: Food. [*Student does not integrate the teacher's definition with her own understanding.*]

Students: [*side conversations with other students in group who are no longer paying attention*]

Student 2: It's like something that used to be living maybe. [*Another student is off-track.*]

Student 1: Dinosaurs? Like distinct animals. [*another incorrect definition*]

Teacher: All different kinds of animals. So clunk expert, you can remember that as a strategy for next time. Where you can look at the root, prefix, or suffix.

After listening to the nonexample, teachers work together to describe the interaction through a guided discussion. Here, teachers noticed that the teacher in this example "spoon feeds" the answer, that she does not ask the students to explain how they came to their responses, that students have lost attention by the time the teacher has provided the answer, and that the teacher leaves the group with no acknowledgment of understanding by the students. Next, teachers come up with ideas for more productive feedback, such as asking questions of students that would help the teacher understand their thinking (e.g., "How did you come up with your definition?"), providing informative feedback (e.g., "Tell students that their definition is not correct"; "Explain why a CSR strategy works—or does not work—here"), and checking for understanding by asking students to say in their own words the meaning of the word. After teachers have brainstormed features of effective feedback, they then work together to role-play the feedback they could provide in their own classrooms in similar situations. Though it is easier to recognize effective feedback than it is to apply the in-the-moment responses that students need, practice helps. We have seen teachers make great strides in every aspect of their interactions with students during group work. In the next section we discuss how teachers set up the classroom to promote high expectations.

THE TEACHER'S ROLE IN FACILITATING HIGH EXPECTATIONS THROUGH CLASSROOM MANAGEMENT

High expectations are also facilitated through classroom management and clear rules that are explicitly taught and consistently enforced (Weinstein, Curran, & Tomlinson-Clarke, 2003). As CSR teachers have found, high expectations in classroom management are built into CSR through several avenues, including cooperative learning groups and routines. In CSR, this is a necessity, as classroom management lends itself to efficiency and clarity of purpose.

Cooperative Learning

CSR teachers often extol the benefits of cooperative learning groups as a built-in feature that encourages high expectations for students' behavior. Since teachers are not the center of the CSR classroom, they can focus more thoughtfully on the learning and actions of group members. As one teacher put it:

> The other thing I think is really good about it [CSR] is it puts the kids on an even playing field because yes you've got your kids that read at a 12th-grade level, and you've got your kids that read at a 4th, but all of a sudden you've mixed that group together and they have to work together or they're not going to get it done. And so it levels the playing field and so they all get to learn sometime, which is cool. Of probably all of the things I have done, with Pre-AP or the differentiation or the other things the district has thrown at me in 7 years, this is probably the only one I will keep and I'm hard to convince. I'm hard to convince and this one has. (DK, personal communication, 2009)

CSR purposefully creates chances for meaningful interactions. Each group member has a significant role to play in the cooperative learning groups. Having students act as experts in the various stages of CSR increases opportunities for traditionally marginalized students to play prominent roles in CSR (Klingner & Vaughn, 2000). Also built in to CSR is peer support for struggling readers and comprehensible input for English Language Learners (Boardman, Klingner, Boelé, & Swanson, 2010). When cooperative grouping is used, students are allowed ownership over their own behaviors and are treated as experts. Teachers are less constricted by policing the classroom and have more time to focus on the learning of students. One teacher discussed students who were using CSR in two classes, both in a language arts class and in a reading class provided to students with poor scores on state standardized tests. She explained that the students were becoming more confident when using CSR in her language arts class: "I really noticed with our kids that are double-dipped, they are doing really great. . . . I made a lot of those kids leaders in my class . . . the strategies really seemed to be in their mind" (CS, personal communication, 2009).

Whereas traditional classrooms are about hierarchies (McDermott, Goldman, & Varenne, 2006), CSR classrooms are focused on supporting each member of cooperative learning groups. CSR allows teachers to counteract the competition of traditional classrooms, where students are pitted against one another, and it creates a space where the learning and expertise of each group member is valued in authentic ways by the teacher and other students. Strong CSR teachers model and teach respect for their students that students then apply with each other. When peers struggle, CSR group members learn the value of being supportive.

Routines

Classroom management in CSR has multiple facets, including routines. By providing clear instructions on such simple transitions as coming into class, getting into groups, and organizing materials, teachers help students internalize rules for expected behaviors. Routines provide autonomy for students so that they can work independently and open up time for the teacher to attend to learning. These procedures allow for high expectations by establishing clear norms that remove the teacher from the center of the classroom. One teacher noted that CSR provided structure and routine, which reduced off-task behavior:

> I don't structure my group work in my other classes as well as CSR is structured, and I feel like we've got it down to where we know exactly how much time every step needs. So there really isn't time for people to be [off-task]; I just have less wandering, less chit-chat about the weekend, like that kind of thing, whereas with my regular classes with group work it's always a struggle. Somebody's always off-task. [With

CSR] I just feel like it's the perfect amount for them to do in the perfect amount of time. (CB, personal communication, 2009)

It is important to point out that the strategies, structure, and routines of CSR are not the goals of instruction. Rather, they are a means to an end, or a way to help students focus on higher level thinking and learning.

CONCLUSION

Many features of CSR contribute to its success at supporting high expectations. These design features include the following:

- The collaborative group format of CSR
- The materials designed to support students' participation, including cue cards that help students fulfill their roles while working in small groups and learning logs in which students jot down their ideas
- The feedback structure of CSR
- The routines built into CSR
- The reading comprehension strategies themselves

In addition, when we provide professional development on how to implement CSR, we try to convey that it is insufficient to merely go through the motions or apply the steps of an instructional approach without making sure in-depth learning is taking place. We emphasize the importance of high expectations for all students.

NOTE

The research described in this chapter was supported by grant R305A080608 from the Institute of Education Sciences, U.S. Department of Education. The content is solely the responsibility of the authors and does not necessarily represent the official views of the Institute of Education Sciences or the U.S. Department of Education.

REFERENCES

August, D., & Shanahan, T. (2006). *Developing literacy in second-language learners: Report of the National Literacy Panel on language-minority children and youth.* Mahwah, NJ: Lawrence Erlbaum.

Berliner, D. C. (2004). Describing the behavior and documenting the accomplishments of expert teachers. *Bulletin of Science, Technology & Society, 24*(3), 200–212.

Blair, T. R., Rupley, W. H., & Nichols, W. D. (2007). The effective teacher of reading: Considering the "what" and "how" of instruction. *The Reading Teacher, 60*, 432–438.

Boardman, A. G., Klingner, J. K., Boelé, A., & Swanson, E. (2010). Collaborative strategic reading. In T. Scruggs & M. Mastropieri (Eds.), *Literacy and learning: Advances in learning and behavioral disabilities* (vol. 23, pp. 205–235). Oxford, UK: Elsevier Science; Greenwich, CT: JAI; Bingley, UK: Emerald.

Bohn, C. M., Roehrig, A. D., & Pressley, M. (2004). The first days of school in the classrooms of two more effective and four less effective primary-grade teachers. *The Elementary School Journal, 4*, 269–287.

Cazden, C. B. (1988). *Classroom discourse: The language of teaching and learning.* Portsmouth, NH: Heinemann.

Echevarria, J., Vogt, M., & Short, D. J. (2004). *Making content comprehensible for English Language Learners: The SIOP model* (2nd ed.). Boston: Allyn & Bacon.

Ellis, E. S. (2002). *Watering up the curriculum for adolescents with learning disabilities, Part I: Goals of the knowledge dimension.* Retrieved from the LD Online website: http://www.ldonline.org/article/5743/

Fuller, B., Wood, K., Rapoport, T., & Dornbusch, S. M. (1982). The organizational context of individual efficacy. *Review of Educational Research, 52*, 7–30.

Hattie, J., & Timperley, H. (2007). The power of feedback. *Review of Educational Research, 77*, 81–112.

Klingner, J. K., & Vaughn, S. (2000). The helping behaviors of fifth-graders while using collaborative strategic reading (CSR) during ESL content classes. *TESOL Quarterly, 34*, 69–98.

Klingner, J. K., Vaughn, S., & Boardman, A. (2007). *Teaching reading comprehension to students with learning difficulties.* New York: Guilford.

Klingner, J. K., Vaughn, S., Dimino, J., Schumm, J. S., & Bryant, D. (2001). *From clunk to click: Collaborative Strategic Reading.* Longmont, CO: Sopris West.

McDermott, R., Goldman, S., & Varenne, H. (2006). The cultural work of learning disabilities. *Educational Researcher, 35*(6), 12–17.

Palincsar, A. S., & Brown, A. L. (1984). The reciprocal teaching of comprehension-fostering and comprehension-monitoring activities. *Cognition and Instruction, 1*, 117–175.

Piaget, J. (1950). *The psychology of intelligence.* London: Routledge & Kegan Paul.

Rubie-Davies, C. M. (2007). Classroom interactions: Exploring the practices of high-and low-expectation teachers. *British Journal of Educational Psychology, 77*, 289–306.

Topping, K., & Ferguson, N. (2005). Effective literacy teaching behaviors. *Journal of Research in Reading, 28*, 125–143.

Vaughn, S., Klingner, J. K., Swanson, E. A., Boardman, A. G., Roberts, G., Mohammed, S. S., & Stillman-Spisak, S. J. (2011). Efficacy of Collaborative Strategic Reading with middle school students. *American Educational Research Journal, 48*(4), 938–964.

Weinstein, C., Curran, M., & Tomlinson-Clarke, S. (2003). Culturally responsive classroom management: Awareness into action. *Theory into Practice, 42*, 269–276.

CHAPTER 6

Learning to Interpret Texts

Engaging Students in Rigorous Discussion

Sophie Haroutunian-Gordon

For many years, I have studied what I call "interpretive discussion," an example of a high-expectation curricular practice that engages students in rigorous discussions of challenging texts. Interpretive discussion bears some similarity to the Junior Great Books practice of Shared Inquiry discussed in the next chapter, except that it may take place at any level of schooling—kindergarten through graduate school—and in the study of any discipline (see Haroutunian-Gordon, 1991, 2009). Interpretive discussion has as its aim to form a shared point of doubt—a question that all in the group wish to address—and to pursue resolution though discussion about the meaning of the text. Thus the discussion may begin with a question posed by either the leader or a discussant. The text may be a work of fiction or nonfiction, a set of statistical data, a film, painting, piece of music—indeed, any object that has enough ambiguity to justify study of its meaning.

Interpretive discussion does not originate with me. Students of all ages in elite public and private schools and colleges may have regular interpretive discussion-like opportunities. However, for many students, chances for such discussions are few and far between. This is especially true for those in low-level, tracked classes or students in "low-performing" schools, where lecture and worksheet drills prevail. Such students are often thought incapable of developing the skills and habits of mind required for participation in interpretive discussion.

The goal of this chapter is to offer evidence for a contrary claim: Students who might be considered unlikely candidates for success with the activity are able to acquire the requisite skills and habits of mind to participate in interpretive discussions. In what follows, I present a group of high school students from a "low-performing" school learning to engage in line-by-line analysis of a text. Line-by-line analysis is required for interpretive discussion because it involves interpreting passages by saying, in one's own words, no more and no less than the passage says—a challenging task where the lines are ambiguous. These discussants begin to acquire the skills of line-by-line analysis within the space of one discussion and in so doing, help each other to interpret the text. Thus there is good reason to believe that, with further experience, they could develop proficiency and, indeed, become successful discussants.

INTERPRETIVE DISCUSSIONS

The case involves a group of 14 students and a discussion leader (myself) who are conversing about the meaning of the Nobel Lecture delivered by the American writer Toni Morrison on December 7, 1993, in Stockholm, Sweden. It is a challenging text that reflects my confidence that, with the appropriate support, almost any student can participate in rigorous, productive discussions. The students who participated in the discussion had been asked to read the text beforehand and write questions that they had about its meaning.

As the leader, I prepared for the discussion by developing a cluster of questions about the meaning of Toni Morrison's lecture. Like the leader of a Shared Inquiry discussion, the interpretive discussion leader prepares for the conversation by developing a cluster of questions about the text. The cluster consists of a basic question (BQ), which is the question the leader wishes most to resolve, and eight follow-up questions. The follow-up questions point to different places in the text, which, if interpreted in at least one way, have implications for resolving the BQ. All the questions in the cluster are interpretive questions; that is, all are questions about the meaning of the text that may be resolved in more than one way, given the textual evidence. Unlike the Shared Inquiry leader, the leader of an interpretive discussion may never pose the BQ to the group—or any of the follow-up questions, for that matter. The purpose of preparing the cluster is to become familiar with the text and to approach the conversation with the discussants seeking meaning and understanding. Further description of the cluster of questions may be found in Haroutunian-Gordon (2009), particularly Chapters 1 and 5.

Students Finding Their Own Words

I was told that the discussants had never before engaged in an interpretive discussion. They were all about 18 years of age and nearing graduation from an urban high school that had been characterized as low-performing. Some, but not all, were planning to go to college. Some had struggled academically, and most came from lower- to middle-class socioeconomic backgrounds. Prior to the discussion, I had met the group members informally on one previous occasion. So these students and I did not know one another, and the text—a challenging piece of prose—was new to us all.

I began our discussion by learning the names of all 14 students. Then I asked the participants whether they would like to pose questions they had written or whether they would like to hear my question. Not surprisingly, because they did not know me, they opted for the latter.

In her Nobel Lecture, Toni Morrison tells a story: "Once upon a time, there was an old woman. Blind. Wise. One day, she is visited by some young people who wish to disprove her clairvoyance and show her to be a fraud." Let's turn first to some excerpts from the discussion that focus on lines 159–164. Here, the young people in the story address questions to the old woman (each speaker's comments are numbered consecutively throughout the chapter):

Sonya [1]:   *[reading line 159–160 from the text]* "Don't you remember being young when language was magic without meaning, when what you could say could not mean? When the invisible was what imagination strove to see?"

SHG [1]:   Hey, let's wait just 1 second. What about this phrase, "When what you could say could not mean." What does that mean?

Sonya [2]:   I don't know. . . . Like when they were young, like magic was just something that you had to think about and they didn't really know the answers to.

In an interpretive discussion, one often sees the leader repeat back what a discussant has said—what O'Connor and Michaels (2007) call "revoicing" (p. 6). Typically, the leader states, in her own words, what she understands the speaker to mean. The aim in so doing is threefold: (1) to make sure she has understood the speaker correctly; (2) to give the speaker a chance to modify her statement, if needed; and (3) to give all discussants time to grasp and ponder what the speaker has said. However, at this point, I have failed to grasp Sonya's meaning, so I cannot repeat it back to her.

It is not surprising that I cannot grasp what Sonya has intended to say. At SHG [1], I follow another discussion-leading pattern typically observed in an interpretive discussion: I directly ask what specific words mean. In this case, they are words in the text. So I say: "'When what you could say could not mean.' What does that mean?" These are indeed puzzling words, and Sonya [2] declares that she does not understand them.

Sonya tries to interpret the lines to which I have drawn attention not by saying "no more and no less than they say" (line-by-line analysis), but by trying to grasp the meaning of other lines in the passage. Although she does not quote it directly, she seems to focus on the line "Don't you remember being young when language was magic without meaning," for she says, "Like when they were young, like magic was just something you had to think about and you didn't really know the answers to." Here, Sonya has the right instinct—to put the puzzling words into the context where they appear—but she does not fully interpret the line of context that she chose, nor does she return to the perplexing phrase. Hence, her move to grasp the meaning of "When what you could say could not mean" fails. So I try to help her pursue her chosen strategy:

SHG [2]:   Let's go back one phrase: "Don't you remember being young, when language was magic without meaning?" Okay, do you want to say what that sentence means?

Sonya [3]: So when they were younger, like we learn words in school and sometimes we don't really know what it means, but we have it in our minds.

SHG [3]:   So it's like these words are kind of, "Language was magic without meaning." So is that what you're saying? We had the words in our heads, [but] we didn't understand what they meant?

Sonya [4]: Uh-huh. But they were there.

At [3], Sonya tries to state the meaning of the words to which I have directed her attention. Here, she appears to grasp the idea of "language . . . without meaning" when she says, "We learn words in school, and sometimes we don't really know what it means." But what about "Language was magic"? Does she understand that part of the phrase? At SHG [3], I repeat back to Sonya what she has said and then ask her whether my understanding of her meaning is correct. Sonya [4] replies affirmatively.

Still, I am not sure—not sure I have understood Sonya fully and not sure that she has understood the words "language was magic without meaning."

Using Words Precisely

In what follows, Teresa tries to help by interpreting more fully, that is, trying to say more precisely what these words say:

Teresa [5]: I feel like it goes better when you're like . . . like a little toddler and you don't, like you're still communicating with others through language, but like what you're saying isn't really language.

Here Teresa imagines the toddler who communicates with others through language, but what that toddler says is not language. Teresa may mean that the words the toddler utters "communicate" because others respond in particular ways, but the toddler does not understand why the others react to the words as they do. Here, then, may be an interpretation of "language was magic without meaning," as from the child's point of view, the words seem to be "magic." At this point, Larry joins the discussion for the first time and returns to the words that had initially puzzled Sonya:

Larry [1]:   I'm going to say . . .
SHG [4]:   Okay, you want to talk loud so they can all hear you.
Larry [2]:   "What you could say, could not mean"—like you could say a word or someone could say a word and then you don't know what it means, but they do and they can put their own meaning to it . . .

Larry announces his attempt at line-by-line analysis: He quotes a few words from the text and then tries to say, in his own words, what the quoted words mean. Has he said no more and no less than the words say? We continue:

SHG [5]:   So they could put their own meaning to it, but are they communicating in that case?
Larry [3]:   No, I don't think so.
SHG [6]:   Why not?
Larry [4]:   Because I think it's the way you talk there and they don't know [if] the meaning is in there . . .
SHG [7]:   Okay, you throw the word out, you know what it means; they know what it means?
Larry [5]:   You could explain to them what it means.

Notice that in the above excerpt, the referents for *you* and *they* shift. At SHG [5], the first *they* refers to the competent language user, whereas the second *they* refers to both the competent language user and the toddler. At Larry [4], *you* refers to the toddler and *they* refers to the competent language user. At SHG [7], the first *you* refers to the toddler, the second to the competent language user, and the *they* refers to the toddler. And at [5], Larry uses *you* to refer to the competent language user: "You can explain to them what it means." I seem to initiate the shift in referent at [7], when I say "you know what it means; they know what it means?"

In so saying, I use the word *you* to refer to the competent language user, whereas *they* now refers to the child. Despite the shifting that takes place, Larry and I seem to be communicating. We continue:

SHG [8]:   Ah-ha. And if you explain to them what it means, then are you communicating?
Larry [6]: Yes.
SHG [9]:   Why?
Larry [7]: Because you guys know what the word means.
SHG [10]:   Because you have the same meaning for the words?
Larry [8]: If you explain to them.

At this point in the discussion, I wondered whether Larry was making a point similar to the one argued by Wittgenstein in the *Philosophical Investigations*; namely, there is no such thing as private language (Wittgenstein, 1958, section 256). If there is language so that two people are communicating, then the meaning of the utterance is shared by the two speakers. Is that Larry's position? I offer an example to find out:

SHG [11]:   If I say . . . I see a lovely bazoozoo here on this table . . . am I communicating?
Larry [9]: No.
SHG [12]:   No? Don't you see that great bazoozoo? I mean it's right there in front of you.
Larry [10]: If you explain it and then tell them what it is and then . . .
SHG [13]:   So I've got to tell you what it is, okay.
Larry [11]: So if you call that cup a bazoozoo, now we know.
SHG [14]:   Oh, my bazoozoo. Uhm . . . uhm. All right, I didn't even tell you, I just picked it up, right? But you all think this is the bazoozoo?
Larry [12]: No.
SHG [15]:   No? You're not sure. All right. But if I definitely say this is the bazoozoo.
Larry [13]: If you point out that that's the bazoozoo.
SHG [16]:   So the point is here that until we all mean the same thing by "bazoozoo," right, or until you and I mean the same thing by "bazoozoo," you and I can't communicate about the bazoozoo, right? Yes, is that true?
Larry [14]: Yes.

Larry answers my questions about "bazoozoo" without hesitation. In fact, his idea about what is required for communication is quite clear, and he and Wittgenstein agree: There is no language between people until all the language users use the words in the same way (Wittgenstein, 1958, sections 5–10), Having grasped Larry's meaning, I return to focus on the text.

SHG [17]:   All right. So this is a case where these children are saying to the old woman: Wow, don't you remember the time when you used language and you didn't know what it was meaning? I mean, that's what you've been describing here. You used words, or you heard words, but you didn't know what they were meaning, okay?

Finally, I am able to repeat back to the discussants the meaning that they have found in Morrison's lines, "Don't you remember being young when language was magic without meaning, when what you could say could not mean?" Have they interpreted the lines fully—said no more and no less than the quoted words say? My ability to read the lines in question and repeat back the interpretation they have offered without questioning them further suggests that at the moment, I judged them successful. Riding on this success, Larry indicates that he wishes to continue by reading and interpreting the next lines in the text:

Larry [15]:   [reading from the text], "When the invisible was what imagination strove to see. When questions and the demands for answers burned so brightly you trembled with fury and not knowing."
SHG [18]:   Okay, let's see what's in those two sentences. How about, "When the invisible . . ." Just read the whole sentence out loud.
Larry [16]:   Oh. "When the invisible was what imagination strove to see."
SHG [19]:   So what does that mean?
Larry [17]:   So you didn't see nothing, but you wanted to see something. You can see it.

Confirming Understanding

Larry is beginning to do all of the things that are involved in line-by-line analysis. And by following certain patterns, I try to help him. First [15], he reads two sentences. Line-by-line analysis in an interpretive discussion always begins with oral reading of the lines/phrases that are to be interpreted. At SHG [18], I focus him on the first of the two lines, so as to take up a more manageable piece of text, and he reads aloud for a second time [16], "When the invisible was what imagination strove to see."

Second, at [17], Larry tries to state the meaning of the line that he has read using his own words: "So you don't see nothing but you wanted to see something. You can see it." He makes that statement after I ask him directly to interpret the line (SHG [19]).

Third, Larry tries to clarify his interpretation of the line in response to my questions. At [17], he makes a fairly clear interpretation of the quoted words "When the invisible was what imagination strove to see" when he says, "So you didn't see nothing, but you wanted to see something." But what does he intend to say when he adds, "You can see it"? That phrase is unclear to me, so I proceed:

SHG [20]:   Okay, so the invisible . . . when the invisible . . . so that's something you can't see?
Larry [18]:   Yeah.
SHG [21]:   Yeah. "Was . . . what imagination strove to see." So what's going on there?
Larry [19]:   When your imagination wants you to see something invisible.
SHG [22]:   Okay, when your imagination wants you to see something— "when the invisible is what imagination strove to see"—so imagination is trying to see something that's invisible, right?
Larry [20]:   Yeah.
SHG [23]:   Like I tell you there's a beautiful mountain on the other side of those trees and you can't look over and see it.
Larry [21]:   But you can try and picture it.
SHG [24]:   You try to picture it. So your imagination is striving to see it. It's invisible to your naked eye.

At SHG [20], I say back to Larry what I have so far understood him to mean: "So the invisible . . . when the invisible . . . so that's something you can't see?" "Yeah," he tells me (Larry [18]). Then I quote the remainder of the line in question again—"Was what the imagination strove to see"— and ask again for his interpretation (SHG [21]). At [19], Larry's attempt at line-by-line analysis is clearer than at [17], for he says: "When your imagination wants you to see something invisible." At SHG [22], I am able to repeat back Larry's intended meaning and link his interpretation to quoted words. At Larry [20], he confirms my understanding of his interpretation. At SHG [23] and Larry [21], we construct an example to illustrate Larry's interpretation. At SHG [24], I am able to say back to Larry his interpretation of the quoted line. So his words, "you can see it," are understood in the context of the example: "You try to picture it. So your imagination is striving to see it. It's invisible to your naked eye."

Here, we begin to see why line-by-line analysis can be complex and difficult. For it involves not only saying no more and no less than the quoted words say, but, in addition, answering questions that others raise about the meaning of one's interpretation. It also involves persuading others that one has interpreted the quoted words fully. Larry has succeeded with these tasks. Given a demanding task and support from me, Larry is able to work his way through a very challenging text.

Analyzing Together

In the next excerpts, the group considers a passage that begins on line 175: "Our inheritance is an affront. You want us to have your old, blank eyes and see only cruelty and mediocrity. . . . How dare you talk to us of duty when we stand waist-deep in the toxin of your past?" Here, we continue to see the discussants help one another carry out the line-by-line analysis, which they are now doing with greater ease:

Marisa [1]: What's an affront?
SHG [25]:   What's an affront? Any ideas? Go ahead, Dave.
Dave [1]:   I . . .
SHG [26]:   Sometimes . . . if you read a little bit more, "Our inheritance is an affront. You want us to have old, blank eyes and see only cruelty and mediocrity."
Dave [2]:   To think everything was . . . like see only the bad and the negative.
SHG [27]:   Okay. "You want us to have your old, blank eyes." So that sounds like what?
Dave [3]:   To be blind like you and not be able to see . . .
SHG [28]:   Be blind, be not be able to see. See only cruelty and mediocrity. . . . So "Our inheritance is an affront"?
Larry [23]: Well, like maybe what was passed down was negative?
Dave [4]:   Like what we're getting is no good.

Marisa [1] begins by following a pattern I initiated previously—asking directly about the meaning of a word/phrase/line. Her very request suggests to me that the discussants are beginning to feel more comfortable doing line-by-line analysis. Dave [1] starts to answer her but then is unable to proceed, seemingly unclear about the meaning of the word. So I suggest that he try to grasp the meaning of *affront* by reading the word in context and then reading the words that follow it [50]: "Our inheritance is an affront. You want us to have old, blank eyes and see only cruelty and mediocrity." When Dave next speaks [2], he makes an interpretation of the words I have read, saying, "See only the bad and negative." Here, he seems to have focused on and tried to interpret the words "see only cruelty and mediocrity." So I then ask him to focus on the words earlier in the same line, "You want us to have your old, blank eyes," which he does do when he says, "To be blind like you and not be able to see" [3]. At SHG [28], I repeat his interpretation of these words and add them to the words he had interpreted previously: "Be blind, be not be able to see. See only cruelty and mediocrity."

My sense at the time was that Dave had said enough about the meaning of the line "You want us to have your old, blank eyes and see only cruelty and mediocrity" to now be able to interpret "Our inheritance is an affront." Indeed, the evidence from the transcript suggests that both Larry [23] and Dave [4] were relatively successful in interpreting that line. Dave's dialogue with me seemed to have helped Larry, and his interpretation seemed to help Dave. For Larry at [23] says, "Well, like maybe what was passed down was negative." And Dave at [4] says, "Like what we're getting is no good." They are getting the hang of it!

Saying Just Enough

In what follows, the discussants take yet another step in learning to do line-by-line analysis: They begin to see that some interpretations are better than others because they do a better job of saying no more and no less than the quoted words in the question say. We turn to the last line in the quoted passage:

SHG [29]:   *[reading from the text]* "How dare you talk to us of duty when we stand waist-deep in the toxin of your past?" How about that, Judy, what do you think?

Judy [1]:   I think they're saying that she's trying to tell them what's wrong when in her past she's done wrong. And like she like wants them to take responsibility, but she's not talking about how she has responsibility for what she has done.

Does Judy say no more and no less than the quoted words say? At [1], she may mean: The young people object because the old woman is trying to tell them about the things that need fixing in the world ("tell them what's wrong") when she and her generation have created the problems. And when Judy says, "She's not talking about how she has responsibility for what she has done," she may mean that at the same time, the old woman is not discussing the obligation she has to help alleviate the hardship to which she has contributed. I respond:

SHG [30]: What do you think of this? *[pause]* Well, what do the rest of you think about [Judy's] interpretation? Folks, you're all looking at me. *[pause]* Hello, I have no privileged access to this [text]. I'm about as new to it as you are. What do you think of that interpretation?

Sonya [5]: I think they're saying that like, why should they have to carry on and do anything to change [things] when they've got stuck with all the bad things from her past and from her own generation. Yeah?

Alan [1]: Yeah.

SHG [31]: Yeah, you like this, Alan, no?

Alan [2]: Yeah.

Do Judy and Sonya interpret the passage the same way? And if not, which one has done the best job of saying no more and no less than the quoted words? In fact, their interpretations differ somewhat, it seems. At [5], Sonya says the young people object to being told that they have an obligation—"a duty"—to change things since the old woman and her generation have created the current problems. So while both Judy and Sonya say the young people fault the old woman for failing to take responsibility for a negative situation she helped to create, Judy says that therefore the young people believe that the old woman has no right to tell them to be responsible—a case of the pot calling the kettle black. In fact, Judy's inference is not justified by the words "How dare you talk to us of duty when we stand waist-deep in the toxin of your past?" So Sonya's interpretation is closer to the meaning of these words, and it wins approval from Alan [1, 2], who seems to find it more convincing.

CONCLUSION

As argued in Haroutunian-Gordon (1991, 2009), skill in line-by-line analysis—saying no more and no less than quoted words say—enables discussants to cultivate questions about the meaning of texts and pursue their resolution. For as they work to say no more and no less than quoted words say, the discussants discover points of ambiguity—words, phrases, or passages that could have more than one meaning, given the textual evidence. And as they study the text to determine the interpretations it best supports, they come to care about resolving the questions and arrive at conclusions about the answers.

However, line-by-line analysis is not easy to do and takes practice, patience, and the desire to understand what other speakers and the text itself intend to say. As we have seen, these discussants, who had had no previous experience with interpretive discussion, made progress toward all of these goals in the space of one discussion as they gained skill in pursuing line-by-line analysis.

Thus it is reasonable to conclude that given opportunities to participate in interpretive discussion, these students might develop the skills and habits of mind that it helps to foster.

REFERENCES

Haroutunian-Gordon, S. (1991). *Turning the soul: Teaching through conversation in the high school.* Chicago: University of Chicago Press.

Haroutunian-Gordon, S. (2009). *Learning to teach through discussion: The art of turning the soul.* New Haven, CT: Yale University Press.

O'Connor, C., & Michaels, S. (2007). When is dialogue 'dialogic'? *Human Development, 50*(5), 275–285.

Wittgenstein, L. (1958). *Philosophical investigations* (3rd ed.). (G. E. M. Anscombe, Trans.). New York: Macmillan.

CHAPTER 7

Shared Inquiry

Making Students Smart

Curt Dudley-Marling
Sarah Michaels

American schools tend to make hierarchies out of "any differences that can be claimed . . . to be natural, inherent, and potentially consequential in school" (McDermott, Goldman, & Varenne, 2006, p. 12). Moreover, in American schools and classrooms, *difference* is typically equated with deficiencies that are "located in the individual who becomes subject to classification, regulation and treatment" (Slee, 1998, p. 130).

> Yet, the problems many people have in the American School stem only incidentally from what they can or cannot do and much more radically from the way they are treated by others in relation to the designation, assignment, and distribution of more or less temporary or partial difficulties interpreted as success or failure. (Varenne & McDermott, 1999, pp. 134–135)

Paraphrasing Ray Rist (1970), there is a greater tragedy than being labeled a low achiever, and that's being treated like a low achiever. Typically, students who are deemed to be *deficient* are treated to a basic skills curriculum focused on remediating deficits in skills presumed to be associated with educational failure. This focus on basic skills is underpinned by a behavioral theory of learning that defines human learning in terms of the mastery of hierarchies of skills and subskills and struggling learners as people in need of these skills—if they are going to succeed in school. For instance, from a behavioral perspective, learning to read is a matter of mastering a scope and sequence of skills (e.g., phonemic and phonological awareness) that are presumed to be foundational to learning to read. Therefore, instruction for students who are defined as *deficient* focuses mainly on these supposedly foundational skills.

No one argues that phonics and other word- and letter-focused skills aren't part of what readers draw on in the process of reading. The problem is when an overemphasis on basic skills denies students opportunities to read authentic, connected texts— a crucial experience in learning to read (Allington, 2005). In these instances, students with presumed deficiencies are presented with an impoverished curricula that denies them the rich, meaningful learning opportunities common in high-achieving classrooms (Anyon, 1980; Bartolomé, 1994; Kozol, 2005). Even in the same classroom, students in low-level reading groups typically experience a reading curriculum qualitatively different from—and inferior to—that of students in higher level reading groups. For instance, there is an abundance of evidence that good readers are more likely to be presented lessons that emphasize meaning, while poor readers' lessons more often emphasize words, sounds, and letters, often out of context (Allington, 1980; Alpert, 1975; Gambrell, Wilson, & Gantt, 1981; McDermott, 1976). Similarly, good readers have been found to read more words than poor readers, in part because poor readers are often asked to read material that is, for them, comparatively more difficult than the reading selections assigned to good readers (Allington, 2005). Since reading development has been linked to the number of words children read, students who read fewer words, either because their instruction is focused on low-level skills or because they read material that is too difficult for them—or both—will be seriously disadvantaged (Allington, 2005).

Circumscribed literacy curricula that limit students' opportunities to learn to read and, therefore, ensure that students who are the victims of impoverished curriculum will never catch up with students who experience richer, more engaging curricula. In other words, low-achieving students learn less because they are taught less, making it likely that they will fall farther and farther behind as they pass through the grades.

In this way, learning doesn't reside in the heads of individual learners; instead, learning is situated in a complex dance between teachers and students, mediated by the curriculum that creates certain affordances for learning. Offering low-achieving students the sort of rich, engaging curriculum commonly provided for high-achieving students can change the shape of this instructional dance and, in the process, transform students' identities as learners.

This chapter draws on data collected during a study of a practice called "Shared Inquiry" in a 4th-grade classroom in a high-poverty, underperforming school in New York City that we call Lexington Elementary. This classroom served a high proportion of poor students of color, many of whom were second language learners and/or had special needs. Our analysis of these data illustrates how students with a history of educational failure can learn to engage in high-level literacy discussions and construct the kinds of arguments that are the hallmark of academic discourse if given challenging texts and supportive "talk moves" by their teachers and peers. In this way, the students at Lexington Elementary were transformed from educational failures—as determined by standardized test scores—into highly competent readers.

PRACTICING SHARED INQUIRY

The overall goal of Shared Inquiry, an element of the Junior Great Books (JGB) program (Great Books Foundation, n.d.), is for students to engage in rigorous discussions of challenging texts by responding to teachers' questions by making claims, backing up those claims with textual evidence, and, if necessary, explicating the link between the textual evidence and the claim. Specifically, Shared Inquiry is a recurring set of tasks, lasting roughly an hour a day over the course of a 5-day cycle, and typically enacted through a teacher-guided, whole-group discussion format. The tasks provide a sequence for practicing intellectual moves and positions, scaffolded by teachers, to help students learn how to build, explicate, and weigh academic arguments—a hallmark of academic discourse. The first day of the cycle features an expert reading of the text, usually by the teacher. Students are given copies of the text and typically read along, sometimes highlighting sections or making marginal notes as they follow along. Students are then asked to generate and discuss questions they have about the text. The goal of Day 1 activities is to ensure that *all* students, regardless of their reading levels, understand the text well enough to engage in a thoughtful discussion. Day 2 focuses on an activity called "Directed Notes" where the text is read out loud a second time, followed by an activity in which students have an opportunity to practice making claims about the text and citing textual evidence to support their claims. Day 3 is typically devoted to something called "interpreting words" but some teachers choose instead to do a 2nd day of Directed Notes. Day 4 is devoted to Shared Inquiry. To prepare for Shared Inquiry, the teacher selects a text for which there is some ambiguity and then prepares an interpretive question that has more than one possible answer and for which there is textual evidence. Teachers are also encouraged to develop follow-up questions that maintain the rigor of the discussion (e.g., asking for textual evidence; clarifying or verifying; soliciting additional viewpoints). Crucially, the teacher draws on a set of tools (talk moves) to orchestrate the discussion. Teachers are discouraged from using any sort of evaluation, on the assumption that teacher evaluation limits real discussion by leading students to believe there really is a right answer. On Day 5 students translate the Shared Inquiry discussion into a piece of persuasive writing.

MAKING STUDENTS "SMART"

Our attention was drawn to Lexington Elementary when we heard reports of dramatic gains in test scores following the implementation of Shared Inquiry. Lexington Elementary had been just another urban, high-poverty school with low test scores and a scripted, basic skills curriculum. However, in the year following the adoption of Shared Inquiry, students at Lexington Elementary made dramatic gains on the district reading assessments. The graph in Figure 7.1 illustrates these gains.

Levels 1 and 2 correspond to "far below standards" and "below standards." Levels 3 and 4 indicate that students "meet" or "exceed" standards. In the year before Shared Inquiry was introduced, fewer than 25% of the students at Lexington Elementary achieved Levels 3 or 4; however, after the implementation of Shared Inquiry over 50% of the Lexington students met or exceeded standards on the district reading assessments. Unexpectedly, there was also a modest increase in test scores in math and science at Lexington Elementary.

We believe that higher test scores at Lexington Elementary can be linked to the implementation of Shared Inquiry, since the introduction of this practice was the only thing that changed at the school during this period of time. However, we are less interested in the effect of Shared Inquiry on state and district test scores than the effect of this practice on students' learning identities. The higher test scores signal improved academic skills. Something about the practice of Shared Inquiry made the students at Lexington Elementary "smarter." What interests us is what there is about Shared Inquiry discussions that makes students smarter—or, alternatively, what the practice of Shared Inquiry reveals about the intelligence students already possess.

We addressed this question by examining the process by which students in one 4th-grade class at Lexington Elementary discussed the story "Cedric," one of the stories in *Tales from Moominvalley* by Tove Jansson

Figure 7.1. Gains on District Reading Assessments After Shared Inquiry Intervention

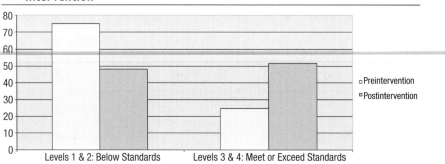

(1962). Specifically, we wanted to know how the practice of Shared Inquiry made students appear "smart" or competent. Overall, our analysis of this single discussion, which is representative of other discussions we observed at Lexington Elementary, indicates that students took much more active roles in the discussion of "Cedric," in contrast to the more passive roles typically ascribed to children in many urban schools where the emphasis is on basic skills instruction (Anyon, 1980; Haberman, 1991; Kozol, 2005). More significantly, our analysis shows that Shared Inquiry discussions created affordances that enabled Lexington Elementary students to display a high level of academic competence, as students constructed sophisticated academic arguments while discussing challenging texts.

"Cedric"—the Story

Readers will find it helpful to have some familiarity with "Cedric," so here we provide a brief synopsis of the story. "Cedric" is about a boy named Sniff who has a stuffed animal named Cedric who has topaz eyes and a moonstone on his collar. The text says, "Possibly the moonstones were more important to Sniff than the dog's inimitable expressions." Sniff gives Cedric away because a character in the story told Sniff that, "if you give something away that you really love, you'll get it back ten times over." Sniff immediately regrets giving Cedric away "to desperation." Sniff visits Snufkin who tells him a story about a woman who had beautiful things that she collected and took care of, to the exclusion of friends or travel. She gets a bone stuck in her stomach and thinks she has only a few weeks to live. She has the idea to give all her stuff away (because she's suffocating), sending just the right thing to different people in anonymous parcels. She starts to feel better and gets nicer. Friends start to visit, and one day she laughs so hard that the bone comes out. She's changed, has friends, and goes off to travel the world. Eventually, Sniff finds Cedric, but the topaz eyes have been removed and made into eardrops and the moonstone on the collar has been lost. But, as the story says, Sniff loves Cedric "all the same," but now "only for love's sake."

The discussion begins with an interpretive question framed by the teacher: "Why at the end of the story does Sniff love Cedric 'only for love's sake'?"

Activating "Passive" Learners

In the context of the basic skills instruction that dominates in many urban schools, especially in low academic tracks, students are constructed as passive learners (Bartolomé, 1994) who need to be filled with skills and subskills before they are ready to engage in serious interpretation of texts.

In these settings, teacher talk dominates. In contrast to this pattern of quiet, passive students, our analysis indicates relatively high levels of student participation in Shared Inquiry discussions, as measured by the amount of student talk (overall number of turns and words per turn) relative to teacher talk. In our analysis of one 54-minute Shared Inquiry discussion at Lexington Elementary, relative to their teacher, students took more turns (268 versus 182) and longer turns (18 words per turn versus 15 words per turn). Overall, students did nearly two-thirds of the talking in these discussions, a complete reversal of the pattern found in typical classroom discussions (Cazden, 2001). Higher levels of participation at least suggest increased student engagement that has been linked to success in school.

Even more impressive than the quantity of student participation in the Shared Inquiry discussions was the quality of their engagement. In the rest of this chapter we present evidence from our qualitative analysis of a 54-minute discussion in one 4th-grade classroom that, given the opportunity, students at Lexington Elementary were able to construct sophisticated arguments that included claims, textual evidence, and evidentiary warrants while they discussed a challenging text. We show that, given a challenging task and a supportive and effective teacher, these students transformed their academic identities from failing readers to highly competent interpreters of texts.

Making Sense of "Cedric"

In the context of Shared Inquiry discussions, the 4th-grade students at Lexington Elementary responded to the teacher's interpretive question—"Why at the end of the story does Sniff love Cedric 'only for love's sake'?"—by making claims, supporting those claims with textual evidence, and, if necessary, explicating the link between the claim and the evidence (i.e., the warrant). Consider the following excerpt about halfway into the discussion of why Sniff loves Cedric "only for love's sake." In the transcripts, ". . ." indicates a measurable pause, and "—" indicates a false start, interruption, or break in timing. For ease of reference, we have numbered each of the turns.

1 Derrick: Um . . . I think he loved him, like I said before, like, because if like, if Cedric because if he had the jewelry back, I think he would still miss Cedric.
2 Teacher: If he had the jewelry back, he would still miss Cedric?
3 Derrick: If they gave him the jewelry and not Cedric, I think he would still miss Cedric.
4 Teacher: Oh, and what makes you think that? I—uh everyone heard what he said? [Students: No] If they had just given him the

jewelry back, go ahead, Derrick. Keep on from there. They didn't hear you.

5 Derrick: Like because on page 80, he regret giving Cedric away. . . . So that's what caused me to think that.

6 Teacher: But tell them what. They didn't hear the first part.

7 Derrick: Oh. If they might give him the jewelry back, he might still miss Cedric.

8 Teacher: Meaning, you know, if he just had the jewelry by itself, without Cedric?

9 Diarra: I understand what Derrick is saying. He's saying that that . . . if they gave him the jewels as a souvenir, then he—then it would remind him [Sniff] so much of him [Cedric] and he would miss him more and more all the time.

10 Teacher: What would make you think he would miss him more and more?

11 Diarra: Um, I think he would miss more miss him more and more because he didn't . . . maybe since—

12 Teacher: No "maybe." What in the story do you think it might—What makes you believe from the story, that it might?

13 Diarra: On page 79, it—it says, "Now, afterwards, it is hard to understand how that small beast, Sniff, could have ever been persuaded to give that small—to give Cedric away."

14 Teacher: So what does that—okay?

15 Diarra: That shows that he—he loved—he loved him so much and he'd miss him if he ever got lost. . . . But since he didn't um, really, she gave him away instead of losing it, uh she's [Teacher: he] he um he's prob—he's probably more angry at himself because, um he really loved him . . . and nobody has ever persuaded him, so he really regretted it. And he was probably um, taking it on himself a lot.

16 Teacher: So then if he really loved and him and we don't understand how he could have been persuaded, then why is it . . . that he gives him away to begin with then?

17 Diarra: Oh. Because he—he didn't understand, on page 80 and 81, he didn't understand what Moomintroll meant when he said . . . "He told him that if one gives away something, then one will get it back ten times over and feel wonderful afterwards." And he probably thought that it meant that if he gave away the um the most precious thing, then he'll get—then he'll um then he'll gain something that he'll that he'll need, or something. . . . So he misunderstood what Moomintroll was saying.

Over a couple of turns, Derrick makes the claim that if Sniff had the jewels but not Cedric, he would still miss Cedric (Turns 1–3). He then references page 80 of the text, which he glosses as "he regret giving Cedric away" (Turn 5) to support his claim that it was Cedric, not the jewels, that Sniff cared about. Diarra restates and expands Derrick's claim in her own words (Turn 9), arguing that if Sniff had the jewels and not Cedric, it would only cause him to miss him more. Moreover, she quotes directly from the text to support her claim (see Turn 13). But Diarra goes further. On prompting from the teacher (Turn 14), Diarra explained how the textual evidence she offered supported her claim: "That shows that he—he loved—he loved him so much and he'd miss him if he ever got lost." (Turn 15). Specifically, Diarra made explicit the evidentiary warrant for her claim—a very sophisticated interpretive move. When the teacher asks a follow-up question (Turn 16), Diarra cites additional textual evidence along with an explanation of how this evidence further supports her claim: "He misunderstood what Moomintroll was saying. . . ." (Turn 17). Over the course of the "Cedric" discussion—and, indeed, all of the discussions we observed—students made claims, cited textual evidence to support their claims, and, if asked, made explicit the warrant for their claims.

What's particularly striking about the Shared Inquiry discussion of "Cedric" is how the students and the teacher worked together to construct arguments that many students may not have been able to construct on their own. Consider the following exchange in which the teacher and three students scaffold attempts by Cory, a student who had been identified as having a severe learning disability, to make a sophisticated claim that he was unable to make on his own. Again, we've numbered the turns to make it easier for readers to reference.

1 Teacher: Cory, what do you want to add?
2 Cory: I . . . I think . . . um I think it's because, I think he loves for love's sake, it's because, on page 85, [Teacher: uh huh] 'cause it's telling you, on page 80—on page um 84 and 85. On 84 it says, "An idea . . . came. She w— [the aunt]. And she was gonna give away everything she owned." [Teacher: uh huh] Also, on page 85, it says, "She thought wisely and she gave um, um, what everybody um would want." So . . .
3 Teacher: So what does that have to do with um Sniff loving Cedric only for love's sake?
4 Cory: It means that, it's telling, 'cause that's how he um loves Cedric for, for who he, for who he is because when he [Snufkin] told him [Sniff] that part of the story, um he's telling him that, that that she didn't, that she loves him for— that she um, if you love . . .

5 Student: . . . for who he is, not like what he got on.

6 Cory: It tells me that, that um . . . she . . . that um if he loved him,
             then she wouldn't give away her jewels, 'cause she didn't
             really care about the jewels. So . . . so that means that if she—
             she didn't care about the jewels, she just cared, cared about
             the um, about her friends, the person, not the jewels.

7 Teacher: She cared about the persons there?

8 Cory: Uh huh. It's sort of like that . . .

9 Students: [overlapping] Her friends, the person, her friends . . .

10 Cory: It's sort of like she loved, she loved the um that, that he
             taught him to love somebody for who they are, instead of,
             for the jewels.

11 Teacher: So how did he teach him that? I'm still not understanding
             that.

12 Cory: He teached him—he teached him that because—

13 Teacher: With the story, you're saying that he taught him something.
             So how did he teach him that with the story?

14 Cory: He taught him that in the story because in this part of the
             story it's telling her that, telling her that she didn't really like
             the jewels if she would've gave it away, if she would've gave
             it away for her friends.

15 Teacher: Does she not really like the jewels? I mean her material
             things?

16 Cory: Yeah, she likes them, but then, but then after, when you read
             on, she didn't really like them 'cause she liked her friends
             better.

17 Student: [softly] She—she—she liked 'em before she had friends.

18 Cory: Yeah, because she didn't know all that was gonna happen
             and death was gonna happen and stuff.

19 Diarra: I get—I understand what um, what Cory is saying. Cory
             is saying that um if it hadn't been for the bone, then she
             would've never changed . . . her manner. And she would've
             never met so many friends.

20 Teacher: Is that what you're trying to say, Cory?

21 Cory: Yeah, yeah, that part if she—if sh—if that— if that part
             wouldn't have happened then she wouldn't change.

22 Teacher: So what does that have to do with Sniff?

23 Cory: So that means, it's telling him, it's telling him that she didn't
             really, care about, care about (that like if). Like if you really
             love something, that um you wouldn't love something
             for the jewels, the jewels it has. 'Cause, on page 80 it says,
             "Possibly the jewels were more important to Sniff than
             expressions." [Teacher: Uh huh] "But . . . but um, but in any

case he loved, he loved Cedric." [Teacher: uh huh] So, so that
means that um . . . that he—he loved, that he's sp—you only
s'posed, he um posed to—he's teaching him to love someone
for who they are.

It appears that Cory recognizes the parallels between Sniff giving away
Cedric and the "story within a story" about the woman who found happi-
ness only after she gave away all the possessions that were "suffocating her."
He seems to be arguing that since she recognized that people, not possessions, are what mattered, Sniff also learned that it was Cedric, not the jewels,
that were important. Indeed, in his final turn (Turn 23), Cory says that when
Snufkin tells Sniff the story about the woman who gave away all her beautiful things, "he's teaching [Sniff] to love someone for who they are."

Recognizing the parallelism in these two stories is a remarkable
achievement for any 4th-grader, but particularly for a student who has
been designated as a *disabled* reader. But, of course, to make his claim and
provide supporting evidence from the text, Cory needs the support of his
teacher and classmates. For instance, it isn't at all clear how Cory's comment in Turn 2 addresses the teacher's interpretation question, "Why at
the end of the story does Sniff love Cedric 'only for love's sake'?" So she
first asks Cory what his answer has to do with the question (Turn 3). Then,
in a series of moves over several turns, she pushes Cory to clarify his re-
marks. In Turn 7, for example, she asks a question ("She cared about the
persons there?") to see if she has gotten his meaning. In other turns, she
pushes Cory to be more explicit (e.g., in Turn 13, "With the story, you're
saying that he taught him something. So how did he teach him with the
story?"). Various students also provide additional details (e.g., in Turn 5,
"For who he is, not what he got on") to help Cory make his claim more
explicit, and finally, Diarra offers her sense of what she thinks Cory means
(Turn 19) and Cory verifies that this is what he's trying to say. With the
support of the teacher and his classmates, Cory is able to construct a clearer, more explicit claim (Turn 23).

What's particularly noteworthy about this excerpt is how much time
and effort the teacher devoted to helping Cory make his claim and provide
relevant textual evidence to support his claim. When the teacher is unsure of
what Cory is trying to say (Turn 3), she could have just moved on to another
student, which is what often happens in classroom discussions. Instead, she
presumed Cory had something worthwhile to contribute to the discussion
and made a series of moves to help him articulate his claim. She also afforded other students the opportunity to support Cory. But, notably, their
support wasn't about giving Cory the right answer because there was no
right answer. Instead, they helped Cory make his claim intelligible and, in

the process, helped transform Cory from a student with a reading disability to a thoughtful interpreter of the text. They helped make Cory "smart."

CONCLUSION

James Gee (2004) asks, "What is it about school that manages to transform children who are good at learning . . . into children who are not good at learning, if they are poor or members of certain minority groups?" (p. 10). In the case of students from Lexington Elementary, how is it that a group of children who were so good at learning before they came to school—as all children surely are—consistently failed at learning once they entered school? Our experience with Shared Inquiry indicates that a rich curricular practice, augmented by thoughtful, strategic scaffolding by the teacher, provided conditions for learning that enabled students to read and interpret challenging texts in ways most often associated with the most successful learners. Shared Inquiry didn't *make* the Lexington students smart, but it did afford students the opportunity to reveal their natural competence for learning and, in so doing, allowed the teacher to build on that competence as they learned a sophisticated reading practice rarely seen in underachieving schools like Lexington Elementary. The lesson here is that all children—whether they are poor, Black, Hispanic, second language learners, or students with disabilities—require a high-expectation curriculum if they are to achieve a high level of success in school.

REFERENCES

Allington, R. L. (1980). Poor readers don't get to read much in reading groups. *Language Arts, 57*(8), 872–877.

Allingon, R. L. (2005). *What really matters for struggling readers: Designing research-based programs* (2nd ed.). Boston, MA: Allyn & Bacon.

Alpert, J. L. (1975). Do teachers adapt methods and materials to ability groups in reading? *California Journal of Educational Research, 26*, 120–123.

Anyon, J. (1980). Social class and the hidden curriculum of work. *Journal of Education, 162*, 67–92.

Bartolomé, L. I. (1994). Beyond the methods fetish: Toward a humanizing pedagogy. *Harvard Educational Review, 64*, 173–194.

Cazden, C. (2001). *Classroom discourse: The language of teaching and learning.* Portsmouth, NH: Heinemann.

Gambrell, L. B., Wilson, R. M., & Gantt, W. N. (1981). Classroom observations of task attending behaviors of good and poor readers. *Journal of Educational Research, 74*, 400–404.

Gee, J. P. (2004). *Situated language and learning: A critique of traditional schooling*. New York: Routledge.

Great Books Foundation. (n.d.). *Junior Great Books*. Retrieved from http://www.greatbooks.org/programs-for-all-ages/pd/what-is-shared-inquiry.html

Haberman, M. (1991). The pedagogy of poverty versus good teaching. *Phi Delta Kappan, 73*, 290–294.

Jansson, T. (1962). Cedric. In *Tales from Moominvalley* (T. Warburton, Trans.; pp. 150–61). New York: Farrar, Strauss, & Giroux.

Kozol, J. (2005). *The shame of the nation: The restoration of apartheid schooling in America*. New York: Crown.

McDermott, R. (1976). *Kids make sense: An ethnographic account of the interactional management of success and failure in one first-grade classroom* (Published doctoral dissertation). Stanford University, Stanford, CA.

McDermott, R., Goldman, S., & Varenne, H. (2006). The cultural work of learning disabilities. *Educational Researcher, 35*, 12–17.

Rist, R. C. (1970). Student social class and teacher expectations: The self-fulfilling prophecy in ghetto education. *Harvard Educational Review, 40*, 411–451.

Slee, R. (1998). The politics of theorising special education. In C. Clark, A. Dyson, & A. Millward (Eds.), *Theorising special education* (pp. 126–136). New York: Routledge.

Varenne, H., & McDermott, R. (1999). Disability as a cultural fact. In H. Varenne & R. McDermott (Eds.), *Successful failure: The school America builds* (pp. 131–156). Boulder, CO: Westview Press.

PART III

MATH AND SCIENCE CURRICULA

This section of the book presents high-expectation curricula and programs in math and science. In Chapter 8 Chapin and O'Connor describe an innovative math program, "Project Challenge," for students in grades 4–7. The program combines rigorous mathematics and discourse-intensive pedagogy, in which students are called upon to externalize their mathematical understandings and conjectures, listen carefully to one another, and build on the thinking and arguments of their peers. In Chapter 9 Sohmer describes an alternative to textbook science. Middle school participants in the Investigators Club build upon their embodied knowledge of the world as they reason their way through compelling demonstrations of concepts central to physics. In both chapters, we see examples of the remarkable student achievement made possible by high-expectation curricula and well-structured discussion practices.

CHAPTER 8

Project Challenge

Using Challenging Curriculum and Mathematical Discourse to Help All Students Learn

Suzanne H. Chapin
Catherine O'Connor

Mathematics instruction in urban middle schools is often numbingly predictable—and not particularly effective; poor students and students of color significantly underperform more affluent White students in mathematics (National Assessment of Educational Progress, 2009). Typically, mathematics instruction in low-income urban schools is characterized by the following pattern: Teachers present new content, followed by student repetition of algorithms and rules and, finally, independent practice by students. Moreover, instruction in these classes tends to focus on lower level arithmetic skills (as opposed to higher level mathematical reasoning). This approach, sometimes referred to as the "pedagogy of poverty" (Haberman, 2010), offers few opportunities for students to engage in the kind of high-level mathematical reasoning or creative problem solving frequently seen in schools serving more affluent students. Arguably, the problem is that educators believe that students from low-socioeconomic-status (SES) backgrounds are in need of the "basics" and, therefore, are not expected or encouraged to do higher level work in mathematics.

But what happens when poor urban students are presented with a program that uses instructional strategies and content often found in high-SES communities? This chapter presents data from Project Challenge, a collaborative intervention project (funded 1998–2002) designed to develop elementary and middle school students' talent in mathematics. It describes features of the Project Challenge curriculum that not only helped students

High-Expectation Curricula, edited by Curt Dudley-Marling and Sarah Michaels. Copyright © 2012 by Teachers College, Columbia University. All rights reserved. Prior to photocopying items for classroom use, please contact the Copyright Clearance Center, Customer Service, 222 Rosewood Dr., Danvers, MA 01923, USA, tel. (978) 750-8400, www.copyright.com.

learn content but also assisted them in developing the reasoning skills, dispositions, ways of thinking, and creative mind-sets that are essential for entry into the intellectual world beyond secondary education.

SEEKING TO IDENTIFY TALENT

Project Challenge, funded by the Jacob K. Javits Gifted and Talented Students Education Program (Grant No. R206A980001, U.S. Department of Education, with Chapin as Principal Investigator [PI] and O'Connor as co-PI had two goals: to identify diverse elementary and middle school students (English Language Learners, minority, and economically disadvantaged) with potential talent in mathematics, and to provide them with a rich, challenging program that would prepare them to continue with the study of advanced mathematics. Project Challenge was situated in Chelsea, Massachusetts, an urban community that ranked in the bottom 20% on the state accountability tests when they were introduced in 1998. During the intervention (1998–2002), approximately 84% of students in the community belonged to minority groups: 70% were Hispanic, 6% were Asian American, and 7% were African American. In addition, 78% of the student population was poor, receiving free or reduced-price lunch assistance. It is a community that has historically served immigrants: 65% of students came from households where English was not the primary language. The district was typical of other urban districts in that the mobility rate ranged between 25 and 35% each year.

This district did not have any programs in place for "gifted and talented" students. Indeed, several administrators informed us that our intervention would not succeed, as their district did not have any gifted students. Our approach, however, was quite different from a traditional gifted and talented program. Those often identify only the students who score in the top 1 or 2% of each grade on aptitude or achievement tests and fashion a pullout program for them. This approach has proven problematic in low-income settings. The identification of talented or potentially talented students from diverse backgrounds is a well-documented challenge. At-risk students as groups have historically performed poorly on standardized tests of achievement and intelligence (Ford, 2011; Secada, 1992); many reports have suggested that using only these types of measures for identification purposes is problematic (Frasier & Passow, 1994; Renzulli, 2011; Sheffield, 1994). Furthermore, at the time the project started, the district did not administer individual standardized tests or intelligence tests.

Renzulli (1988) recommends that there be a shift in "emphasis from the absolute concept of 'being gifted' (or not gifted) to a concern with developing gifted behaviors in those youngsters who have the highest potential for benefiting from special educational services" (p. 61). Since our goal was in line with Renzulli's, the selection of students was based on a range of criteria including grades in mathematics in grade 3, student work samples, and teacher and parent recommendations and referrals. We wanted to identify 100 students to participate in the program, in line with Renzulli's recommendation to develop talent in large groups of students.

However, one of the difficulties with our identification process was that the sample of 600 students whom we evaluated using beginning-of-the-year 4th-grade work samples did not exhibit much of a range of abilities. Students had had limited opportunities with open-ended questions or with justifying their thinking. For example, only 5% and 3%, respectively, correctly answered the two questions used in the selection process (see Figure 8.1). Most students did not exhibit characteristics of even very bright students, let alone characteristics of those gifted in mathematics, such as logical reasoning about quantitative relationships, flexibility in applying mathematics, and energy and persistence in solving problems (Krutetskii, 1976).

Since the majority of materials used to select students for Project Challenge in the first year did not easily identify children who might have greater than average talent for mathematics, we needed additional data to use in the selection process. Thus, following the first year of the project, scores on the Naglieri Nonverbal Abilities Test (NNAT; Naglieri, 1996) were used to identify students with "above average" abilities regardless of their limited or emerging English language skills. (Sample questions from the NNAT are displayed in Figure 8.1.)

Additionally, an attempt was made to match the representation of ethnolinguistic minorities in Project Challenge to the incidence of these

Figure 8.1. Sample Questions Used for Selecting Students

Draw this shape:
I have four sides.
Two of my sides are the same length.
I have no right angles.

Does this picture show two eighths?

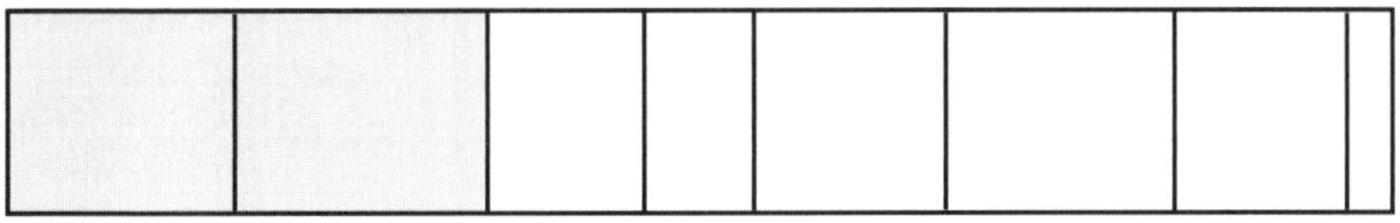

Explain.

minorities in the larger community. Using the NNAT, teacher recommendations, and work samples, we filled approximately half of the 100 places. To fill the remaining 50 slots, we chose students from the "average" NNAT category based on race/ethnicity and gender to maintain the same balance as the district as a whole.

In its first four years (1998–2002), four cohorts of 100 students each, starting in 4th grade, were instructed daily in mathematics in classes of approximately 25 students each. Each subsequent year a new cohort was selected, as previous cohorts moved to the next grade level.

THE MATHEMATICS CURRICULUM AND INSTRUCTION

The mathematics content in Project Challenge's curriculum aligned with the Massachusetts Mathematics Frameworks and the National Council of Teachers of Mathematics standards documents. The core materials were units from *Investigations in Number, Data, and Space* in grades 4 and 5, and units from *Connected Mathematics* (CMP) in grades 5 through 7. Since the goal was to have students enroll in Algebra I in 8th grade, we started some relevant topics in grade 5, a year earlier than suggested in either curriculum. For example, *Prime Times* (CMP), a 6th-grade unit on primes, composites, and factors, was used in 5th grade. These curricular materials supported the development of sense making and the building of connections among ideas.

Assessment included weekly quizzes and unit tests in order to build accountability. Students were coached on how to study, practiced writing explanations about problem solutions, and were held to high standards in terms of retaining and utilizing previously learned content. All students were expected to participate in respectful discourse about mathematical ideas. Getting students to talk about academic ideas or procedures brought to the surface their gaps in understanding; they realized when they didn't fully understand and teachers were able to adjust instruction to address misconceptions and confusion.

In other classrooms in the schools in which we worked, there was a focus on procedural skills at the beginning of each school day. However, in Project Challenge classrooms, early morning work focused on building mathematical reasoning skills. Starting in 5th grade, students were given a packet of five tasks every Monday; they worked on one task/problem each day during the designated "review" period. Many of the problems included an application of skills or introduced students to new vocabulary, and, in most, the solution process also involved inductive, deductive, algebraic, or spatial reasoning. Then at the start of their mathematics period, a discussion was held about the problem. An example from the 6th-grade curriculum illustrates some features of these problems: "What digit is in the ones place in 9^{25}? Look for patterns in easy powers of 9. Explain your reasoning."

This problem requires students to apply their knowledge of exponents and multiplication facts and procedures, and to use induction to generalize to find an answer. Students found the values for some of the powers of 9 ($9^1 = 9$, $9^2 = 81$, $9^3 = 729$, $9^4 = 6561$, $9^5 = 59,049$, . . .) and through discussion were able to articulate how the ones digit would always be a 9 or a 1 since each subsequent power was multiplied by an additional 9. They were able to reason that 9^{25} had to have a 9 in the ones place since there were an odd number of nines multiplied together. Assisting students in making mathematical generalizations is one instructional emphasis that is often missing from urban classrooms. Furthermore, the idea that one must practice reasoning skills in order to improve one's ability to think in this manner is often ignored, because "it takes too long and there are so many skills to cover." Yet by talking daily about problems of this sort, students were required to practice reasoning.

Project-based learning was another feature of the Project Challenge mathematics curriculum. Students in urban districts rarely have opportunities to work on projects that focus extensively on higher level cognitive tasks where they must analyze and synthesize material. Each year students completed at least three projects, the final end-of-year project being the most extensive and time-consuming. For example, in the 4th grade, students explored measurement topics by figuring out the average weight of a 4th-grade sneaker. Their final project involved researching bridges and building a model bridge from toothpicks. They tested designs to find the style that would hold the greatest possible weight. In the 5th grade, students learned about M. C. Escher and the mathematics behind tessellations. They were challenged to create a unique tessellation that was then used to cover the surface of a three-dimensional box. Students in 6th grade developed and analyzed games of chance following a unit on probability. Their final project involved designing and building a miniature house to scale, complete with roof, windows, and doors. Seventh-grade students completed algebra projects where they analyzed a pattern, identified the 100th term, determined recursive and explicit rules, and represented the relationship with tables, graphs, and equations. Their final project involved geometry, with the students designing, building, and flying actual kites.

Overall, projects supported creativity, extended mathematical content in other areas of the curriculum, and required students to work together collaboratively. But more important, students always had to produce something, such as a written report, model, poster, or game, and time was always allocated for the students to present their projects orally to an audience of parents, teachers, students, and administrators. Specific questions were given to students to help guide them in making these presentations and explaining their work.

High-level mathematics achievement involves more than computation. Conceptual development is central, as is the acquisition of skills and practices that support sustained exploration of complex ideas and their consequences. Along with these, however, comes the obligation to explain: to explain one's thinking; to explain to another how a problem was set up or solved; and to explain how one idea is related to another idea. The ability to use language to externalize one's thinking to a partner, teacher, and parent was an important goal of Project Challenge.

THE PROFESSIONAL DEVELOPMENT COMPONENT

Mentoring and coursework for teachers were the basis of the professional development for the project. In-class mentoring supported teachers in using discourse to develop students' understanding. Starting with the 4th grade in the first year, one master teacher worked side by side with the classroom teachers from one grade level, modeling specific pedagogy and team teaching, and coaching them in specific strategies such as the use of wait time. The next year, this teacher would move up to the next grade and work with teachers there. Teachers in the previous grade, who had been trained the year before, mentored new colleagues.

In addition, each year Project Challenge provided teachers with an after-school course designed to update and extend their knowledge of mathematics, mathematics curriculum including pedagogy, and the particular ways that talent might be developed in students. These courses met for over 45 hours (including summer workshops) and focused on mathematics topics specific to the grade level, pedagogical issues (e.g., classroom discourse, worthwhile mathematical tasks, the role of the teacher, the social culture of the classroom), and issues germane to talented students. Unfortunately, the yearly attrition rate of Project Challenge teachers was high. Over 60% of the teachers who received professional development through Project Challenge were not with the program at the end of 4 years.

In light of the high attrition rate, the new teachers joining Project Challenge did not have professional development opportunities; therefore, support materials were produced by project faculty for teachers. For every instructional unit, project staff produced written "crib sheets" that explained the important mathematical ideas and connections, listed the key discussion topics, and provided justification for why these specific topics and ideas needed to be discussed. These materials helped teachers frame their classroom discussions and kept them focused on talking about the "big" ideas.

MEASURED OUTCOMES OF PROJECT CHALLENGE

A variety of achievement data was collected on Project Challenge from the fall of 1998 through 2003 in order to monitor the progress of students in the program and provide formative assessment feedback to teachers and project faculty. Students' gains on the norm-referenced California Achievement Test (CAT) were considerable. Table 8.1 compares Project Challenge students to the national norming sample in terms of percentile scores. After 2 years in the project, students were scoring better than 87% of the students in the national sample.

Another measure that was used to monitor Project Challenge students was their results on the high-stakes state test—the Massachusetts Comprehensive Assessment System (MCAS). The MCAS in mathematics is used to check students' use of algorithms and computation, and their knowledge of concepts and applications, using multiple-choice, short-answer, and open-response questions. Student scores are reported as: Advanced, Proficient, Needs Improvement, and Failing. At the time of the intervention, students in Massachusetts were given the MCAS in mathematics in the 4th, 6th, 8th, and 10th grades. (Coincidentally, the first year it was given was 1998, the first year of Project Challenge.) We were able to get information about Project Challenge students' mathematics learning as measured by the MCAS after about 9 months in the program and after almost 3 years in the program. After one academic year, at the end of 4th grade, over half (57%) of each Project Challenge class scored Advanced or Proficient on the MCAS mathematics test, where the state average was 38% (see Figure 8.2). Few Project Challenge students fell into the Failing category.

Table 8.1. California Achievement Test of Mathematics (Total) Mean Percentile Rank

	4th Grade Cohorts I–IV	5th Grade Cohorts I–IV	6th Grade Cohorts I–III	7th Grade Cohort I
Number of months in Project Challenge	3	15	27	39
Percentile rank	75	78	87	90
n*	304	261	176	70

*Only students who started Project Challenge in grade 4 and remained in the project were included.

At the end of 6th grade, over three-fourths (82%) of each Project Challenge class, averaging across cohorts, scored Advanced or Proficient on the MCAS mathematics test—again, significantly better than Massachusetts as a whole, at 38% (see Figure 8.3).

Project Challenge students also scored better, on average, than students in Newton, one of the highest-ranked cities in the state (see Figure 8.4).

Figure 8.2. 4th-Grade MCAS Scores in 1998 Compared with Massachusetts State Average

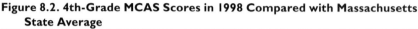

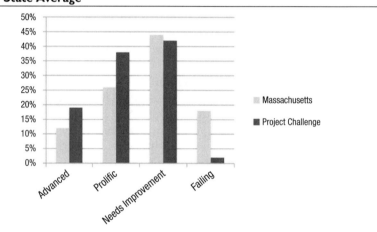

Note: Percentages are pooled from Cohorts I through V.

Figure 8.3. 6th-Grade MCAS Scores in 2001 Compared with Massachusetts State Average

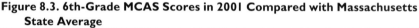

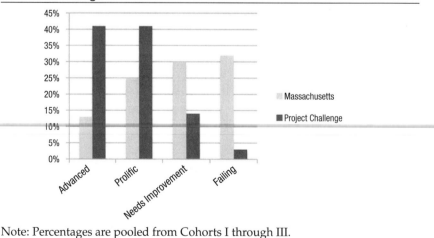

Note: Percentages are pooled from Cohorts I through III.

Figure 8.4. 6th-Grade MCAS Scores in 2001 Compared with High-SES District in Massachusetts

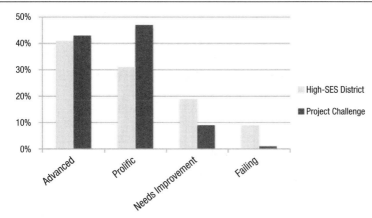

SEEKING FURTHER EVIDENCE

Although our study was not originally designed in this way, we were able to construct a post-hoc, quasi-controlled comparison that allowed us to address the hypothesis that all of our students did well simply because they were "gifted." As we indicated above, half of the students in our beginning cohort were identified through the use of the Naglieri Nonverbal Abilities Test (NNAT). The other half of the cohort was essentially selected at random from students scoring in the average range on the NNAT. Eventually, we had a total of 106 such "average" students in the Project Challenge cohorts and 140 such "average" students in the regular classes in the corresponding years. We compared the performance of these two "average" groups after 1 and 2 years to determine whether the outstanding test scores of the Project Challenge students were completely due to a preponderance of gifted students or whether the program was actually benefiting average students more than the instruction they would receive in a regular classroom. After one year in the program, we compared the two groups' performance on the MCAS. Using a factorial analysis of variance, we showed that the Project Challenge "average" students significantly outperformed the regular post-hoc control group in mathematics ($F = 74, p < .0001$) and in English language arts ($F = 84, p < .0001$). (See Figure 8.5.) Both comparisons yielded large effect sizes: Both were over 1.1 (Cohen's d).

We also tested whether the effects persisted after the first year, using the CAT (the MCAS in math was not administered in 5th grade). Again, the results were significant. The Project Challenge students outperformed the regular controls on the mathematics portion ($F = 50$, $p < .0001$). Using normal curve equivalent scores we could see that the Project Challenge students were over one standard deviation higher (Effect size: $d = 1.36$). (See Figure 8.6.)

CONSIDERING A RANGE OF EXPLANATIONS

These results indicate that the Project Challenge results were not simply due to a preponderance of "gifted" students in the program. Moreover, we believe that multiple features of the intervention benefited students of both "high" and "average" abilities. One factor was the curriculum: It provided Project Challenge students with daily experiences that are found more commonly in affluent schools. The focus on challenging material, in the form of complex problems and projects, prepared students to deal with more complicated materials. The Project Challenge students seemed less likely to be "thrown" by encountering something beyond a one-step problem. They became accustomed to making sense of content. Another feature related to curriculum was the emphasis on building understanding by asking students to

Figure 8.5. 4th-Grade MCAS Results (Scaled Scores) in Post-Hoc Controlled Comparison

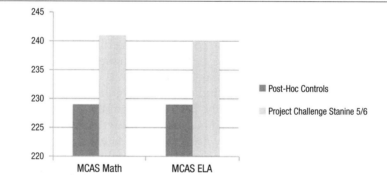

Figure 8.6. 5th-Grade California Achievement Test Math Results (Normal Curve Equivalent) in Post-Hoc Controlled Comparison

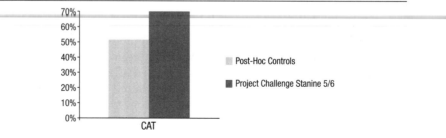

compare and contrast ideas. Discussions focused on helping students categorize knowledge and generalize across topics. Students discussed and debated high-level questions that helped them build and connect knowledge.

Another factor was the emphasis on accountability in terms of homework and tests. When Project Challenge began, elementary school classes in Chelsea generally did not give quizzes. By learning how to study for biweekly quizzes, students gradually internalized their own responsibility for academic achievement and gained an understanding of how much effort was required. Yet another factor was improved teaching. Although the teachers who agreed to participate in Project Challenge generally started out with relatively low levels of understanding of mathematics and of how students learn mathematics, they either received intensive professional development or were given focused support materials. Based on pre- and post-test surveys of teachers, we know that their knowledge of mathematics, how students learn, and how to teach mathematics effectively all improved. (And as evidence of their accomplishment, a number of the Project Challenge teachers moved on to better jobs in more affluent districts, where their skills and knowledge made them valuable commodities.)

An interesting hypothesis voiced by a number of the participating teachers is that the intensive use of classroom talk played a major role in student achievement. We strongly emphasized classroom discussion, in which teachers asked students to provide reasons for their answers and explanations for their solutions. This seems a reasonable hypothesis, particularly given the fact that student achievement in English language arts rose along with mathematics (refer to Figure 8.5). This outcome, along with our analysis of written work and videotapes of classroom discussions (e.g., O'Connor, 2001), led us to believe that our emphasis on productive classroom talk played a role in fostering students' ability to reason and express their reasoning coherently.

Often classroom discussions consisted of an overt and prolonged struggle to understand difficult ideas, with many such ideas embodied in difficult texts. It seems likely that as teachers encouraged students to struggle with understanding, the students took on a productive disposition towards such struggles. They learned that it often takes more than a few minutes to figure something out—sometimes it takes days. They learned that it takes time and effort to be sure that you understand someone's idea. They learned that they did not have to have the right answer immediately, and that sometimes the content of one's reasoning was the most important issue. These dispositions undoubtedly would affect a student's performance on a standardized test. For one thing, such students would be less likely to panic or give up. They would be more likely to reread and try to understand. This "communicative stamina" in itself could account for some of our results on standardized tests. But there are other possible mechanisms.

One is increased intelligibility of the content through repeated reformulations. Teachers frequently "revoiced" student utterances (O'Connor & Michaels, 1996) and asked the other students to do so as well. This led to more linguistic input for the second language learners, and also led every student to have more time to process the complex material that was being presented. It put pressure on students to clarify their ideas, and let them know that they had both the right to be heard, and the corresponding obligation to listen carefully and respectfully to others.

Another mechanism is a focus on greater depth and coherence of reasoning, leading to better understanding of the mathematics content itself. There was interplay between the content of the discussions, which focused on mathematical connections and generalizations, and the emphasis on focused reasoning and justification brought about by the talk moves themselves, as used by the teacher. Students internalized mathematics into a framework of key ideas that were each supported by facts and knowledge and that were highly connected to other ideas. Their ability to work with these ideas and explain their reasoning about these ideas was strengthened by the inclusive practice of discussion.

In what follows, we present an example for readers to think with. In the example in Figure 8.7, the teacher has presented one of the morning "logic problems" described above.

Finding the solution to this problem involves the use of deductive reasoning. Students must reason based on specific given facts. The problem is also challenging because it uses a negation—what can we conclude if we know that Santiago's specialty is *not* orthopedics? Through discussion, students started to follow the logic that since Santiago was not an orthopedic doctor, he must be either a pediatrician or a surgeon, but since each doctor's last name begins with a letter that is different from her specialty, Santiago cannot be the surgeon.

What follows is a constructed example, not an actual transcript. It reflects the range of talk moves used in the Project Challenge pedagogy, and it reflects the kinds of responses students might give. It is based on the kinds of teaching and student responses we have seen many times, in many classrooms. Of course in actual transcripts exchanges like those below might take longer, with students providing partial or incomplete answers and with the

Figure 8.7. Logic Problem Example

Doctors Pierce, Otis, and Santiago specialize in pediatrics, orthopedics, and surgery.

Santiago's specialty is not orthopedics.

None of the last names of the doctors begins with the same letter as that doctor's specialty.

Question: What is the specialty of each doctor?

teacher relying more on "partner talk" or other moves that cannot be illustrated here due to space considerations. Nevertheless, we intend this constructed example to provide a sense of the kind of talk the Project Challenge teachers elicited during at least part of every lesson. Consider what benefits might accrue as students engage in such talk every day.

(The class has discussed the meaning of "surgery," "orthopedics," and "pediatrics.")

Teacher: Now that we have established what each of these doctors do, let's talk about the information. Eduardo, tell us a fact from the problem.

Eduardo: Santiago is not the orthopedic doctor.

Teacher: Okay, so what does that mean?

Eduardo: It means he doesn't fix broken bones.

Teacher: He doesn't fix broken bones. Well, what else does that clue tell us? Why don't you all turn to your partner and come up with one other fact using the information that Eduardo just shared. [Teacher waits 90 seconds while students talk together.] Okay, Ramona, what did you and your partner think?

Ramona: Well, we think Santiago has to be, like, the surgeon or the other one?

Teacher: Okay, Ramona and Kelsey, you think Santiago might be the surgeon or "the other one"? What does "the other one" mean?

Kelsey: He might be a pediatrics. The kids' doctor.

Teacher: Right, a pediatrician is a doctor who takes care of children. And Ramona, why do you and Kelsey think that Santiago is either a surgeon or a pediatrician?

Ramona: Because he's not an orthopedic doctor and he has to be one of the other kinds.

Kelsey: But I said I don't think he can be a surgeon.

Teacher: Why do you think that?

Kelsey: Because it says right here that none of the last names begin with the same letter.

Teacher: Okay, hmm. Let's make sure we all follow this. Joseph, can you say what Kelsey just said in your own words?

Joseph: She said that Santiago is not the surgeon, but I'm not sure why.

Teacher: Okay, Kelsey, can you help us figure this out? Why don't you think Santiago can be the surgeon?

Kelsey: It's the other clue. [reads] "None of the last names of the doctors begins with the same letter as that doctor's specialty."

Teacher: Talk to your partner. Put the meaning of that clue into your own words. [One minute later.] Julia, what do you think?

Julia: Does it mean that since Santiago begins with an *s* that he
            can't be the surgeon?
Teacher: Wayne, do you agree or disagree with Julia and why?
Wayne: Umm, I agree with her. Because . . . Santiago's name starts
            with an *s* so that doctor can't be the kind that starts with an *s*.
Lillian: I agree too. You can cross out two doctors. Can I show you?
            [Comes to the board and writes:]
            Santiago   orthopedics   x
                          surgery   x
                          pediatrics   ✓
Teacher: Okay. Lillian has used what we call in mathematics
            the "process of elimination." She *eliminated* two of the
            possibilities, leaving just one possible choice. Can someone
            explain why Lillian put Xs next to two specialties and a check
            next to pediatrics? Okay, Maurice.

This process of drawing conclusions from specific givens is especially difficult for students, yet it is an essential step in reasoning. Discussions like the one above provided the students with many opportunities to engage with the ideas. Notice how students' attention was focused on key pieces of evidence when a statement was repeated or when they were asked to talk with their partners about the statement. Furthermore, students deepened their own reasoning when asked to explain why they made particular statements or if they agreed or disagreed with another's conclusions. When students are repeatedly pressed to provide evidence for their conclusions, they soon naturally provide this information on their own. Finally, discussion of these types of problems built students' flexibility in using a variety of types of reasoning as they were exposed to other students' strategies and approaches.

CONCLUSION

Many of the students in our project did not come from homes where a great deal of time was devoted to externalizing one's thinking. Even in homes where that does happen, the obligation and privilege to do so are often not evenly distributed. For example, in some cultures it is considered unseemly for girls to make presentations and talk about their reasoning, even if boys are encouraged to do so. We noticed from the beginning that it was difficult to get some girls to speak in front of the class, and thus we built this component into the project-based work. Students had opportunities to practice their presentations prior to the actual event and then to present to an audience of parents, teachers, and peers. Over the years of the project we watched as formerly silent students became energetic and enthusiastic contributors within this special context of school. The unfamiliar activity of externalizing one's reasoning and talking at length about academic content became available to all students in the project.

Project Challenge is an example of what is possible when poor urban students are afforded a different type of learning environment. The sustained nature of the intervention, the emphasis on reasoning and generalizing, and the opportunity to reflect on and articulate one's thoughts through discussion all contributed to the development of students' robust learning.

REFERENCES

Ford, D. (2011). Closing the achievement gap: Gifted education must join the battle. *Gifted Child Today, 34*(1), 31–34.

Frasier, M. M., & Passow, A. H. (1994). *Toward a new paradigm for identifying talent potential* (RM94112). Storrs, CT: The National Research Center on the Gifted and Talented.

Haberman, M. (2010). The pedagogy of poverty versus good teaching. *Phi Delta Kappan, 92*(2), 81–87. (Original work published 1991)

Krutetskii, V. A. (1976). *The psychology of mathematical abilities in schoolchildren.* Chicago: University of Chicago Press.

Naglieri, J. A. *(1996). Naglieri Nonverbal Ability Test.* San Antonio, TX: Harcourt Brace Educational Measurement.

National Assessment of Educational Progress (NAEP). (2009). *The nation's report card.* Washington, DC: National Center for Educational Statistics. Retrieved from http://nces.ed.gov/nationsreportcard/

O'Connor, M. C. (2001). "Can any fraction be turned into a decimal?" A case study of a mathematical group discussion. *Educational Studies in Mathematics, 46,* 143–85.

O'Connor, M. C., & Michaels, S. (1996). Shifting participant frameworks: Orchestrating thinking practices in group discussion. In D. Hicks (Ed.), *Child discourse and society learning: An interdisciplinary perspective* (pp. 63–103). Cambridge, UK: Cambridge University Press.

Renzulli, J. S. (1988). The three-ring conception of giftedness: A developmental model for creative productivity. In R. J. Sternberg & J. E. Davidson (Eds.), *Conceptions of giftedness* (pp. 53–92). Cambridge, UK: Cambridge University Press.

Renzulli, J. S. (2011). More changes needed to expand gifted identification and support. *Phi Delta Kappan, 92*(8), 61.

Secada, W. G. (1992). Race, ethnicity, social class, language, and achievement in mathematics. In D. A. Grouws (Ed.), *Handbook of research on mathematics teaching and learning* (pp. 623–660). New York: Macmillan.

Sheffield, L. J. (1994). *The development of gifted and talented mathematics students and the National Council of Teachers of Mathematics standards.* Storrs: University of Connecticut, National Research Center on the Gifted and Talented.

CHAPTER 9

The Investigators Club

A High-Expectation Alternative to Textbook Science

Richard Sohmer

All students come to school with well-developed theories of how the world works. Students are already dedicated and successful investigators of the physical world. They know how to jump out of the way of an oncoming bus, transfer liquids, move heavy or clumsy objects around, and deal with friction and force. They have theories (largely implicit) of invisible causes (suction, heat, pressure, gravity) underlying apparent effects in their environments. Note that "all students" is meant to emphasize that it isn't just children from wealthy or middle-class families who come to school with "well-developed theories"—ESL students and children from impoverished families also enter school with complex and useful knowledge (often exceeding that of their more privileged or monolingual peers) of how the world works.

The way science is typically taught in schools—"textbook science"— disparages students' already-existing knowledge. The extent, complexity, and workaday utility of student knowledge are rarely appreciated; and even when students' ideas *are* taken into account, they are framed as pernicious, a snarl of misconceptions—useless impedimenta that are to be extracted and replaced by canonical prosthetics (think dentures!). In short, textbook science privileges and rewards the memorization and regurgitation on command of (putatively canonical) texts, formulas, and procedures. The problem is that memorization is not understanding. Memorizing a text which has the potential to evoke a specific concept is in no way the same thing as understanding the concept in such a way that it becomes a productive, usable tool—linked to others in the cognitive toolkit.

The textbook approach to science education—in poor and economically privileged schools alike—routinely incapacitates students. For one thing, it disparages students' workaday knowledge of the world as "unscientific." This is incapacitating in that students take it as an authoritative diagnosis that their own minds and bodies are unsuited to engaging with and learning about the world and how it works. Then simultaneously, textbook science assures students (of the unmitigated falsehood) that the mass of texts, formulas, and procedures that they are force-fed is "real" science. Since this force-fed mass (aka "content") is undigested and uncomprehended, students are unable to put it to any productive use.

A reasonable response from those who have been subjected to this studied practice of incapacitation would be extreme and justifiable *anger*—along the lines of "How is it possible that I have *wasted* all these months and years studying 'science' without knowing any science?" Unfortunately, since the institutional participants in the textbook science hoax seldom cast any doubt upon its authenticity, students generally conclude that their failure to comprehend and profit from textbook science is proof of their own inadequacy.

More research is *not* required. "Textbook science" is efficacious, in a horrible way. What most students take away from their years of exposure to the textbook science scam is two conclusions—*about themselves*: (1)"I don't like science," and (2) "I'm no good at it."

We can do little about those we have already maimed. But we owe it to the children who continue to show up every year—bright-eyed, inquisitive, ready and able to learn—to teach them or, at the very least, not to maim them.

The Investigators Club (I-Club, for short) is a high-demand, high-expectation science curriculum, originally designed as an after-school program for inner-city, low-SES students from a wide range of cultural and linguistic backgrounds who were struggling or failing in school. (It has since been adapted for use as an in-school program in elementary and middle schools, as preservice teacher training, and as a prekindergarten curriculum.)

This chapter describes the talk, tools, and tasks that are interwoven in the Investigators Club, illustrated through an example of physics learning taken from the middle school after-school program. By drawing on the knowledge about the world that students bring to school, the Investigators Club enables previously failing middle school students to understand and use complex physics theories, to resee the world conceptually, and to identify themselves as competent and powerful agents within it.

EFFECTIVE SCIENCE LEARNING FOR *ALL* STUDENTS

Over the past 10 years the Investigators Club has worked with researchers, teachers, and students to integrate the best practices of science education (e.g., Arons, 1997; Freier & Anderson, 1996; Liem, 1991; Minstrell, 1989), studies of scientific cognition (e.g., Hutchins, 1995; Latour, 1986; Polanyi, 1962), and seminal linguistic, psychological, and sociocultural research (e.g., Gee, 1996; Grolnick, 2003; Lave & Wenger, 1991; Rommetveit, 1974; Wertsch, 1985) anatomizing the processes of primary and secondary discourse acquisition (aka successful apprenticeship).

The Investigators Club (I-Club) is designed to provide students with a successful apprenticeship into science. To that end, the I-Club makes use of students' everyday ways of speaking about and interacting with the world as the basis for scaffolding them into the use of new discursive and representational tools—more effective ways of understanding, perceiving, and manipulating the world. The focal experimental setups ("demos") are, by design, assembled from recognizable, everyday materials (no "black boxes") so that students can anticipate, predict, and argue for multiple possible outcomes. Arbitration is administered by the actual outcome of the demo, not the teacher's say-so.

> Instead of ignoring the alternative frameworks that children have developed, science teaching programmes could benefit by taking greater account of them. By making their theories more explicit in the formal learning situation children are able to explore their implications and make comparisons between one "framework" or "theory" and another. They can also be given experiences which serve to develop their ideas or, if necessary, to challenge them. (Driver, 1983, p. 76)

Making one's best argument is the heart of the I-Club game. If a student's prediction or theory (or both) are, in the end, disconfirmed by the evidence, that is okay. The job of the scientist—which the members of the I-Club are apprenticing to be—is not to be *right* "by rote," but to make cogent predictions and theories, so that they may be cogently confirmed or disconfirmed. The goal, then, is to make one's claim as explicit and persuasive as possible. Everyone benefits from seeing the best theory prevail against the field of contesting, arguably possible—though ultimately less effective—theories, and everyone can and is expected to appropriate the results in their consideration of the next demo.

MODELING HOW SCIENTISTS TALK, THINK, AND ACT

As they analyze and explain contesting predictions and theories about physical events that they observe together, the I-Club students are scaffolded toward the "Discourse" of physics. The notion of a "Discourse" (with a capital *D*) has been central to the design of the I-Club and stems from Gee's seminal work (Gee, 1989, 1992, 1996). Gee's *Discourse* refers to the ways in which people align language with ways of acting, interacting, thinking, valuing, and feeling, as well as ways of coordinating (and getting coordinated by) people, objects, tools, and technologies, *so as to display different socially situated identities*. We are all members of many Discourses—sometimes compatible, sometimes conflicting.

Note that the Discourse of physics is not anybody's *primary* Discourse. For instance, most people see, use, and accept "suction" as a perfectly adequate explanation of ordinary actions like using a vacuum cleaner to clean a carpet or drinking a milkshake through a straw. An ordinary person drinking a milkshake through a straw sees *sucking* (or, what sounds more scientific, a "vacuum") at work. A physicist, in contrast, sees *pushing*. The actual forces of pulling and pushing are both invisible, but practitioners of physics see pushing—atmospheric pressure pushing the milkshake up into the straw.

In the process of doing science, the I-Club participants take on a new identity (Science Investigator is how the students refer to themselves and each other), which does not conflict with their current understanding and ways of speaking. This new identity builds upon (and transforms) their current understandings as the basis for new ways with words and new ways of "seeing" the world.

Investigators Club activities ("tasks") are embedded in a set of participant structures and expectations that model the way scientists actually talk, think, and act. In Circle-Up Time, the central event in the I-Club, students engage in a powerful whole-group talk format that we characterize as a "position-driven discussion." Students focus on a single problem (see Figure 9.1) or question—embodied in a discrepant-event demo assembled from everyday or hardware store components—with multiple outcomes that are arguably possible. [See http://www.investigatorsclub.com for details.] Everyone is encouraged—indeed, at strategic points in the debate, *required*—to commit to one position or another and to justify his or her respective predictions or theories. As the debate continues, participants are free to change their positions on the basis of another's evidence or arguments, with the proviso that they explain what it is in the other's position that they find useful or persuasive.

HELPING STUDENTS EXPLICATE THEIR REASONING

With rare exceptions, the I-Club teacher's job is not to provide "right answers" during position-driven discussions. "Telegraphing" (indicating in any way) which argument or theory is closest to being canonically correct inhibits position-driven discussions. Instead, the teacher scaffolds the ongoing multiparty discussion by asking specific students to "say more about that," or to repeat in their own words what another student has said; encouraging others to say whether (and why) they agree or disagree with a specific claim; or "revoicing" student contributions—pushing for clarification—so that everyone has access to everyone else's reasoning.

Revoicing

In regard to the problem shown in Figure 9.1, the teacher might say, "Okay, so let me see if I've got your theory right. Are you saying that the volleyball will weigh less [when we put more air into it] because a balloon falls slower when it's full of air?" The teacher *revoices* to help the student construct the claim, prediction, or theory the student envisions and is struggling to put into words. When students register that the teacher is exerting her or his skills in their service, they typically respond forthrightly to skillful revoicing, with responses running the gamut from "No, that's not what I said" to "Yeah, that's it" to "Yeah, but I also want to say . . ." and everything in between.

Getting teachers to use talk moves such as revoicing without "editorializing" on the correctness or likelihood of the student's claim has turned out to be a tougher job than we anticipated. Part of the difficulty is that revoicing runs counter to the received model of "teacher equals provider and enforcer

Figure 9.1: A Circle-Up Problem for a Position-Driven Discussion

The two volleyballs balance on the scale, initially. When more air (ten strokes of a bicycle pump) is put into the ball on the left, what will be the result? Will the ball with more air go up? Go down? Stay the same?

of right answers." Another part of the problem is that revoicing requires the teacher to sustain a very high level of awareness and self-discipline, because there is little or no margin for error. Students *cannot* ignore correctness cues from teachers; when the teacher emits one—as happens inadvertently on occasion even to skilled discussion facilitators—the students' investigations are summarily terminated. Learning to revoice as a matter of habit is like learning to ride a bicycle. Initially, it seems to entail rude halts, crashes, and scrapes. With repeated attempts and the observation of others' successful performances, however, one "gets the hang of it"—and can go places and do things easily that were previously inaccessible and impossible.

Revoicing and related discussion-facilitating tools have been written about as "Accountable Talk" (Michaels, O'Connor, Hall, & Resnick, 2002) and "Academically Productive Talk" (Chapin, O'Connor, & Anderson, 2009). This work identifies a small set of talk moves ("talk tools") for teachers that have been shown to be effective for orchestrating multiparty talk in culturally complex and/or noisy classrooms. These talk tools are "follow-up moves"—teacher responses to students' contributions. Each is a productive alternative to the default "Evaluation" move (as in I-R-E recitation). The tools position students as thinkers, reasoners, and holders of positions. The net effect is to create an environment in which engaged argument (from multiple points of view) is the valued norm—and in which students do the "heavy lifting" in reasoning through complex problems.

Michaels and O'Connor (2011) characterize these talk moves as tools that help teachers accomplish four critical goals in guiding discussions (see Figure 9.2).

These talk tools and goals are critical in the Investigators Club—because having multiple, "sayable" theories (positions, predictions) is more important for student discussion and real learning than rote arrival at the "right answer."

Only when all predictions and theories have been put on the table in their strong forms, with evidence and arguments marshaled in their support, is the demo allowed to run its course. Nature speaks and settles the argument. At that point, the teacher's role is to facilitate the debriefing process. What happened? What have we learned? What's still undetermined, unknown, ambiguous? What ways of thinking about the problem were fruitful? Here, again, the teacher's job is not to bludgeon the students out of their home-based knowledge and the theories implicit in that knowledge, but rather to help them explicate and clarify competing ideas and their implications in light of the demo's outcome in order that more effective, more canonical ideas emerge as motivated matters of personal importance.

In the I-Club, where the teacher's goal is to facilitate a genuinely position-driven discussion, heterogeneity of students' experience and cultural background is a valuable resource. I-Club members can readily

Figure 9.2. Goals for Productive Discussion with Associated Talk Tools

Goal One: Helping students share, expand, and clarify their thinking

1.	**Time to Think:** Partner Talk Writing as Think Time Wait Time
2.	**Say More:** "Can you say more about that?" "What do you mean by that?" "Can you give an example?"
3.	**Verifying and Clarifying by Revoicing:** "So, let me see if I've got what you're saying. Are you saying . . . ?" (always leaving time for the student to respond—to agree or disagree and say more)

Goal Two: Helping students listen carefully to one another

4.	**Who Can Rephrase or Repeat?:** "Who can repeat what Javon just said or put it into their own words?" (Variant after a partner talk: "What did your partner have to say?")

Goal Three: Helping students dig deeper into their own reasoning

5.	**Asking for Evidence or Reasoning:** "Why do you think that?" "What's your evidence?" "How did you arrive at that conclusion?" "What do you see in the text [the data, the demo] that made you think that?"
6.	**Challenge or Counterexample:** "Does it always work that way?" "How does that idea square with Sonia's example?" "What if it had been a copper cube instead?"

Goal Four: Helping students engage with others' reasoning

7.	**Agree/Disagree and Why?:** "Do you agree/disagree? (And why?)" "Are you saying the same thing as Jelya or something different, and if it's different, how is it different?" "What do people think about what Vannia said?" "Does anyone want to respond to that idea?"
8.	**Add On:** "Who can add onto the idea that Jamal is building?" "Can anyone take that suggestion and push it a little further?"
9.	**Explaining What Someone Else Means:** "Who can explain what Aisha means when she says that?" "Who thinks they could explain in their own words why Simon came up with that answer?" "Why do you think he said that?"

Note. Adapted from *Talk science primer* by S. Michaels and C. O'Connor, 2011, p. 11 (http://inquiryproject.terc.edu/shared/pd/TalkScience_Primer.pdf).

predict the outcome of discrepant-event demos, using their diverse, culturally derived, everyday locutions, *because* the demos are made from everyday objects (balloons, soda cans, drinking glasses, candles, water, fire, etc.). Nonetheless, the underlying realities instantiated by the demos are the laws of physics, which are the same across cultures. When the student evaluates competing theories in their most persuasive forms in the shared context of the demo at hand, cognitive growth in the form of movement toward more effective, more canonical ways of seeing and talking is self-motivated and self-enhancing, grounded in and assimilated to experience, and driven by the desire to know and make things happen in the world, rather than by a concern for the "right" answer.

Strategic Use of Explanatory Tools

At strategic points—when experience has demonstrated their effectiveness and when it would be unproductive to demand that students "reinvent the wheel"—the I-Club teacher provides new "explanatory tools," often in the form of analogies and/or narratives. The "Air-Puppies" story (Sohmer & Michaels, 2005), for example, is a narrative form of the Ideal Gas Law. In the "Air-Puppies" story, the puppies referred to are mythical or fictional beings combining *some* of the properties of real puppies with the behavioral characteristics of the molecules that make up air. The air-puppies are the bumbling (mindless) agents in a modifiable story with a particular setting (always including two rooms separated by a moveable wall-on-wheels), participating in a series of events, always resulting in some kind of lawful effect—that is, the wall moves as it *must*, given the air-puppies' opposing impacts upon both sides.

We typically introduce the "Air-Puppies" story to the students in a 10- to 20-minute session by telling them the basic story, followed—always—by several variations. As the story progresses, the situation and changes in it are illustrated with simple, freehand drawings (on whiteboard, paper, or chalkboard).

We begin by asking the students to imagine a big room divided into two smaller rooms by a wall on frictionless wheels (like roller skates). In each of the rooms on either side of the wall-on-wheels there are air-puppies—initially, equal numbers and kinds—mindlessly bumbling around. (Figure 9.3 shows a top-down view of the situation.) The dividing wall-on-wheels moves whenever a puppy bumps into it (not intentionally, just mindlessly moving around). As the puppies bumble around and mindlessly bump into things (all the walls and each other), "What," we ask the students, "will happen to the *wall*?" In this first session, one or more students will confidently "read" the situation to predict that "the wall will stay in the same place."

Figure 9.3. The View from Above at the Beginning of the "Air-Puppies" Story

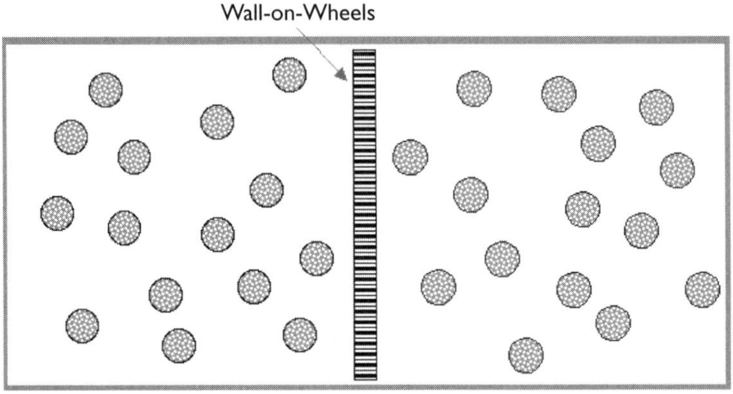

Wall-on-Wheels

Once the scenario in Figure 9.3 is set in motion, the wall-on-wheels (or, as the students refer to it, simply "The Wall") is pushed a little bit to one side or the other each time a puppy bumps into it. Because the wall gets, on average, the same number and kind of bumps from each side, the wall stays over time in approximately the same place, oscillating about the centerline (see Figure 9.4).

A number of variations on this basic story are examined and discussed.

Variation 1: Few Air-Puppies vs. Many Air-Puppies

Storyteller: "What if we start out with 20 air-puppies on this [right-hand] side of the wall, and more air-puppies—say, 100—on the other [left-hand] side? What do you think will happen to the wall-on-wheels?"

Students will say something like: "The Wall's gonna move toward the 20-puppies side [the wall will move to the right] because there's more puppy hits on the other [100-puppy] side."

Variation 2: Fast [Hot] Air-Puppies vs. Slow [Cold] Air Puppies

Storyteller: "What if we start out with the same number of air-puppies on both sides of the wall, but we get the puppies on one side really excited—so that they bumble around much faster than the puppies on the other side? What do you think will happen to the wall-on-wheels?"

Students will say something like: "The fast puppies are gonna bump into The Wall faster and more times and harder, so The Wall is gonna be pushed away, toward the slow puppies."

Figure 9.4. Equal Numbers and Kinds of Air-Puppies on Each Side of the Wall on Wheels

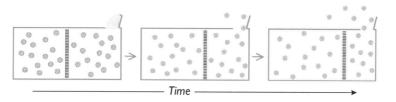

With equal numbers and kinds of air-puppies on each side, the wall-on-wheels is continually bumped from side to side. The net impact of the puppies on one side of the wall-on-wheels is, on average, equal to the net impact of the puppies on the other side, making the wall oscillate about the centerline.

Variation 3: Air-Puppies on One Side of the Wall-on-Wheels Escape

Storyteller: "If we start out with the same number and speed of air-puppies on each side of the wall, and then a door opens, so that some of the air-puppies on the right side of the wall bumble out—what will happen then?" (Figure 9.5 illustrates this situation.)

Figure 9.5. Three Views as Time Progresses

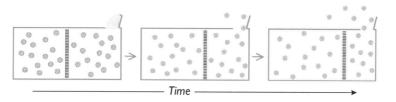

As air-puppies in the right room "bumble" out the open door, there are fewer and fewer air-puppy impacts from the right upon the wall-on-wheels. Increasingly, unopposed air-puppy impacts from the left push the wall away to the right. In this case, the wall-on-wheels is pushed to the right, as puppy bumps on the left side are, over time, decreasingly opposed by puppy bumps on the right side.

The "Air-Puppies" story has been a spectacularly useful tool to children and adults alike. Presenting it to a group takes about 15 minutes, starting with "All you have to do to have your thinking transformed by this story is to tell it to someone else." It then, like any tool, has to be practiced extensively, with support and guidance, with many different air pressure demos. (Demos and animations of the Air-Puppies scenarios are available at the Investigators Club website: http://www.investigatorsclub.com)

The I-Club members take on new tools such as the "Air-Puppies" story and new ways of arguing—building and weighing scientific arguments. They learn new ways to model and theorize about complex phenomena and new ways to make their thinking visible to their peers and to themselves. In short order, their ability to understand and explain physical phenomena scientifically positions these children—once school failures—as *experts* in the eyes of their peers, their teachers, younger students, and science fair judges.

EVIDENCE OF SIGNIFICANT RESULTS

From a variety of perspectives and using a number of indicators, we have been able to show that students who were failing in school became increasingly capable over the course of their participation in I-Club activities, demonstrating impressive intellectual abilities—in understanding and theorizing difficult problems in physics and in demonstrating their understanding to others. Evidence includes, but is not limited to, pre- and post-tests of science knowledge; questionnaires of I-Club students and matched controls' motivation, participation, and sense of efficacy in school; teacher judgments of students in school; Investigators' successful participation in the school science fair; and Investigators' demonstrated ability to present, conduct discussions about, and teach the physics of air pressure to younger (5th-grade) students.

We have both quantitative and qualitative evidence that these students took on expanded identities as "Science Investigators." They participated as effective members of a specific Discourse, the Investigators Club, which embodies skills, attitudes, and knowledge valued by the Discourses of science and school. We can also show that the I-Club Discourse did not resonate with their previous negative experiences in school, and that it consisted of practices that allowed these students to voluntarily acquire and demonstrate competence in knowledge, skills, and attitudes valued in scientific contexts (and schools).

We also assessed changes in students' scientific reasoning. Repeated measures analyses showed that I-Club students increased in the complexity of their responses over time relative to control children, who decreased. I-Club students were less likely than control participants to use anthropomorphic or volitional causes (e.g., "the fire wanted to escape from the bottle and so it sucked the egg in") as explanatory devices.

Our studies of the motivational structure and impact of the I-Club have also provided significant results. Relative to their matched controls, the I-Club participants increased more from pre- to post-assessments in school engagement and learning orientation (working to actually learn something rather than just to look smart) and decreased more from pre- to post assessment in their performance orientation and external motivation for school (doing schoolwork just to look smart or because they "have to"). Additionally, the I-Club students described their teachers and parents as more supportive of their autonomy over time relative to the controls, indicating that the I-Club was successful in creating positive changes that were evident even outside of the I-Club setting.

CONCLUSION

In the Investigators Club, students are invited to make use of their embodied knowledge and home-based ways of speaking, in a range of talk formats (such as partner talk, whole group, position-driven discussions, and student presentation/critique sessions). At the same time, they are introduced to a new set of discursive norms and forms (Accountable Talk), to help them take up and work with a set of symbolic tools (such as the Air-Puppies model). These tools give them purchase on a complex set of relationships that make it possible to re-see the world—"seeing" air pressure phenomena as physicists do, as the cumulative effects of air molecules pushing rather than sucking. Here, successful learning is a function of the Discourse itself coming to be (1) shared, (2) assumed as common knowledge, and (3) serving as a carrier of intelligence as it speaks through the I-Club members. Who or what is doing the guiding? Participation in the talk, tasks, and tools of (the Discourse of) physics enables the Investigators to "re-see" the world in more powerful ways than their peers (and their parents) and and thereby to experience a change—an upgrade—in their social status: They are seen by others as "scientists." They see themselves (often for the first time) as competent, powerful learners.

Implementing such a "high-expectation" practice or curriculum, as is the case in the Investigators Club, is not easy. Norms for respectful and equitable talk must be established, not assumed, and carefully socialized (over a period of months) in order to ensure participation by all. Teachers need deep knowledge of the intellectual domain (physics, in this case) in order to recognize and then scaffold learners' initial, ill-formed forays into successful enquiries. Sequences of rigorous, generative tasks must be cultivated and archived (as at http://www.investigatorsclub.com)—as they are in the Japanese practice of "lesson study"—so that teachers do not have to "reinvent the wheel." With time and intent, rules of thumb about which talk format is best at any particular point emerge. When is partner talk appropriate? When is it likely to waste time? What questions launch effective position-driven discussions? How can productive tools like the Air-Puppies model be generated? (We have yet to find one that works as well in supporting students in "seeing" density or gravity, for example.)

When we began developing the Investigators Club, many argued that "lower-class" children's learning was irremediably limited by their putatively "restricted linguistic code." We were intent on demonstrating that all children are capable learners of physics. We believed that children would respond to a high-expectations environment designed and implemented to apprentice them into the practice of physics by learning—not memorizing—physics. Our experience in the Investigators Club has repeatedly and absolutely confirmed that belief.

At present, implementing a high-expectations science curriculum (like the Investigators Club) at scale runs up against a formidable obstacle. Put briefly, the existing teacher corps is fundamentally unable to apprentice students into the practice of science. Why? Because the teachers—with rare exceptions—have themselves never experienced anything other than textbook science. What we need are high-expectations professional learning opportunities, experiences, and curricula for *teachers*—so that they can embody and implement the kinds of high-expectations programs that we know can be successful with children.

Marty Rutherford (the author of Chapter 3) was an inner-city teacher in Alameda, California, when I worked with her and her 1st-graders on the physics of air pressure and the Air-Puppies model, as a visiting science teacher. Rutherford read a draft of this chapter and, in a personal response to my rather harsh, but honest concern about "the existing teacher corps," wrote:

> As one of those teachers you are talking about I think it is fair to say—
> we cannot teach what we do not know. Most of us did not take science
> courses—much less physics courses—beyond high school. And
> while I learned from you that physics was the most fundamental—
> foundational of the sciences . . . I did not know this before you taught
> me, so how could I possibly have taught my kids?
>   You are right to call for high-expectations curricula for kids. We
> need to simultaneously call for a great change in teaching credential

programs and professional development so that ALL teachers have the opportunity to acquire the deep knowledge needed in order to teach young people what they need to know and understand. One thing cannot happen without the other. (Marty Rutherford, personal communication, April 10, 2012)

In the Investigators Club, I've characterized the apprenticeship structure as an environment where everyone is "on the same page." Teachers and students have different roles, but they are focused on, and building, an intersubjectively shared world. Rutherford refers to this in her final comment:

When we worked together, you were always talking about "creating a page so big that no one can fall off." That page we have to build must include every single person—including teachers! (Marty Rutherford, personal communication, April 10, 2012)

In this description of the Investigators Club, we have suggested (concurring with the latest research and human history) that apprenticeship is the educational environment best suited to maximize motivation and real—not rote—learning. We have targeted three components—"talk, tasks, and tools"—that figure as key notions in constructing and sustaining high-demand and high-expectation guided knowledge construction. As always, there is much that we don't know and plenty to learn, but the time for excuses is over. We know enough *now* about how to engineer successful learning for all students. It's up to us to act on what we know. Let's do it.

REFERENCES

Arons, A. B. (1997). *Teaching introductory physics*. New York: Wiley.

Chapin, S., O'Connor, C., & Anderson, N. C. (2009). *Classroom discussions: Using math talk to help students learn* (2nd ed.). Sausalito, CA: Math Solutions.

Driver, R. (1983). *The pupil as scientist?* Philadelphia: Open University Press.

Freier, G. D., & Anderson, F. J. (1996). *Demonstration handbook for physics*. College Park, MD: American Association of Physics Teachers.

Gee, J. P. (1989). Literacy, discourse, and linguistics: Essays by James Paul Gee. *Journal of Education, 171*(1).

Gee, J. P. (1992). *The social mind: Language, ideology, and social practice*. New York: Bergin & Garvey.

Gee, J. P. (1996). *Social linguistics and literacies: Ideology in discourses*. London: Taylor & Francis.

Grolnick, W. S. (2003). *The psychology of parental control: How well-meant parenting backfires*. Mahwah, NJ: Erlbaum.

Hutchins, E. (1995). *Cognition in the wild*. Cambridge, MA: MIT Press.

Latour, B. (1986). *Laboratory life: The social construction of scientific facts*. Princeton, NJ: Princeton University Press.

Lave, J., & Wenger, E. (1991). *Situated learning: Legitimate peripheral participation*. Cambridge, UK: Cambridge University Press.

Liem, T. L. (1991). *Invitations to science inquiry*. Lexington, MA: Ginn Press.

Michaels, S., & O'Connor, C. (2011). *Talk science primer*. Cambridge, MA: TERC. Also available on the Talk Science and Inquiry Project website: http://inquiryproject.terc.edu/shared/pd/TalkScience_Primer.pdf

Michaels, S., O'Connor, C., Hall, M., & Resnick, L. (2002). *Accountable talk: Classroom conversation that works* (CD-ROM set). Pittsburgh, PA: University of Pittsburgh.

Minstrell, J. (1989). Teaching science for understanding. In L. B. Resnick & L. Klopfe (Eds.), *Toward the thinking curriculum* (pp. 133–149). Alexandria, VA: Association for Supervision and Curriculum Development.

Polanyi, M. (1962). *Personal knowledge*. Chicago: University of Chicago Press.

Rommetveit, R. (1974). *On message structure: A framework for the study of language and communication*. New York: Wiley.

Sohmer, R., & Michaels, S. (2005). The "air-puppies" story: The role of narrative in teaching and learning science. In U. Quasthoff & T. Becker (Eds.), *Narrative interaction* (pp. 5–91). Philadelphia: John Benjamins.

Wertsch, J. V. (1985). *Vygotsky and the social formation of mind*. Cambridge, MA: Harvard University Press.

SECOND LANGUAGE LEARNERS, STUDENTS WITH DISABILITIES, AND STRUGGLING READERS

The chapters in Part IV shift the gaze from particular programs or curricular practices to what research suggests we ought to be doing in order to provide high-expectation learning opportunities for all students, including English Language Learners, students with disabilities, ethnolinguistic minorities, and struggling readers.

In Chapter 10 Ruiz critically examines the research findings on English Language Learners from the past 40 years. She argues that the assumption that English Language Learners are "pretty much" like native speakers, just a bit behind, is tantamount to adopting a deficit perspective. Instead, she suggests a range of approaches that provide high expectations and high support for English Language Learners, building on findings in the literature where ELLs make significant and rapid progress.

In Chapter 11 Kliewer brings us into the world of young children with and without disabilities constructing meaning together. He provides rich descriptions of these children, through play, imaginatively constructing meaning, creating (instead of acquiring) literacy with the support of the adults around them. Kliewer uses the metaphor of "flow" to conceptualize the manner in which children, some with severe learning disabilities, create complex literacy profiles as they develop symbolic and written language.

In Chapter 12 Urbach and Klingner argue that high-expectation pedagogy involves recognizing and building upon the knowledge, experiences, and background that students bring to class. They describe the early literacy competencies of several African American 1st-graders, as seen through their quite remarkable oral storytelling performances. They put forward a view of literacy both as a socially constructed concept and a dynamic, living, and protean art that is experienced and drawn on differently by different students. Educators, they argue, must seek to engage children's many different ways of knowing and challenge the dominant view of literacy as a narrow set of skills.

In Chapter 13 Allington and McGill-Franzen summarize the literature on struggling readers and the achievement gap that has accumulated over the past 20 years, revisiting the research on effective reading instruction, including early intervention programming, high-success reading, comprehension development, the use of running records, and tutoring. They argue persuasively that the problem is not a lack of money or knowledge, but rather a "long-standing set of professional beliefs, practices, and programs that fail to reflect what we have learned in the past 20 years about teaching all children to read."

Taken together, these chapters support the view that high expectations are required for both students *and* teachers (and the policy makers and administrators who support them), if we are to put into practice what we know works, and if students are to be given the opportunities they deserve.

CHAPTER 10

It's Different with Second Language Learners

Learning from 40 Years of Research

Nadeen T. Ruiz

A recently published book (California Department of Education, 2010) on instructed English Language Development, which historically has been called English as a Second Language (ESL), highlights two contrasting ideas about the instruction of English Learners. The first proposition appears in a chapter by Snow and Katz (2010), and I call this stance on language and literacy instruction "It's Different for English Learners." Here, Snow and Katz describe the stance in terms of teacher education:

> Two basic assumptions guide many current teacher preparation programs: (1) that the needs of English learners do not differ significantly from those of other diverse learners; and, (2) that the discipline of ESL is primarily a menu of pedagogical adaptations appropriate for a variety of diverse learners. These faulty assumptions . . . are reflected in the following teacher's statement: "It's not all that different" (the process of second language learning). Such assumptions lead to the beliefs that the learning of a second language simply requires exposure to and interaction in the target language and that all English learners will learn English in the same way. (pp. 134–135)

The second, contrasting proposition appears in a chapter by August and Shanahan (2010). I have labeled their perspective, following the teacher's quote above, "It's Not All That Different for English Learners." They comment:

> Generally, this research suggests that a sound literacy curriculum for English learners will focus on the same components of literacy as a curriculum geared

for English-proficient students. The following section further elaborates on this guideline. *Guideline 1: Effective instruction for English learners is similar to effective literacy instruction for native speakers.* From the first guiding principle, it is evident that English learners have to focus on the same components of literacy as monolingual students. What needs to be learned to read in English is largely the same whether one is a native speaker of English or an English learner. (p. 220)

Though the authors do raise the possibility of adaptations of instructional approaches for English Learners, that point is watered down by the much greater number of statements purporting that teachers can use strategies developed and tested on monolingual English speakers with English Learners (Ruiz & Gold, 2011).

Whether or not one looks at these stances as polar opposites or as degrees of difference along a continuum of beliefs and practices regarding English Learner instruction, I would contend that underlying differences, or degrees of difference, can make a significant impact on the instruction that we offer English Learners. Considered in light of this book's guiding premise, degrees of difference along the continuum can affect whether English Learners are "treated like a poor learner" (Rist, 1970) or offered "high-expectation" curricula (see the Introduction to this volume).

Viewing English Learners as "almost the same" as English monolinguals is a deficit perspective couched in subtlety. The thinking goes something like this (when avoiding polemic terms): "English Learners are very similar, but you know, not quite, because of the language learning challenge. We may have to do some adapting for that challenge." The alternate perspective views English Learners not as something different from the norm, but as representative of *diversity as the norm* in schools. This perspective also views English Learners as bringing distinct and substantial resources to literacy learning. I would further contend that the way to help researchers and teachers change their views and classroom practices that are anchored in the "It's Not All That Different" paradigm is to acknowledge the 40-year research base on second language acquisition and instruction that shows "it's different."

In this chapter I illustrate the connection between these stances and the nature of English Learner instruction. I first take a quick look at an English Learner's literacy development in 2nd grade to consider how different and how similar literacy processes and instructional practices look in the case of English Learners. I then discuss some instructional strategies that reflect 40 years of research in the area of English Learner instruction, and, consequently, enact high-expectation curricula and instruction. In the last section, I contrast these classroom practices with what seems to be a return to 1960s-era second language instruction, a step backwards due to the downplaying of differences between native English speakers and English Learners with little attention to the research-based practices emanating from the second language field.

ENGLISH LEARNERS' LITERACY DEVELOPMENT

Diana (a pseudonym) arrived at Carolina Oropeza's bilingual 2nd-grade classroom an emergent writer. Almost 8, she had gone to school in a school district some 80 miles away, but had not learned English, or beginning English literacy skills, despite being in an all-English classroom. Carolina asked her 2nd-grade students to write in student-teacher interactive journals, very cognizant of their use since the late 1970s with English Learners and deaf students from elementary to university levels (Peyton & Straton, 1993). She knew that interactive journals were an effective strategy for English Learners to develop writing conventions, to encode sound-symbol relationships, and to increase their range of language functions. She also knew that her English Learners brought a rich set of lived experiences with them to the classroom—even those children at very emergent stages of literacy development, like Diana—and that offering them a choice of writing topics was essential to create a space for them to write about those experiences. The first image in Figure 10.1 shows an example of one of Diana's first interactive journal entries. Written in Spanish, it shows a 2nd-grader who is using letter strings and drawing to convey meaning.

In September, Diana told Carolina that she had written about going to school with her brother. (Notice that in the response to Diana's journal entry in September, the teacher asks Diana what grade her brother is in, and Diana replies "6S." The teacher replies, "Ah, in sixth." Over the course of the next 8 months, Carolina involved Diana and her other students in a high-expectation curriculum, using instructional strategies from the Optimal Learning Environment (OLE) Project (Ruiz, Vargas, & Beltrán, 2002). The OLE Project is firmly grounded in research on second language acquisition and instruction and creates instructional contexts that look like classrooms for gifted and talented programs (Ruiz, 1989; Ruiz, García, & Figueroa, 1996). In May of Diana's 2nd-grade year, she wrote an entry in her interactive journal telling of a frightening encounter she and her brother had, not long after an anti-immigrant proposition was passed by California voters (but later overturned by the courts). Written in Spanish, the entry was 62 words long. All words are segmented correctly, and 58 out of 62 (94%) are spelled correctly (see the first page of the May interactive

Figure 10.1: Diana's Interactive Journal Entries in September and May

Diana's September Entry, in dialogue with her teacher.

Diana's May Entry, in dialogue with her teacher.

journal entry at the bottom of Figure 10.1). Here is an English translation of her May entry:

> Yesterday my father told me that I shouldn't play with my friend who is White. One day my brother and I went to the neighborhood store and a White boy said to him that the police were going to come and take us because we are Mexican. He was the one who heard it. I didn't.

The second page of this interactive journal includes the teacher's response to Diana. In OLE classrooms, all entries receive a response, either from a teacher or a peer, following the research on interactive journals with English Learners. In this case Carolina's focus in writing to Diana, however, is less about Diana's literacy development and more about helping her process a difficult experience. Here is an English translation of the response with Diana's answers:

Carolina: Diana, how did you feel when the White boy said that about Mexicans?
Diana: Terrible, and when I got home, I wanted to cry.
Carolina: The boy who said that is a racist. Do you remember that we have talked a lot about that?
Diana: Yes.
Carolina: Racist people are ignorant. All humans are the same inside even though we are different colors on the outside. If you were to see that boy again, what would you tell him?
Diana: That he's ignorant.
Carolina: We Mexicans need to be proud because we are very intelligent.

I invite readers to first consider whether there was anything distinct in what Diana brought to her literacy lessons in relation to a native English speaker, and whether there was anything different in the way Carolina designed her instruction to Diana in comparison to a native English speaker. The second observation I would like readers to make is regarding the pace of Diana's spelling and writing development. For any primary grade child, moving from letter strings to conventional spelling of long texts in 8 months is impressive. Yet, in high-expectation curricula, based on 40 years of research with English Learners, my colleagues and I have seen similar progress repeatedly (e.g., Ruiz & Enguídanos, 1997; Ruiz, Vargas, & Beltrán, 2002). As we will see in the next section, Carolina solidly built her instruction of English Learners upon the foundation of 40 years of research.

ACKNOWLEDGING THE 40-YEAR RESEARCH BASE IN OUR INSTRUCTION OF ENGLISH LEARNERS

As a member of a group of teaching and research colleagues, I am currently engaged in a project that focuses on Indigenous students from Mexico in California (Ruiz & Barajas, 2012). Indigenous migrants from Mexico often speak as their first language Mixtec, Zapotec, or one of the many Indigenous languages of Mexican states like Oaxaca. As the numbers of Mexican Indigenous migrant families have increased, especially in California and the Pacific Northwest, so have the challenges facing their children in U.S. schools. Indigenous children have been the objects of a number of acts of intolerance by U.S. school peers. In response to these acts, my colleagues and I were asked to bring nine Indigenous teachers from Mexico to study English for a month at our university. After their intensive English program, the teachers traveled to various regions in California that have large numbers of Mexican Indigenous migrant families to work in Migrant Education summer school programs.

From Here to There Lesson Sequence

In order to integrate content learning with the teachers' English Language Learning—an instructional strategy emanating from research on instructed English Language Development (Echevarria, Vogt, & Short, 2010)—we asked the Mexican teachers' English instructor to incorporate lessons on literacy instruction for K–8 students as "content" for the Mexican teachers. One of the lessons involved using the book *From Here to There* (Cuyler, 1999) to teach several language and academic objectives, such as present tense, reporting, survival English, and geographic vocabulary, to English Learners with beginning proficiency. The first pages of the book contain this text:

> My name is Maria Mendoza (pp. 1–2). I live with my father, my mother, my baby brother, Tony, and my older sister, Angelica, (pp. 3–6), at number 43 Juniper Street, (pp. 7–8), in the town of Splendora (pp. 9–10), in the county of Liberty (pp. 11–12), in the state of Texas (pp. 13–14), in the country of the United States (pp. 15–16), on the continent of North America (pp. 17–18) . . .

The book continues to follow the pattern of ever-increasing geographical units until it reaches "the universe and beyond." The book closes with a return to the child protagonist and the beginning of the book, "From here to there, my name is Maria Mendoza."

One of the Mexican educators in our project, Santiago Gabriel Dolores, is a native speaker of Triqui from Oaxaca. Maestro Santiago (*Maestro* is an honorific term in Mexico that means "teacher") participated in this activity as a beginning English Learner, and also as a teacher constructing a model for teaching this lesson to his own students in California's migrant regions and Mexico. Figure 10.2 is a series of the first six pages of Maestro Santiago's self-illustrated book in English. He also translated the book into Spanish and Triqui.

In designing this activity, we did not simply decide that a literacy approach often used with English-speaking children, Shared Reading, should work with English Learners, although Shared Reading was developed by Don Holdaway (1979) with Maori English Learners in New Zealand and Australia. Instead, we first considered how the activity would reflect the literature on second language acquisition (SLA). Just to name a few SLA findings that come into play in this lesson, we know that, in acquiring a

Figure 10.2. Excerpt from Maestro Santiago's Book

second language, the present tense is often acquired later than the past and present progressive (Lightbown & Spada, 2007). Having a focused lesson on present tense usage, then, was important to help English Learners through texts written solely in the present—texts that students will encounter frequently because of the underlying belief by textbook publishers that literacy tasks are simplified for native English speakers by using the present tense only.

The lesson also reflects SLA research in that it supports the use of formulaic phrases, a common strategy of beginning English Learners (Snow & Katz, 2010). Formulaic phrases are memorized, unanalyzed "chunks" of language that English Learners use to communicate, often with the effect of making them sound more proficient than they are, and thereby attracting more interaction with more proficient speakers of English. "My name is" and "I live" are useful formulaic phrases.

One more finding from SLA research that I highlight here comes from a series of case studies and qualitative research that showed that the more socially distant language learners felt from the target language group, the greater their difficulty in acquiring the second language (Schumann, 1976). Currently, it is difficult to call to mind a more "socially distant" group than Indigenous Mexican students in U.S. schools, frequently criticized by peers from all peer groups, including Mexican American students who do not self-identify as Indigenous, for their physical characteristics, language, socioeconomic status, and farm-worker backgrounds. In fact, the word *oaxaca* or *oaxaquito*, deriving from one of the most beautiful and linguistically rich states in Mexico—Oaxaca—has become an insult among schoolchildren for bullying purposes. The fact that this lesson, then, purposely incorporated an original book with illustrations of a family of color, and most important, asked students to insert their names, their significant others, and their locations in the universe as a requirement for successfully completing the lesson, is another one of many possible examples of the active connection between SLA research and instruction that went into the creation of this lesson.

The research links to instructed English Language Development (ELD) are equally strong. Before even opening the book, we made links between the themes of the book (e.g., We have unique families and homes; we share our geographical settings; and so on), and the teachers' background knowledge. Of course the literature on the importance of background knowledge and reading is clear for monolingual English speakers' reading comprehension, as well. Specific research with English Learners and background knowledge shows, however, that it has a distinct function with second language learners. For example, research by Hudson (2007) showed that students with more beginning English proficiency could perform as well as those with more advanced proficiency on language and literacy tasks when background knowledge activities occur at the start of the lesson. Support for this finding came from the Mexican teachers themselves, whose language proficiencies ranged from Level 1 on the Michigan Test of Language Proficiency (the majority had no English instruction before our program) to one teacher's score at Level 7 (Advanced). Careful planning based on SLA research made this an activity in which teachers at either end of the continuum of language proficiency engaged, performed well, and committed to use the lesson with their students in California migrant regions and at home in Mexico.

Other research-based strategies enacted in the *From Here to There* lesson included *communicative language teaching* (Richards, 2006), where the focus was language as a tool for authentic social and academic needs. The Mexican teachers were alternately asked to work in pairs, small groups, and the whole class within highly interactive participant structures that depended on English language use to carry out the communication and academic objectives. The ELD instructor delivered *comprehensible input* to the English Learners (Echevarria et al., 2010), but also implemented tasks that asked the Mexican teachers to produce *comprehensible output* (productive speech and written language), to put the press on their linguistic resources needed for deeper second language processing and growth (Gibbons, 2002).

Concurrently, as instructed ELD research would suggest, form-based instruction occurred during the lesson sequence, resulting in accurate usage of language frames and presentation language and in the publication of their personalized books with standard grammar and spelling. Careful use of feedback on the teachers' oral and written English usage was implemented, relying on the research promoting judicious error-feedback to enhance second language development (Ellis, 2005). The instructor knew that either too much error correction, or insufficient correction, or correction at the wrong time during the lesson sequence could have deleterious effects on second language growth. Furthermore, all of these carefully considered and implemented research-based instructional strategies occurred within a print-based lesson sequence. Once again, the instructor enacted what the research base of instructed ELD has supported for years, namely that early introduction of print with even beginning-level English Learners is related to enhanced second language development (Hudelson, 1984).

There are several other areas of SLA and instructed ELD research that were taken into account in the planning and implementation of the lesson sequence, which I have not pointed out here. Still, my hope is that readers have begun to see that high-expectation curriculum for English Learners very much relies on the past 40 years of research. In terms of Carolina's work with Diana in interactive journals, the high level of interaction, authentic communicative contexts, a focus on comprehensible input and output, primacy of students' background knowledge, and early introduction of print also supported Diana's rapid growth in literacy.

"Honoring Our Families and Communities" Lesson Sequence

One other example of a lesson sequence may even more firmly establish this point. In the next lesson, Maestro Santiago participated in an instructed ELD lesson sequence that forms part of our professional development module for U.S. teachers of Mexican Indigenous students (Ruiz, Barajas, McGinty, & Romo, in press). This particular lesson came from an intermediate grade (grades 3–6) unit in the module called "Honoring Our Families and Communities." Once again, the Mexican teachers participated in this lesson sequence as a way to connect their second language instruction to academic content—here, lessons that they could use with Indigenous students both in migrant communities in California during the summer program of teacher exchange and, once back in Mexico, in their teacher and administrator positions.

In this unit, my colleagues and I wanted to directly address in several ways the prejudicial attitudes and bullying behaviors directed towards Mexican Indigenous students in the United States and in Mexico. One tack we took was to focus on the wise words of all of our families. Again, the research on English Learners permeated our approach, recognizing the influence of González, Moll, and Amanti's (2005) work in documenting the "funds of knowledge" within poor immigrant families, and the learning that happens when those funds are brought into classrooms as units of study.

Figure 10.3 presents an essay written by Maestro Santiago. In this writing and art piece, he tells us of a member of his family who has guided him. Maestro Santiago wrote the piece in Triqui, Spanish, and his brand new language, English.

Expecting a multiparagraph expository essay from an English Learner in a 4-week, first-time, intensive English program certainly captures this book's theme of what is possible through high-expectation curricula. Of course the instructional scaffolds put into this lesson sequence were extremely strong in guiding the writing of this piece (Gibbons, 2002). Besides those research areas cited above—taking into account developmental sequences, integrating formulaic phrases through oral and written language frames, recognizing social distance as an acquisition factor, the use of background knowledge activities to raise the language functioning of students with beginning proficiency, the authentic communicative intent in lesson activities, the high degree of interaction, the integration of form-based instruction, comprehensible input and output, judicious error correction/

feedback, and the early introduction of print—there are others significantly undergirding this lesson sequence and Maestro Santiago's work, such as the use of students' primary language in instruction.

The effectiveness of primary language instruction is, at least in the research arena, almost without debate (Lindholm-Leary & Genesee, 2010). With regard to making a case for the "It's Different" position, English Learners' proficiency in their first language has to figure prominently. Overwhelmingly documented by research, a well-developed first language is an asset to second language learning and academic achievement, as well as responsible for the social benefit of bilingualism and biliteracy. While it is true that bilingual teachers are trained to implement primary language instruction, there are concrete ways that monolingual teachers can also integrate students' first languages into literacy and academic content lessons. As an example of that approach, Maestro Santiago's English instructor did not speak Spanish or Triqui or any of the other Indigenous languages represented by the Mexican teachers in her ELD classroom. Yet all of her students, the majority with no previous English language instruction, were able to write an expository essay about a significant elder

Figure 10.3. Maestro Santiago's Essay

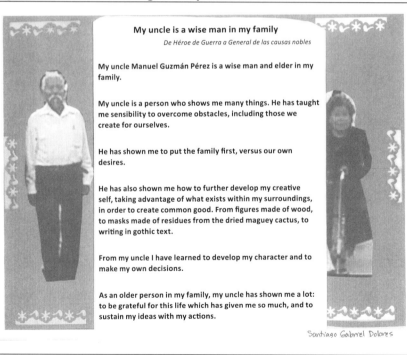

My uncle is a wise man in my family
De Héroe de Guerra a General de las causas nobles

My uncle Manuel Guzmán Pérez is a wise man and elder in my family.

My uncle is a person who shows me many things. He has taught me sensibility to overcome obstacles, including those we create for ourselves.

He has shown me to put the family first, versus our own desires.

He has also shown me how to further develop my creative self, taking advantage of what exists within my surroundings, in order to create common good. From figures made of wood, to masks made of residues from the dried maguey cactus, to writing in gothic text.

From my uncle I have learned to develop my character and to make my own decisions.

As an older person in my family, my uncle has shown me a lot: to be grateful for this life which has given me so much, and to sustain my ideas with my actions.

Santiago Gabriel Dolores

in their family or community at the end of 4 weeks of language instruction. In terms of Carolina's interactive journal work with her student Diana, the high-expectation instruction also included Diana's native language. Without the primary language component, we would not have known about Diana's struggle (and high-level processing on many levels) about whether playing with a White friend is advisable in anti-immigrant times. There is certainly a press on one's linguistic and literacy resources— comprehensible output—when there are such important topics to talk about in a high-expectation curriculum. If there continues to be an overinsistence on the position, "It's Not All That Different," powerful lessons on English language acquisition—ones that address social justice issues for groups that suffer extreme hardships in our schools and communities— are not heeded and built upon.

A brief recounting of some of the additional research-supported instruction present in the "Honoring Our Families and Communities" lesson sequence includes scaffolding reading and writing with graphic organizers (Gibbons, 2002). In this particular sequence, the instructor offered the Mexican teachers sentence frames for an expository paragraph, such as "_____ is a wise person in my family." Part of the next scaffolded section continued: "_____ taught me _____. She/he also taught me _____. In addition, I learned how to _____ from _____." One of the scaffolds provided for a closing sentence was "As a wise elder in my family/community, my _____ has taught me many things." Interestingly, Maestro Santiago and many of the other Mexican teachers chose to go beyond the assignment of a single expository paragraph and created short essays. He also chose not to use the scaffold and instead crafted his own sentences. This was possible because Maestro Santiago had the opportunity to write and share his essay first in Spanish, before working on the Triqui and English versions.

One additional research area reflected in this sequence—and highlighted here—is the instruction of academic English to English Learners. Academic language can be viewed as one end of a language continuum, with conversational language occupying the opposite end, and most of our actual language use running from one side of the continuum to the other in dynamic ways. Readers of this chapter can study the construct of academic language as connected to English Learners in texts by leading theorists and researchers such as Schleppegrell (2004), but for our purposes here, I rely on Pauline Gibbons's (2002) very accessible work, theoretically undergirded by systemic functional linguistics. We designed the sequence of lessons leading to the expository paragraph or essay purposively, giving the Mexican teachers opportunities to communicate using conversational English. In contexts where conversation-like English is sufficient to accomplish tasks, participants relied on shared background knowledge and the immediacy of the situation to convey meaning. In addition to using conversational

English, however, the Mexican teachers were called upon to use academic English. For example, the teachers employed very specific language forms and vocabulary to express meaning, especially when an individual teacher was the sole possessor of the information (e.g., the wise elder in his or her family, and that elder's guidance) and had to use language without the aid of shared experience to convey meaning. The teachers also put into practice other features of academic language: long turns of talk and writing; a range of language functions such as comparing, describing, and reporting; organizational features of both oral and written language that are associated with different genres or text types; and many more. Making the English Language Development instructor's job much easier in this context, of course, was the fact that the Mexican educators controlled academic Spanish extremely well; theirs was a task of learning the specific conventions of English academic language, not the overall purpose or usage of academic talk. This same advantage would hold for immigrant students who arrive with many years of formal schooling. U.S. classroom teachers of very young English Learners, however, would most likely not have that advantage, and therefore need to know the recent research on acquisition and instruction of academic language to English Learners. One critical aspect of that instruction is to include the research findings that have been cited thus far in the chapter. In other words, it is not enough to say, "English Learners need instruction on academic English." Without the support of that body of research, a laudable goal—academic English for English Learners—can turn into an anachronistic, ineffective approach to instructed ELD. The next section gives an example of what happens when we do not keep in mind 40 years of research on SLA and ELD.

IGNORING THE RESEARCH

One common approach emanating from the "It's Not All That Different" stance in English Learner instruction is the use of highly scripted reading programs that were developed for monolingual English speakers (Dutro & Kinsella, 2010). Figure 10.4 shows an example from one program, reprinted from a local newspaper touting the unveiling of a new scripted reading program for 9th-graders in urban schools (DeFao, 1999).

The stilted nature of the text, constructed to use as many words with short vowels as possible, starkly contrasts with the authentic texts being used or produced by the Mexican teachers in the intensive English program, or by young Diana in Carolina's classroom.

Most scripted reading interventions developed for monolingual English speakers clearly do not reflect the SLA and ELD research. As Dutro and Kinsella (2010) point out, these intensive reading programs do not

Figure 10.4. Example from a Local Intensive Reading Program

"You were the best class, and I think you should have a big picnic," Miss Pitt said to the kids. "But I must admit that I cannot plan it. Could you help?"

Dan sprang up and said, "Miss Pitt, I will plan the spring picnic for us. I can tell it's a lot of stress for you. You were strict, but you were the best, Miss Pitt."

High school freshmen in the program have progressed to reading short books like "The Spring Picnic," with two to three sentences per page telling the story of sixth-graders planning a picnic.

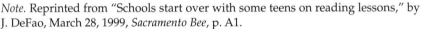

Note. Reprinted from "Schools start over with some teens on reading lessons," by J. DeFao, March 28, 1999, *Sacramento Bee*, p. A1.

give English Learners opportunities for oral language interaction that are needed for second language development. Furthermore, the artificial texts are often accompanied by workbook exercises that focus on discrete phonics and spelling skills that are infrequently linked to any real communicative function other than completing the worksheets.

I would like to close this chapter with a more complex example of what happens when we do not pay attention to SLA and instructed ELD research. *Frontloading* (California Reading and Literature Project, 2005) is an instructional approach for English Learners that is currently very popular in California. The good news about frontloading is that, unlike the intensive scripted reading programs discussed above, it was precisely developed as explicit language instruction for English Learners. Most important, it helps teachers carefully consider the language demands of their English language and content instruction in terms of the grammar, vocabulary, and language functions. But when recently developed programs or approaches for English Learners do not take into account what we have learned about SLA and ELD over the past 40 years, even a specifically designed approach to ELD instruction—one that clearly says, "It's Different for English Learners"—can lapse into mistakes of the past.

A teacher recently recounted her experience in bringing a 4th-grade student with Asperger's syndrome to an ELD lesson using frontloading. The student was Spanish-dominant. The classroom teacher had chosen a language frame that the students were to repeat several times, "I like _____ more than _____." After being asked to repeat the sentence many times from a limited number of word choices, this student loudly said, "¡Ya no! No lo voy a decir otra vez. ¡Ya lo he dicho muchas veces!" (Enough already! I'm not going to say it again. I've already said it a lot!)

To those of us in the field of SLA and ELD for a long time, this recounting takes us immediately back to either the foreign language instruction of the 1960s, or the subsequent research that showed that students did not make good gains in language proficiency with exercises disassociated from language with real communicative intent (Brandl, 2008). Unless we pay attention to the rich SLA and ELD research base at our disposal and offer evidence-based instruction to English Learners, the achievement gap—which is actually created by a research and instruction gap—will continue.

CONCLUSION

English Learners arriving to U.S. schools face a daunting task: acquiring a full linguistic repertoire of English while simultaneously learning academic content. These students are *not* "almost the same" as monolingual English students. When English Learners begin schooling behind their native-speaking peers on language and academic achievement assessments, their learning has to happen at a pace faster than for monolingual English speakers; that is, they need to make greater gains within a series of years to eventually "catch up" with their peers. The only way that accelerated language and academic development can happen is through enriched, high-expectation curriculum—distinct instruction developed for them over the course of 40 years or so of research in second language acquisition and instructed English Language Development. Our task as educators is to make sure we continue to share what we know about the body of literature that can help guide instruction tailored to the unique resources and needs that English Learners bring to our classrooms.

REFERENCES

August, D., & Shanahan, T. (2010). Effective literacy instruction for English learners. In California Department of Education (Ed.), *Improving education for English Learners: Research-based approaches* (pp. 209–250). Sacramento: California Department of Education.

Brandl, K. (2008). *Communicative language teaching in action: Putting principles to work*. Upper Saddle River, NJ: Prentice Hall.

California Department of Education. (2010). *Improving education for English learners: Research-based approaches*. Sacramento: Author.

California Reading and Literature Project. (2005). *A focused approach to frontloading English language instruction for Houghton Mifflin reading, grades K–6*. Sacramento: California Reading and Literature Project, Sacramento State University.

Cuyler, M. (1999). *From here to there*. New York: Harcourt Brace.

DeFao, J. (1999, March 28). Schools start over with some teens on reading lessons. *Sacramento Bee*, p. A1.

Dutro, S., & Kinsella, K. (2010). English language development: Issues and implementation at grades six through twelve. In California Department of Education (Ed.), *Improving education for English learners: Research-based approaches* (pp. 151–208). Sacramento: California Department of Education.

Echevarria, J., Vogt, M. E., & Short, D. (2010). *Making content comprehensible for elementary English learners: The SIOP model*. Boston: Allyn & Bacon.

Ellis, R. (2005). Principles of instructed language learning. *System, 33,* 209–224.

Gibbons, P. (2002). *Scaffolding language, scaffolding learning*. Portsmouth, NH: Heinemann.

González, N., Moll, L. C., & Amanti, C. (2005). *Funds of knowledge*. Mahwah, NJ: Erlbaum.

Holdaway, D. (1979). *The foundations of literacy*. Sydney, Australia: Ashton Scholastic.

Hudelson, S. (1984). Kan yu ret anrayt en ingles: Children become literate in English as a second language. *TESOL Quarterly, 18*(2), 221–238.

Hudson, T. (2007). *Teaching second language reading*. Oxford, UK: Oxford University Press.

Lightbown, P., & Spada, N. (2007). *How languages are learned*. Oxford, UK: Oxford University Press.

Lindholm-Leary, K., & Genesee, F. (2010). Alternative educational programs for English learners. In California Department of Education (Ed.), *Improving education for English learners: Research-based approaches* (pp. 323–382). Sacramento: California Department of Education.

Peyton, J. K., & Staton, J. (1993). *Dialogue journals in the multilingual classroom: Building language fluency and writing skills through written interaction*. Norwood, NJ: Ablex.

Richards, J. C. (2006). *Communicative language teaching today*. Cambridge, UK: Cambridge University Press.

Rist, R. C. (1970). Student social class and teacher expectations: The self-fulfilling prophecy in ghetto education. *Harvard Educational Review, 40,* 72–73.

Ruiz, N. T. (1989). An optimal environment for Rosemary. *Exceptional Children, 56,* 29–41.

Ruiz, N. T., & Barajas, M. (2012, April). *Multiple perspectives on the schooling of Mexican indigenous students in the U.S.* Paper presented at the annual conference of the American Education Research Association, Vancouver, British Columbia.

Ruiz, N. T., Barajas, M., McGinty, I., & Romo, D. (in press).*Weaving learning communities across borders: Mexican indigenous students and families in California.* Sacramento: California Department of Education, Office of Migrant, Indian and International Education.

Ruiz, N. T., & Enguídanos, T. (1997). Authenticity and advocacy in assessment: The case of bilingual students in special education. *Primary Voices, 5*(3), 35–46.

Ruiz, N. T., García, E., & Figueroa, R. A. (1996). *The OLE curriculum guide.* Sacramento: California Department of Education.

Ruiz, N. T., & Gold, N. (2011, June 7). Review of Improving education for English learners: Research-based approaches by California Department of Education. *Education Review/Reseñas Educativas, 14,* 1–13. Retrieved from http://www.edrev.info/reviews/rev1091.pdf

Ruiz, N. T., Vargas, E., & Beltrán, A. (2002). Becoming a reader and writer in a bilingual special education classroom. *Language Arts, 79*(4), 297–309.

Schleppegrell, M. (2004). *The language of schooling: A functional linguistic perspective.* Mahwah, NJ: Erlbaum.

Schumann, J. H. (1976). Social distance as a factor in second language acquisition. *Language Learning, 26*(1), 135–143.

Snow, M. A., & Katz, A. (2010). English language development: Issues and implementation in kindergarten through grade five. In California Department of Education (Ed.), *Improving education for English learners: Research-based approaches* (pp. 83–150). Sacramento: California Department of Education.

CHAPTER 11

Creating Literacy

Young Children with and Without Disabilities Constructing Meaning Together

Chris Kliewer

Sixteen 4- and 5-year-old children comprised the student population of the Moon Room in the Prairie Early Childhood Center. Four children had Individualized Education Programs (IEPs), including LaShawn, who was 4.5 years old on a January afternoon when I sat quietly in the library corner of the classroom conducting a participant observation. LaShawn, small for his age with bright brown eyes and curly black hair, had experienced perinatal trauma, and was born with severe physical disabilities. When he was 2, LaShawn entered an inclusive toddler program 3 days a week. I began following his progress when he joined an inclusive full-day class for 3-year-olds.

During my visit on that cold January day, two of LaShawn's classmates without disabilities, Jay and Stephen, raced across the classroom, each with a blanket attached around the neck. "Superman," Jay yelled as he pointed, "I seen the Bane attacking the city." Stephen's hand reached out and held Jay as he responded, "Right, Batman. We got to stop his evil." Stephen rubbed his chin in a classic "pondering" pose. He then thrust an arm up, finger pointing, and proclaimed, "To the Bat Cave, Batman. We need the maps of the city."

The boys quickly moved past other busy children to a pretend kitchen area in a corner of the room. Earlier, Jay and Stephen had together drawn and then cut out a representation of a computer, which they taped to the plastic stove. The boys gathered at their computer, poking at the buttons. Stephen said, "Okay, we need the map readout." They raced to the classroom writing center and began to draw a map.

Through all of this activity, LaShawn lay sprawled on his stomach on a wedge-shaped blue mat near the middle of the room. His arms hung over the edge and he used his curled left fist to nudge several toy cars on the floor in front of him. He appeared less interested in the cars than his peers' movements around the room. With effort, he moved his head from side to side. A teacher's aide, Jordan Peters, entered the classroom carrying a stack of papers. He immediately focused on LaShawn and approached him saying, "LaShawn, my man, had enough of the cars? What? You want to do something different? Music? The writing center?" LaShawn, who did not have any understandable spoken language, lifted his head and looked in the direction of Jay and Stephen. To communicate, he made use of sound, eye gaze, body posture, and certain written words and symbols, many of which were contained in a symbol book kept near his side. Jordan Peters said, "It looks like we got some Supermen over there? You want to help battle crime? You want to be Superman?" Stephen (aka Superman), overhearing the conversation, approached Peters and LaShawn. He said, "I'm Superman and Jay is Batman. LaShawn gots to be someone else. He can be like Spider-Man or the Hulk or . . ." Jay interrupted, "He can be Bane when we battle!" Peters said, "LaShawn don't want to be evil. He's on the good team." Stephen nodded and replied, "Yeah, on the good team."

Peters opened LaShawn's symbol notebook. The first laminated sheet had a large "yes" and "no" printed on it. With Jay and Stephen watching, Peters asked LaShawn, "You want to be a superhero now?" Peters's intention was for LaShawn to either use eye gaze or a gesture to indicate "yes" or "no" to the question. Instead, LaShawn thrust his head back with his mouth open wide in a smile. Peters said, "That's an affirmative. Let's see who you want to be." Grabbing a small whiteboard, he asked, "Let's see, what are our options? We have Spider-Man." He wrote the name on one corner of the board. Jay interjected, "The Human Torch." Peters put an H and a quick representation of a flame in a second corner saying, "What else?" Stephen said, "The Hulk?" Peters wrote out, "Hulk." Peters held the board close to LaShawn, who laboriously reached his left hand out and touched the word *Spider-Man*. Peters said, "Spider-Man it is. Let's get you a blanket." With an annoyed tone, Jay said, "Spider-Man don't got no cape!" Peters said, "Well, he's got something. Like an S on his chest?" Stephen said, "No, he has a spider on his chest." Peters said, "Oh, that's right. Let's go get you a spider on your chest."

With Jay and Stephen following, Peters carried LaShawn to the writing center. Peters drew, then cut out a spider and attached it to LaShawn's chest. Stephen said, "I need an S on me." He carefully drew a large looping S that covered an entire sheet of paper. Jay said, "Batman—b-b-b-Batman. B is for Batman. I need a B on me." Stephen said, "Batman gots a bat not a B." Jay responded, "I'm going to have a B and a bat." He drew a large B but did not try to make a bubble letter. He then drew a small squiggly shape in the little room remaining below the B and said, "That's the bat. That's Batman's bat sign."

The dramatic superhero play of Stephen, Jay, and eventually LaShawn neatly framed a range of fundamental dynamics central to early literacy and the children's developing literate profile. I observed young children with and without disabilities in symbolic-rich environments determinedly and imaginatively *creating* as opposed to *acquiring* literacy through their efforts to construct meaning of their surrounding worlds. They were far from passive recipients of an arbitrary code. I was witness to adults who took this creative and social work of young children seriously and entered into the children's lifeworlds and zones of proximal development to push, prod, and pull them in further directions of increasingly sophisticated literate citizenship.

PARTICIPATION OF YOUNG CHILDREN WITH DEVELOPMENTAL DISABILITIES

The superhero play of Stephen, Jay, and LaShawn, and numerous other vignettes I observed over the year in the Moon Room captured young children's initial literacy emanating from their passions, whether derived from their self-created narrative trajectories or brought to their attention by an adult. From these determined, active, and social efforts, thoughtful teachers were able to draw out substantive and, importantly, procedural aspects of various sign systems that furthered children's symbolic-based meaning making. LaShawn's participation in the swirl of sign systems clearly showed that, at the least, certain young children with significant developmental disabilities, often cast as intellectually hopeless, are able to engage literacy as they work to make meaning of their surrounding world.

My data, however—in direct contradiction to socially ensconced myths that act as evidence-based belief systems—overwhelmingly suggest that LaShawn's example is far less the exception than it is the rule (see also Erickson & Koppenhaver, 1995; Koppenhaver & Erickson, 2003). Young children with significant developmental disabilities are able to profoundly grow in their literate profiles. Thoughtful teachers foster this development in rich environments that promote what I term the *four currents of early literacy*:

1. Making sense of the visual-tactile, pictorial, and orthographic sign-based narratives of others
2. Finding and expressing meaning in one's own experience through narratives crafted from visual-tactile, pictorial, and orthographic sign systems

3. Developing complexity with visual-tactile, pictorial, and orthographic sign systems to construct increasingly sophisticated narratives

4. Deriving joy and other affective forces from critical, reflective engagement with visual-tactile, pictorial, and orthographic sign systems

These currents, exemplified in the superhero data vignette, are again illustrated in a second series of observations (culled from thousands of such examples contained in my field notes and dozens of hours of digitized video libraries of participating early childhood inclusive programs) that occurred in lead teacher Pat Ricer's Sun Room at the Shoshone School, an inclusive early childhood center. For her class of primarily 4-year-olds, Ricer and her teaching team designed a thematic unit around the classic picture book *Brown Bear, Brown Bear, What Do You See?* (Martin & Carle, 1967). Among the 17 participating students was just-turned-4 Jo, a girl labeled with severe autism on the autism spectrum (whom I ethnographically documented over 3 years, from age 3 through 5). When Jo had first entered Shoshone at age 3, medical records detailed severe delays across the developmental spectrum, including significant cognitive and communication impairments. Developmental scores then procured out of bureaucratic necessity by Shoshone did not contradict the medical records, though the results did evoke skepticism among the staff, who recognized the restrictive nature of developmental screenings in general.

One of the unit activities that Jo participated in included a *Brown Bear* adventure walk along a recently designed nature trail that ran through a small wooded area behind the Shoshone School. Ricer arranged downloaded pictures of the animals from the book on paper sheets that were then laminated and labeled with print captions. Two children shared a single sheet. A classroom aide had earlier arranged matching pictures in various locations (e.g., tacked to trees) along the path. As children discovered the pictures in the forest, they used oversized water-based markers to check the particular animal off their laminated sheets. For the nature walk, Jo was partnered with a favorite peer while an adult remained in the vicinity. Jo carried her laminated sheet with the downloaded pictures. When she and her partner came upon matching pictures in the wooded area, the adult as well as her partner assisted Jo in checking off the captioned picture on her sheet. In one instance, three peers had gathered around the image of *yellow duck* from the story peeking from behind a branch. Jo hurried toward the excited group with her partner in tow and spun several times beneath the yellow duck image. She then made a beeline for the assisting adult as her partner laughed, shouting, "Would you wait for me?" The adult held the laminated sheet toward Jo and placed a stabilizing hand on Jo's forearm. The adult asked, "What'd you find, Jo?" Jo slapped toward the paper in the direction of the matching yellow duck.

Prior to the *Brown Bear* nature walk, Ricer had on several occasions read *Brown Bear, Brown Bear* to her students, who sat in a large-group circle. Jo had always struggled to join circle times. Most often she paced on tip-toe just outside the group, seemingly keeping a peripheral eye on the unfolding events while her hands flapped and she let out brief squeals and other assorted sounds. However, for some of the *Brown Bear, Brown Bear* readings, Jo had actually accepted an aide's invitation to sit on her lap as part of the group.

In addition to the nature walk and the group reading of the book, Ricer had designed several other thematic activities. For instance, at one learning center, children organized and glued downloaded, captioned pictures from the book in the correct sequence. Jo participated, with an adult providing her two choices and asking, "Which comes next?" With facilitated support at the wrist, Jo pointed to her choice. With hand-over-hand support, Jo used a glue stick to glue the pictures to her sheet. At a second center, children were provided with cover sheets that included two blank lines on which to write one's name (twice, in keeping with the spirit of the book) followed by the preprinted text, "What do you see?" Copied digital photos of each child were provided and children glued their photos to the cover after writing their name. Text sheets were provided, preprinted with the text, "I see a [blank] looking at me." Children drew pictures or clipped pictures from available magazines and glued them to the text sheets. Children colored the pictures. Some children added text to the blank on their own. Some children added text with adult support. Some children chose not to add text. The children's pages were stapled and each child read his or her book to the group.

In this second center, Jo participated with adult support. From a group of four photos, she correctly chose her picture and glued it to the cover sheet. Shown a letter board, Jo was asked to point to the first letter of her name. She then drew a J with hand-over-hand support. The process was repeated for the O. Using old issues of *National Geographic*, Jo chose three pictures of animals to complete a three-page book. Using a color choice-board, Jo chose the color she wanted for each picture. With prompts, Jo colored over the pictures. The adult asked, "What's the first letter of the word 'blue?'" The adult then wrote out the complete color and animal word for Jo. Ricer then read Jo's book to the group as Jo paced nearby.

As described in Tables 11.1–11.4, both LaShawn's participation in the superhero drama and Jo's participation in the thematic unit demonstrate how thoughtful teachers, recognizing *all* children's social drive to make meaning of the surrounding world, engaged the four currents of literacy to promote the developing use of visual-tactile, pictorial, and orthographic sign systems

Table 11.1. Description of Current 1 with Examples

Current 1	Description	LaShawn Data Vignette	Jo Data Vignette
Making meaning of the visual-tactile, pictorial, and orthographic sign-based narratives of others.	Fundamental to literate citizenship is the developing understanding that others have meaningful narratives to express. Young children with significant developmental disabilities must be exposed to, and actively connect with, others' symbolic presence, meaning making through narrative, and construction of sign systems. This of course requires that children be in environments swirling with stories expressed by peers, heard on tape, CD, and DVD, run on the computer, read, collaboratively created, played and acted, told by teachers, danced, drawn, retold, remembered by visiting grandparents, and so forth.	Exposed to child-initiated dramatic play narrative involving visual-tactile, pictorial, and orthographic signs. Presumed by adults and peers to be capable of making meaning of other children's flowing narrative structures and use of visual-tactile, pictorial, and orthographic sign systems. Presumption on the part of adults to the importance of participation in dramatic play. Presumed by adults and peers to be motivated to join dramatic play and option of joining provided [visual-tactile, pictorial, and orthographic]. Seamlessly integrated into ongoing narrative augmented by visual-tactile, pictorial, and orthographic signs. Development of a logical and valued role in ongoing narrative that furthered narrative.	Exposed to the repetitive text, narrative sequence, and simple illustrations of the picture book. Saw that text and pictures could augment one another to convey ideas. Experienced clipped text and pictures from the book being used to create related, but new, narratives. The cutout pictures actually form a sort of three-dimensional sign from the original two dimensions [visual-tactile, pictorial, and orthographic]. Motivated to move closer to the group through the reading of the picture book. Provided with other children as models for her own efforts. Heard other children's created book narratives read. Interacted around sign systems with peers on the nature walk.

Table 11.2. Description of Current 2 with Examples

Current 2	Description	LaShawn Data Vignette	Jo Data Vignette
Finding and expressing meaning in one's own experience through narratives crafted from visual-tactile, pictorial, and orthographic sign systems.	Important to literacy development is the need for a child to understand that her or his own experiences, ideas, and emotions are worthy of expression and can be conveyed through visual-tactile, pictorial, and orthographic sign systems. Children with significant developmental disabilities must be understood as full and valued citizens of the classroom with rich experiences, ideas, and stories to share.	Looking toward peers interpreted by adults as signal of interest and intention.\n\nBoys join aide to support LaShawn's role development using pictorial and orthographic signs as well as body language.\n\nVisual-tactile, pictorial, and orthographic signs provided for LaShawn to indicate choices and enrich role in play.	Jo designed a personalized, repetitive book similar to *Brown Bear, Brown Bear* making choices in terms of pictures to include and colors to use.\n\nJo was supported to mark off the animal pictures found on the nature walk indicating her progress and success.

Table 11.3. Description of Current 3 with Examples

Current 3	Description	LaShawn Data Vignette	Jo Data Vignette
Developing complexity with visual-tactile, pictorial, and orthographic sign systems in constructing narratives.	Efforts to foster the literate citizenship of young children with developmental disabilities must go beyond rudimentary stages. Movement toward increased complexity with visual-tactile, pictorial, and orthographic signs must always be the goal of literacy opportunities. Importantly, opportunities with text must be a part of the child's inclusive experience.	Exposed to the construction and use of previously used and new (to him) orthographic and pictorial and signs that allow for participation in a flowing, imaginative narrative. Presumed by adults and peers to be capable of making meaning of other children's flowing narrative structures and use of visual-tactile, pictorial, and orthographic sign systems.	While Jo's participation in group reading varied from her peers', it was presumed that she was making meaning of the picture book. Jo was exposed to the rhythm and sequence of the picture book and participated in retelling the sequence. Jo was provided options through which she made imaginative choices when constructing her own book, which was presented to the class as Jo's own effort. Jo was included in all extending activities based on the picture book and was supported according to her needs to effectively construct visual-tactile, pictorial, and orthographic signs. Jo was given opportunities to make use of letters in the construction of text with the full expectation that this was a meaningful endeavor.

Table 11.4. Description of Current 4 with Examples

Current 4	Description	LaShawn Data Vignette	Jo Data Vignette
Deriving joy and other affective forces from engagement with visual-tactile, pictorial, and orthographic sign systems.	Developing sophistication with sign systems for children with significant developmental disabilities is most effective when children experience the tremendous intellectual and emotional thrill that occurs while discovering the narratives of others and in sharing and connecting their own narratives. For children without disabilities, the emotions and cognitive energy associated with getting lost in a story (or art or play) are recognized and valued in terms of promoting a motivating context for literate development. This must be a part of all children's experience.	LaShawn's interest in joining peers was recognized. LaShawn provided sign-based supports to join dramatic play as a full member. LaShawn's competence was demonstrated to his peers who fully accepted his participation. According to grandma, LaShawn was exposed at school to a personal interest from home.	Jo was drawn toward the group by the particular reading. With adult support, Jo appeared to make sense of the related activities and remained engaged with the expectations. The nature walk provided Jo with a structured format within which to interact with a valued peer and other friends.

as metaphoric-creative acts and as tools for social connectedness on the part of young children with significant developmental disabilities.

Teachers involved in my research formally measured children's developmental and curricular growth through a variety of means, including the following:

1. Developmental evaluation tools
   ➢ Brigance Early Preschool Screen and Preschool Screen
   ➢ Bracken Basic Concept Scale Test of Early Reading Ability
2. Ongoing evaluation of IEP/IFSP objectives
3. Portfolio development

Certainly, this is not a study aimed to *prove* causality nor correlation, but it is of note that students with significant developmental disabilities consistently made enormous developmental strides within these currents of literacy. LaShawn, for instance, was considered untestable (e.g., at infant stages) across the developmental domains on any screens available to the Prairie School staff when he first entered the program. "Now," lead teacher Vivian Gray told me in reference to the Test of Early Reading Ability, "he's off the charts. Particularly with, like, letter recognition, word recognition. He's maybe the highest in the class." Pat Ricer's three students labeled with severe disabilities, including Jo, had over the course of 10 months gained on average 18 developmental months according to Bracken-assessed skills related to recognition of letters, shapes, colors, and other dimensions constituting what was described as a School Readiness Composite. By the time Jo exited Shoshone School to begin kindergarten, she had gone from the status of nonverbal to limited spoken language. Interestingly, and not inconsistently with other young children with significant developmental disabilities, Jo's initial efforts with speech centered entirely around voicing words she had read.

THE EARLY CHILDHOOD LITERACY FLOW

From the infinite potential of the inclusive terrain, children actively construct, transform, and create a sign-based literate community out of visual-tactile, pictorial, and orthographic signs. They do so as metaphoric-creative acts and as social tools for connection (Paley, 2004). Four-year-old Jasmine, for example, in interaction with a shifting group of children, actively constructed a visual-tactile three-dimensional sign by donning a plastic construction hard hat to serve as an astronaut's helmet during a dramatic outer space play scenario. Her quick shift, from dramatically playing space traveler to drawing a spaceman to writing out the word *spaceman*, metaphorically captured in a snapshot the child's epic story of literacy development itself. Gallas (2003) has described this movement as evoking symbols "from playing to drawing to writing" (p. 42). This path is most often (mis)conjectured as a disconnected shift from the dominance of the representational and subjective form (i.e., visual-tactile and pictorial) to an arbitrary, objective, mechanistic form (i.e., orthographic text).

In the child's construction of visual-tactile and pictorial signs, their meaning and chosen form are considered integral. The sign is meant to *look like* the object or idea represented. This makes signs representational but also clearly unstable and nonmechanistic in that they are context-bound or, put another way, highly influenced by the specific social network in which they are crafted. For instance, Jasmine's use of a plastic construction helmet during the space traveler play was meant to *look like* an astronaut's helmet and was made meaningful by the direct context of the narrative. Apart from the students in the play, other people might or might not understand its meaning. Further, that same helmet might take on very different meanings as the children alter their narratives and thus the context within which the signs are constructed.

In contrast, text is formed from a set of simplified, seemingly arbitrary shapes that *do not look like* the object or idea being described. Alphabetic letters represent the sounds of language. For instance, the written word *spaceman* does not look like an astronaut. It is composed of particular letters arranged in a conventional and rule-laden sequence and structure that does not reveal its meaning without the help of an adult to initially point it out to children. The presumption pervades that in written language, unlike in other early childhood sign systems, form and meaning have no intrinsic connection that children might link. Form, then, is said to be arbitrary, plucked from the great ether. Further, the word *spaceman* in one setting is commonly considered to be *spaceman* in all settings that share in the English language. As such, spelling out or deciphering *spaceman* is said to be an abstraction or, put another way, is context-free. The sign is commonly thought to transcend individual or collective imagination and therefore might be considered stable or mechanical.

This rigid conceptualization of literacy development, from representational to arbitrary and sound-based with little connection or relevance between the forms, has resulted in early reading programs that essentially act as literacy boot camps. This has the effect of stripping children of their individual literate profile constructed over their brief lifetime through experience, and, we hope, rich symbolic opportunity, motivation, and play within thoughtful early childhood programs. These conventional literacy efforts ignore individual histories, acting as if the child has no capacity to engage nonrealistic symbols and recasting the child in a mass mold that is reflective of the misconstrued adult belief that literacy is an arbitrary, objective enterprise that must be drilled in from on high.

For the young child, the metaphor of flow serves as a better conceptualization of the development of their literate profiles. The literacy flow is a seamless movement, albeit one filled with rapids, countercurrents, eddies, vortexes, and an occasional hurricane. Within the flow, the young child progresses from particular representational forms not to arbitrary ones, but to other particular representational forms. As my examples to this point have shown, children do not approach text as a near-impenetrable code existing in detached, objective fashion, far apart from their world. In the rich, inclusive early childhood educational setting, orthographic text in combination with other sign forms swirl around the child and he or she creates, constructs, and makes meaning of the text when it matters personally. Systematic efforts at developing the sophistication of young children's literate profiles must make orthographic text matter to the child and take into consideration the following important points that have arisen out of my research on the literacy flow.

First, from a very early age children construct meaning from visual-tactile, pictorial, and early orthographic signs that do not look like that which they are formed to represent. Perhaps the most common example of this is the 2-year-old child who is able to *read* the meaning of the Golden Arches. This is referred to as logographic or idiographic functioning and is commonly, albeit strangely, dismissed as having little relevance to the child's literate profile. The Golden Arches do not look like McDonald's, but the logo/ideogram still has representational impact for the young child who moves directly from visual form to lexical meaning. This is exactly how good readers actually read: In the span of a nanosecond, good readers recognize whole words, word chunks, and even word combinations and phrases, moving directly from visual representation to meaning. In an example from my data, I watched a 4-year-old girl draw the figure of a person. She then wildly scribbled in red crayon over the figure and announced, "Her is really mad." The raging red lines did not look like anger per se, but in the child's mind they were representational and did in fact look like anger. She translated the scrawled lines directly from form to meaning.

Second, early and serious literate efforts with signs emerge from the child's narrative constructions, in interaction with the surrounding rich literate context, as metaphoric-creative acts and social tools for connectedness. The child works between the visual form and the meaning he or she wants to construct. Systematic efforts to foster the child's literate sophistication must be immediate to the child's meaning-making efforts and the surrounding context.

Third, initial orthographic efforts of young children are viewed by the child as representational. They are not strung-together sounds, but are drawings of the ideas and objects represented and are entered into the child's lexicon as such. When Jasmine signed her name to the drawing of the astronaut, she was not stringing together sounds but was drawing a visual representation of herself. The name did not look like Jasmine the person, but in her mind it served as a powerful visual representation of herself. Similarly, when the children recognize the title *Moondogs* (Kirk, 1999), they were not decoding sounds but going directly from visual (orthographic) form to meaning, just as good readers do. In effect, sign systems within the literacy flow build on one another. As Kress (1997) explained,

> The learning of writing proceeds in exactly the same fashion as the development of other sign systems: employing the strategy of using the best, most apt available form of expression of a particular meaning. Children use such representational means as they have available for making that meaning. The child's written signs are the effect of their meaning making actions, arising out of interest, using what they have available as representational means. (p. 17)

And fourth, research indicates that children build and access written language lexicons through both word (and graphemic, morphemic, syllabic, and even written phrase) recognition as well as through decoding skills (Ashby & Rayner, 2006). Currently, to the detriment of the goal of a more critically literate citizenry, nearly all policy focus is being placed on phonetic decoding as the singular entry point to literate citizenship (Stahl, Duffy-Hester, & Stahl, 1998), though we have now been immersed in the "decade of phonics" for nearly 2 decades with little evidence of heightened literacy scores. In no way do I wish to deemphasize the importance of decoding as *one tool* in the child's developing literate profile. Nor do I want to suggest that components of decoding should not be introduced at early ages. As described in the dramatic play data vignette involving LaShawn and superheroes, LaShawn's friend Jay solved the problem of how to orthographically represent Batman by sounding out the name and making use of the alphabetic principle. In effect, Jay had a motivating problem to solve and he accessed tools at his disposal for its resolution. Clearly, the development of phonetic awareness and the alphabetic principle served here as a useful tool. Other children, however, might arrive at a similar resolution by making use of written language lexicons that include entire word recognition of *Batman*, or that contain slots for the word recognition, *bat*, and the word recognition, *man*, that are then neatly combined; indeed, there may be a myriad of other ways that allow for the resolution of that particular motivating problem.

CONCLUSION

Notably, I arrived at my conceptual model of the literacy flow with an initial focus on young children with significant developmental disabilities. I thought I knew what early literacy was when I began these studies, and I intended to describe how children historically excluded from rich literacy opportunities might be supported to fit into the existing framework. Only after I initially began to document what might be considered surprising literate capacities on the part of children commonly cast as hopelessly preliterate did I begin to systematically explore the symbolic and written-language worlds of their nondisabled peers. Out of this undertaking emerged my understanding of the literacy flow through which all young children, with or without significant developmental disabilities, create their complex literacy profiles. Looking at students with disabilities with a broadened definition of literacy reveals the underlying competence that these children actually possess. In the context of high-expectation curricula, all children, whatever labels we may assign to them, possess fundamental language and literacy competence.

REFERENCES

Ashby, J., & Rayner, K. (2006). Insights from research on skilled reading. In D. K. Dickinson & S. B. Neuman (Eds.), *Handbook of early literacy research* (Vol. 2, pp. 52–63). New York: Guilford Press.

Erickson, K. A., & Koppenhaver, D. A. (1995). Developing a literacy program for children with severe disabilities. *The Reading Teacher, 48*, 676–684.

Gallas, K. (2003). *Imagination and literacy: A teacher's search for the heart of learning.* New York: Teachers College Press.

Kirk, D. (1999). *Moondogs.* New York: Putnam's.

Koppenhaver, D. A., & Erickson, K. A. (2003). Natural emergent literacy supports for preschoolers with autism and severe communication impairments. *Topics in Language Disorders, 23*, 283–292.

Kress, G. (1997). *Before writing: Rethinking the paths to literacy.* New York: Routledge.

Martin, B., & Carle, E. (1967). *Brown bear, brown bear, what do you see?* New York: Henry Holt.

Paley, V. G. (2004). *A child's work: The importance of fantasy play.* Chicago: University of Chicago Press.

Stahl, S. A., Duffy-Hester, A. M., & Stahl, K. A. D. (1998). Everything you wanted to know about phonics (but were afraid to ask). *Reading Research Quarterly, 33*, 338–355.

CHAPTER 12

The Storytelling Playground

Expanding the Definition of Literacy Through Storytelling

Jennifer Urbach
Janette Klingner

Shawn: *[speaking slowly]* One dark night. This one vampire, he turned
into ten thousand million bats . . .
Aisha: Can I stop you for a minute? Are you going to make it long?
Shawn: No, but it's going to be scary.
Aisha: I can handle scary.
Shawn: I have nightmares about scary stuff. I love nightmares.

The above exchange occurred between two students during an oral story-telling project in a 1st-grade, urban classroom. To many, the exchange may seem puerile, two students simply playing, but if we look deeper we can see that Shawn and Aisha are sharing their knowledge of stories—what makes a good story and how to start a story so that it arouses strong emotions. They are demonstrating understandings of literacy that are important to consider when supporting their growth as emergent literary beings. If we are to have high expectations for our students, we must first recognize their strengths and build on what they already know, incorporating their experiences and frames of reference into our instruction. The classroom should be a place where students' competencies are valued and where they are encouraged to draw upon the resources available to them. Yet, in order to see the students' rich knowledge, we must first acknowledge literacy as a socially constructed ideology. Literacy encompasses the social, cultural, historical, and institutional ways literacy is used throughout life (Street, 1995). Literacy, then, cannot be the same for everyone. It is a dynamic and living art (Bakhtin, 1981) where a number of different stances and resources can be utilized by "readers" in order to inform both their literacy knowledge and their daily lives.

However, schools often assume one narrowly defined view of literacy. Throughout the past 3 decades, the marginalization of certain types of literacy has been well documented (Gee, 1996; Heath, 1983; McCabe & Bliss, 2003). Mehan (2000) describes this phenomenon as the *politics of representation*, contending that there are many layers of knowledge, yet social and historical elements help legitimize only certain types of knowledge, thus often leading to a one-dimensional view. In schools, the knowledge that is legitimized is that of the dominant culture (Champion, 1997; Heath, 1983; McCabe & Bliss, 2003). When it comes to what younger students should understand about literacy, this dominant knowledge focuses on phonological awareness and decoding at the expense of comprehension (Gamse, Bloom, Kemple, & Jacob, 2008). When schools do address comprehension, they tend to focus on an analytical understanding or stance toward stories (i.e., the "recall" of a story, structure of the story). Bloome, Katz, and Champion (2003) note that schools emphasize the importance of "narrative as text" (highlighting the structure) over "narrative as performance" (highlighting the audience engagement). In addition, some resources are considered more legitimate than others. Teachers often privilege text-based materials over popular culture resources, deeming the latter to be "low-class" resources (Alverman & Heron, 2001; Alvermann & Xu, 2003).

This narrow view of literacy often leads to the perception that students from backgrounds that diverge from the mainstream lack literacy and language skills (Bliss & McCabe, 2008; Gee, 1996; McCabe & Bliss, 2003), thus lowering teachers' expectations for what students can accomplish. Unless we broaden our view of literacy, many of our students' unique abilities and understandings of story may go undetected in the classroom. We will continue to perpetuate a deficit model of learning instead of creating an inclusive learning environment that provides students with a rich understanding of literacy. Thus, in order to expand the definition of literacy, we must challenge the politics of representation. This chapter attempts to do this by highlighting three students' knowledge of literacy as demonstrated through their oral stories.

THE ORAL STORYTELLING PROJECT

The students highlighted in this chapter were part of an interactive storytelling process that was embedded within the language arts curriculum of an urban 1st-grade classroom at Monte Vista Elementary. Of the 30 students in this classroom, 28 of the students were African American, one was Hispanic, and one was White non-Hispanic. The stories and interactions of three students—Andre, Shawn, and Aisha—are highlighted in this chapter. All three students are African American. These students were purposively picked for the study because their interactions and stories were noteworthy in that they either supported central themes found within the class or diverged from the typical interactions of the class. If we are to expand what literacy means, it is just as important to highlight the latter cases—those that are atypical—as it is the central themes.

Similar to other storytelling projects, interactive storytelling in this classroom gave students opportunities to listen to, tell, and in some cases read and write stories (Cliatt & Shaw, 1988; Palmer, Harshbarger, & Koch, 2001). The class listened to stories from the teacher, teacher assistant, researcher, and community storytellers as well as other students. In addition, students told stories in both large and small groups. When the students acted as the audience members, they were encouraged to ask questions, make comments, and give suggestions to the storytellers. As part of the planning process, students drew story maps, and as the school year went on, some students wrote out their stories.

This storytelling process promotes high expectations by providing a platform for teachers to be able to see the rich knowledge students bring into the classroom. The setting acknowledges the sociocultural importance of learning by allowing children not only to draw on their school-based knowledge but on their home and cultural knowledge as well. Providing a socially interactive setting for learning illuminates many pathways to literacy that are not normally highlighted within the regular classroom. Due to the diversity of the students' backgrounds, the storytelling process becomes an expansive playground where students can discover different aspects of what it means to be literate. It also provides teachers with an understanding of what students *can* do rather than what they *can't* do. If teachers know the rich knowledge that students come in with, they can begin to teach students to use these skills and thus enhance students' literacy knowledge (Lee, 2006; Smitherman, 1994).

In order to highlight the expansive literacy knowledge within the stories, the first author audio recorded and transcribed all of the case study students' stories. In order to see if students valued the performance aspect of a text, we felt it was important to capture prosodic elements in the students' stories. Thus the transcription included a number of voice markers: pitch, stretching of sounds, volume, speed, and pauses (Couper-Kuhlen, 2003). In addition, as the students told their stories, the first author took field notes to describe the interactions of the storyteller and the audience. All of the case study students' stories were analyzed through a number of traditional and nontraditional assessments. Three of these assessments are discussed here. The first is a developmental chart of story structure

(Hughes, McGillivray, & Schmidek, 1997) based on the traditional story grammar elements (see Table 12.1). In addition, we utilized a couple of nontraditional measures, including an assessment of students' use of evaluative devices (Labov, 1972), which are used to create a purposeful and entertaining story, and stanza analysis (McCabe & Bliss, 2003), which is used to uncover structures other than the European linear structure. Using both traditional and nontraditional assessments helps to reveal a broader array of literacy skills that our students may possess.

ANDRE: THE ANALYTICAL STORYTELLER

Andre was a 1st-grader who came to Monte Vista Elementary about a month after school started. Andre transferred to Monte Vista after an altercation with a teacher at his original school. During the 5 months of this study, Andre was suspended twice for fighting. Additionally, while students did not shy away from him, he did not seem to have many close friends. Even though Andre had difficulty with social interactions, his teacher stated that he was a smart student who had the potential to do well in school.

Andre's strengths as a storyteller highlight the skills typically emphasized in a 1st-grade classroom. As Andre told stories, the main focus of the story seemed to be the structure of the story. In the following story, we can see how his story is easy to follow and has a beginning, middle, and end.

Table 12.1. Developmental Story Structure Level

Story Structure Level	Description
Descriptive Sequence (Preschool Age)	Describes characters, habitual action. No temporal or causal actions.
Action (Preschool Age)	Actions are temporally listed but there is not a cause and effect relationship.
Reactive Sequence (Preschool Age)	Actions are causally ordered. No clear goal directs behavior.
Abbreviated Episode (around 6 years)	Goal-directed behavior, but lacks an internal plan or intentional behavior.
Incomplete Episode (7–8 years)	Intentional planning or behavior, but at least one of three elements—initiating event, attempt, or consequence—is missing.

Note. Adapted from *Guide to narrative language: Procedures for assessment*, by D. Hughes, L. McGillivray, and M. Schmidek, 1997, Eau Claire, WI: Thinking Publications.

Andre: Once upon a time there was this red rocket that was so little
             nobody didn't even want to play with it except for his mom and
             dad. Then there was this gray rocket and the red rocket said
             to the gray rocket, "Hey, do you want to play with me?" And
             the gray rocket said, "No." And then the red rocket was sad.
             And then there was a green rocket that came. And they were
             both sad together. And then they follow each other. And they
             said, "Hey do you want to play?" And they both said, "Yeah."
             And then the red rocket said, "Well what can we play?" And
             they turned into little, tiny shapes. And then they flied around
             everywhere. The end.

In addition, his stories often had the majority of story grammar elements
described by Stein and Glenn (1979). Overall, the majority of his stories
were considered developmentally appropriate for 7- and 8-year-olds on
the Hughes et al. (1997) developmental chart (refer to Table 12.1).

Andre's structural knowledge of stories is corroborated through his
discussion of his story.

Urbach: Okay. And then what do you think people liked about your
             story?
Andre: They think . . . They liked about my story because it had rockets
             and it had, and it had nobody to play with and then they, it
             had a problem not being solved . . . being mean. And then the
             problem was solved . . . being good by the green rocket. And the
             red rocket solved it. So the gray rocket was mean.

Andre's answer again focused on the elements of the story. He assumed that students enjoyed the fact that he had the correct elements in
his story. Arguably, Andre saw storytelling as a school-based task with
certain elements that needed to be accomplished, but it is not clear if he
understood how to make a story come alive. He seemingly lacked an ability to arouse his audience's interest. While most students appeared to be
listening to his stories, there was a notable lack of audience laughter and
comments. In the five stories that Andre told in front of the class, the audience did not interact (e.g., laugh, make comments, or ask questions) with
him as he told his stories. They sat politely, but they were not captivated
by the performance. This lack of interaction was in stark contrast to the
interaction found with other students' stories. Even when Andre was in
small-group settings, students still exhibited a lack of interest. In the following excerpt we see how Jordan, a student typically involved in students' stories, expressed disinterest in Andre's story.

Jordan: Hey can I ask you a question? How come you write about rockets so much?

Andre: Because I know about one . . .

[Further on in the story]

Andre: The chief called the red rocket and green rocket like and said to them. . . .

Jordan: But, excuse me. I'd like to say they're all the same. I can stop you if I want. . . .

Andre: Okay. You nearly made me lost my mind. I forgot what I said. *[Argument over what he last said.]* . . . Okay this is about to get very frank. The orange rocket was about to attack with his evil army.

Jordan: Are you done yet?

There are several reasons for the lack of engagement. Andre told all of his stories in a low, monotone voice. In the last story, he raised his voice for exactly one word. In addition, Andre did not pick up on the literary devices that other students used to garner attention for their stories. For instance, while other students tried to gain a reaction by using classmates' names or pop culture items in their stories, Andre used only one popular culture reference in his stories and never used his classmates' names. Furthermore, while other students began playing with creative story starters, Andre used the same standard story start ("Once upon a time . . .") for every story.

Andre's stories clearly matched his interactions within the classroom. His teacher noted that he had the ability to do well in his schoolwork, but his social interactions were lacking. Likewise, he understood how to use the analytic elements within a story, but, just as Andre seemed to have difficulty with social skills in the classroom, he also appeared to have a lack of understanding of the social aspects of telling stories. A traditional analysis of structural elements would recognize (and even favor) Andre's skills, but by employing multiple analyses we were able to see what new skills he could be taught. In order to truly enhance Andre's literacy skills, we can teach him what stories are supposed to do and how this can be accomplished.

SHAWN: THE THEATRICAL STORYTELLER

Our next case study student is Shawn. Similar to Andre, Shawn was often reprimanded in school. Yet unlike Andre, Shawn was a very social student with lots of friends. Shawn enjoyed sports such as basketball and football. He also enjoyed video games and cartoons. Shawn enjoyed being center stage during the storytelling. When Shawn told a story, he often sat in the "storyteller chair" and leaned his body forward, toward his audience. With eyes wide open, as if they were going to pop out of his head, he would often look down at his audience as he started his story. This is when the magic happened. In this case study, we examine Shawn's stories and point to elements that made his stories so compelling.

Shawn did not score well on the traditional measures that evaluated his knowledge of story structure. Shawn's stories were generally hard to score because during some of his stories he focused on fast-paced action rather than developing a plot. In addition, he would skip important details or would often replace words with sound effects:

Shawn: And Goofy hit his head on the wall
And then he picked a . . . (inaudible) up and said oo::h
And a dinosaur [speaking quickly] here comes a dinosaur
UH YO:: UHA AH::
[Shawn is making lots of movements with his arms like he is getting beat up.]
[Audience is laughing, and someone asks, "What happened next?"]
And then he was like, "You want a piece of me?"

In this sequence of events it is not clear what the point is (or if there is one). It appears as if the main character, Goofy, is getting beat up, although Shawn did not explicitly tell us this. The use of sounds instead of actions makes it even more difficult to code because it is not clear what is going on. Due to these characteristics, it was often hard to identify the story grammar elements, so when the stories were rated on the Hughes et al. (1997) developmental chart, four out of six stories were rated as preschool-level stories.

Yet Shawn's purpose was not to tell a linear story, but to use storytelling as a platform for play. With the exception of the fifth story, his stories focused on themes meant to scare his audience (something he found entertaining) or they focused on fast-paced comedic action. Shawn was successful at entertaining himself and his audience. The audience responded throughout his stories with laughter, comments, and questions. Shawn drew on a number of resources to create these stories, yet often these resources are overlooked in schools.

The most obvious resource used in his stories was his knowledge of popular culture. Shawn often used his popular cultural knowledge to develop his story. In fact, Shawn often borrowed characters or ideas from movies, cartoons, and video games. Yet Shawn did not simply borrow these ideas, he took ownership of the items by manipulating and transforming them into a new creative product that had meaning to him and his classmates: "and there was a BIG, BIG big ol' giant . . . it was a Fat Albert giant *[audience laughing]* . . . and then Fat Albert turned into a regular kid and he was skinny too." Borrowing items and transforming them into a new story is a necessary part of understanding the intertextual links in stories. While we create a text, it is paradoxically never ours alone. Text, like language, is a social product that is awash with signs and symbols from our experiences. We are all consumers of cultural signs and symbols around us and it is our job to borrow these and transform them to create a new text (Bakhtin, 1981; Gee, 1996). Thus Shawn understood the necessity of borrowing resources and manipulating them for his own stories.

Besides consciously borrowing and transforming characters from popular culture, Shawn also drew upon a number of resources to create a vivid picture and draw an emotional reaction by using what Labov (1972) calls "evaluation devices." The purpose of evaluation devices is to keep the audience interested in the story: "So what? Every good narrator is continually warding off this question" (p. 366). Specifically, Shawn heavily relies on devices that intensify the action in a story. The intensifying devices Shawn used throughout the study were gestures, expressive phonology, quantifiers, repetition, and ritual comments (see Table 12.2). Of all these intensifying devices, expressive phonology was the most used intensifier.

As evidenced by the chapter-opening quote, by combining his knowledge of both pop culture and intensifiers, Shawn created wonderfully intense and vivid stories that resonated with his audience: "*[speaking slowly]* One dark night. This one vampire, he turned into 10 thousand million bats." This excerpt combines a pop culture item (vampire bats) with devices that intensify the story—a deliberately slow pace that intensifies the words "one dark night" and an exaggerated number of the creepy bats. Thus looking at this excerpt in a new light allows us to see the wonderful literary resources that Shawn employs instead of only seeing his lack of structure.

AISHA: THE STORY MANIPULATOR

Our final case study student was a young girl who was an average student, friendly, sociable, and eager to please. Even though she did not stand out within the classroom, she was a wonderful storyteller. She was the first student to draw a reaction from the audience when telling a story.

Similar to Shawn's, Aisha's stories were difficult to score on measures that focused on traditional story grammar elements. She pulled the audience into the story by using their names, adding cultural references familiar to her audience, and heavily using a number of evaluative devices in her stories. Her stories were met with enthusiasm from the teacher and students. However, one story in particular stood out as having rich

Table 12.2: Intensifying Storytelling Devices

Type of Intensifier	How It Is Used by Shawn	Example
Gestures	To emphasize words (or in place of words), provides a visual for the story	Slapping legs for footsteps as he states: ". . . Then they heard footsteps coming."
Expressive Phonology	Used in a myriad of ways: To speed up, slow down, stretch words (and thus highlights words); sometimes Shawn creates sound effects	"AHHH! MY LEG!" "boing, boing, boing"
Quantifiers	To provide extreme statements	"millions of dragons"
Repetition	Repetition of words or phrases often suspends the action of the story and builds up suspense	"Coming closer and closer and closer"
Ritual Comments	Draws upon the cultural knowledge of the audience	"and his eyes were going all loco"

literacy knowledge not often acknowledged in schools. While this story at first appeared to be wandering and poorly structured, when it was looked at through "stanza analysis," a wonderful structure emerged (McCabe & Bliss, 2003). When the story was broken into stanzas, it appeared to have a "topic associated" structure, in that it was based on episodes or stanzas implicitly linked to a theme, rather than a linear structure (Gee, 1996; McCabe & Bliss, 2003). The story focused on a "predator versus prey" theme. Furthermore, when the story was examined through a topic associative story lens, it became apparent that her use of orientation was masterful: There was a pattern of using minimal orientation (i.e., identification of the character and what they were doing) to introduce similar scenes, yet an entire stanza was used to introduce the audience to each new predator.

Orientation Stanza: Entry of a New "Predator"—Setting the Scene

Aisha: Then! Once there was this (other) lady
           and she was creepy
           and she was creepy

> and she was like [makes growling noise] [audience laughing]
> and then she walked and walked and walked and walked
> (Urbach, 2010, p. 10)

It was clear that Aisha was a master manipulator of stories. She wanted to perform for her teacher and classmates and even changed her stories based on their opinions: "I didn't want to say that in front of my friends—like 'you are talking about the American Dragon we already know about the American Dragon' and I would say—'oh I should have said predator so I changed it into the predator.'" Yet through the course of the study, Aisha's stories changed, as did her identity. Aisha slowly gravitated away from a focus on performance. In the end, Aisha's stories became short with minimal evaluations.

Aisha: The Great Wall of China.
         When I went to China I saw a . . . I saw a girl
         and she couldn't talk.
          So I went up to her
         and I . . . I couldn't see,
         so I went up to her.
         That was not okay because she was evil.
         She tricked me.
         Kicked me in the foot. The end.

Aisha's story, while short, included a title, setting, initiating event, attempt, and consequence. Her story is centered on the topic and does not wander off. Yet there is very little richness in her story. Despite being encouraged to elaborate on her story, Aisha did not. When asked about this in the interview, Aisha stated, "Because I think that people . . . if I read the same words people will understand." Thus her interviews and interactions showed that she was more focused on making sure she told exactly what was on her paper than on the presentation elements. This seemed to relate to her identity as a writer. As the study went on, Aisha was growing as a writer and, instead of making storymaps, was writing simple stories. She began to prioritize the reading of the story rather than the performance; her stance toward telling stories was closely related to her new identity as a writer.

Aisha's stories throughout the year demonstrated her changing understanding of stories. She understood the performative value of stories and, later, the importance of narrative as text. Hopefully, with the help of her teachers, Aisha will eventually realize the importance of those performative aspects she employed early on and combine that knowledge with her new knowledge of text. In the end, Aisha's case study illustrates even more than her changing knowledge. It underscores the fact that literacy knowledge cannot be divorced from what we value.

CONCLUSION

These case studies reveal the rich literacy knowledge that students draw upon when telling a story. Andre, Shawn, and Aisha are three very different students, each of whom has a strong, yet different, understanding of what is important in stories. Their stances toward stories are closely linked to their identities and what they value. As Aisha shows us, what we value can change over time, thus affecting our knowledge. As teachers, it is our job to understand why these changes are occurring and how we can expand out student knowledge in diverse ways. The themes presented here are just a few of the ways students can understand stories. Indeed, we could have even discussed other ways students understood storytelling. For example, Andre's use of a story about a rocket without friends may be his way of connecting with the text. Yet this chapter is not meant to be an all-encompassing description. Since everything we do is socially, culturally, historically, and institutionally constructed, defining all aspects of literacy would be quite impossible. Everything we do is multilayered. Thus each student used a range of skills or strategies when engaging in the processes of negotiating and constructing meaning while reading, writing, drawing, and telling stories. High expectations for literacy would require that students use this wide range of skills.

The vast array of literacy devices used in this study establishes that young students do have the capability of developing the vividness of a story. We were able to see the rich knowledge of the students because they engaged in an interactive process of storytelling, but storytelling is not emphasized in most schools. Storytelling in itself is a true literacy event. And unlike reading a book or writing a story on paper, it allows for an immediate negotiation of the text between the audience and teller. The teller realizes the impact his or her words have on the audience and the audience realizes its power within the story. In addition, performance is highlighted within the storytelling setting. Therefore, just as plays and poetry recitations are viewed as acceptable classrooms literacy events, storytelling should also be acknowledged for its own literacy value.

This chapter focused on highlighting our students' rich knowledge, which is often marginalized in a traditional view of literacy. If we only use traditional ways of evaluating students' stories, we come away with the impression that they are lacking basic skills. High expectations are first and foremost based upon realizing students' potential. Education reform will not occur until we expand our definition of what counts as literacy. If educators seek to engage children's multiple ways of knowing, then they need to begin to challenge the dominant view and acknowledge multiple knowledge sources as legitimate tools for understanding literacy. Wenger (1998) states that "knowledge is a matter of competence within a valued enterprise" (p. 4). If so, we need to first understand what students value about stories before we can understand their knowledge. Only then can we begin teaching students to use a variety of rich knowledge skills. Acknowledging these different views, explicitly discussing the importance of different views, and challenging the students to be self-reflective in their practice can provide students a rich learning experience and a rich literacy life.

REFERENCES

Alvermann, D. E., & Heron, A. H. (2001). Literacy identity work: Playing to learn with popular media. *Journal of Adolescent & Adult Literacy, 45*, 118–122.

Alvermann, D. E., & Xu, S. H. (2003). Children's everyday literacies: Intersections of popular culture and language arts instruction. *Language Arts, 81*(2), 145–155.

Bakhtin, M. M. (1981). Discourse in the novel. In M. Hoquist (Ed.), *The dialogic imagination: Four essays by M. M. Bakhtin* (pp. 259–422). Austin: University of Texas Press.

Bliss, L. S., & McCabe, A. (2008). Personal narratives: Cultural differences and clinical implications. *Topics in Language Disorders, 28*(2), 162–177.

Bloome, D., Katz, L., & Champion, T. (2003). Young children's narratives and ideologies of language in classrooms. *Reading and Writing Quarterly, 19*(2), 205–223.

Champion, T. (1997). Tell me somethin' good: A description of narrative structures among African American children. *Linguistics and Education, 9*(3), 251–286.

Cliatt, M. P., & Shaw, J. M. (1988). The storytime exchange: Ways to enhance it. *Childhood Education, 64*, 293–298.

Couper-Kuhlen, E. (2003). Intonation and discourse: Current views from within. In D. Schiffrin, D. Tannen, & H. E. Hamilton (Eds.), *The handbook of discourse analysis* (pp. 13–34). Malden, MA: Blackwell.

Gamse, B. C., Bloom, H. S., Kemple, J .J., & Jacob, R. T. (2008). *Reading First impact study: Interim report* (NCEE 2008-4016). Washington, DC: National Center for Education Evaluation and Regional Assistance, Institute of Education Sciences, U.S. Department of Education.

Gee, J. P. (1996). *Social linguistics and literacies: Ideology in discourse.* (2nd ed.). London: Falmer Press.

Heath, S. B. (1983). *Ways with words.* New York: Cambridge University Press.

Hughes, D., McGillivray, L., & Schmidek, M. (1997). *Guide to narrative language: Procedures for assessment.* Eau Claire, WI: Thinking Publications.

Labov, W. (1972). *Language in the inner city: Studies in Black English Vernacular*. Oxford: Blackwell.

Lee, C. D. (2006). Every good-bye ain't gone: Analyzing the cultural underpinnings of classroom talk. *Qualitative Studies in Education, 19*(3), 305–327.

McCabe, A., & Bliss, L. S. (2003). *Patterns of narrative discourse: A multicultural, life span approach*. Boston: Allyn & Bacon.

Mehan, H. (2000). Beneath the skin and between the ears: A case study in the politics of representation. In B. A. U. Levinson, K. M. Borman, M. Eisenhart, M. Foster, A. E. Fox, & M. Sutton (Eds.), *Schooling the symbolic animal: Social and cultural dimensions of education* (pp. 259–279). Lanham, MD: Rowman & Littlefield.

Palmer, B. C., Harshbarger, S. J., & Koch, C. A. (2001). Storytelling as a constructivist model for developing language and literacy. *Journal of Poetry Therapy, 14*(4), 199–212.

Smitherman, G. (1994). "The blacker the berry, the sweeter the juice": African American student writers. In A. H. Dyson & C. Genishi (Eds.), *The need for story: Cultural diversity in classroom and community* (pp. 80–101). Urbana, IL: National Council of Teachers of English.

Stein, N., & Glenn, C. G. (1979). An analysis of story comprehension in elementary school children. In R. Freedle (Ed.), *New directions in discourse processing* (pp. 53–119). Norwood, NJ: Ablex.

Street, B. (1995). *Social literacies: Critical approaches to literacy in development, ethnography, and education*. London: Longman Group.

Urbach, J. (2010). Beyond story grammar: Looking at stories through cultural lenses. *Education and Urban Society*. Advance online publication. doi:10.1177/0013124510392567 Retrieved from http://eus.sagepub.com/content/early/2010/12/22/0013124510392567

Wenger, E. (1998). *Communities of practice: Learning, meaning, and identity*. Cambridge, UK: Cambridge University Press.

CHAPTER 13

Closing the Reading Achievement Gap

It's Up to Us to Act on What We Know

Richard L. Allington
Anne McGill-Franzen

The title of this chapter summarizes what research has been telling us for almost 20 years. Still, there are lots of kids who are not reading on grade level. In this chapter we argue that the evidence now available indicates that schools could have all students reading on grade level by the end of 1st grade. Accomplishing this goal requires only that we provide more effective reading lessons and, for some children, more intensive reading lessons. We argue that, in general, it is not the costs of providing such instruction that stands in the way of accomplishing the goal, but rather a long-standing set of professional beliefs, practices, and programs that fail to reflect what we have learned in the past 20 years about teaching all children to read. In the end, it will be up to educators to enact the policies, programs, and practices that thus far have been largely ignored.

WHAT WE KNOW ABOUT STRUGGLING READERS

The most recent National Assessment of Educational Progress (NAEP) for reading (NAEP, 2009) reports that roughly one-third of the students at the 4th-grade level could not read grade-level material and another third could read grade-level material but only with literal and low-level understanding. Moreover, the lowest third is filled largely with children from low-income families, children of color, and children labeled as having a disability. The reading achievement gap between these groups and White, more affluent students has remained stable since 1988. We know less about the reading abilities of children labeled as learning disabled, but we do know that these children read at substantially lower levels of proficiency than children who are not so labeled (Denton, Vaughn, & Fletcher, 2003).

At the same time, we have an extensive research base that suggests that developing all children as grade-level readers is difficult and expensive over the short term. A body of research indicates, for example, that for accelerated reading growth to occur (i.e., more than one and one-half years' growth per year), both expert teachers and very small instructional groups are essential (e.g., Mathes et al., 2005; O'Connor et al., 2002; Scanlon, Vellutino, Small, Fanuele, & Sweeney, 2005; Torgeson et al., 2001). However, it may cost no more to provide high-quality early intervention than it does to provide low-quality reading interventions over the long term.

In addition to expert teachers and small instructional groupings, the studies cited above also engaged students in high-success reading by reading or rereading materials appropriate for their level of development. In these cases, *high-success reading* can be described as reading with at least 98% accuracy, reading in phrases, and reading with 90% comprehension. Ehri, Dreyer, Flugman, and Gross (2007), for instance, found the best predictor of reading gains was the number of texts that students read with 98% accuracy or better. They conclude that, "Higher levels of accuracy may have been achieved either by the tutors selecting easier texts or by the tutors previewing and coaching students more effectively through the texts" (p. 440).

Likewise, O'Connor and her colleagues (2002) found that when expert tutors worked with struggling 6th-grade students (whose average reading level was at the 3rd-grade level), the level of reading accuracy in the materials the students read made a huge difference. In this case, tutors were assigned to work with the struggling readers with either classroom curriculum materials (usually grade-level materials) or with materials selected to match the reading levels of the struggling readers. Minimal progress was observed for many students when classroom materials were used, while the use of high-success, reading-level-matched reading materials produced accelerated reading growth. Notably, none of the expert tutors worked exclusively with a commercial reading program. Instead, the intervention lessons were designed to meet the needs of the struggling reader.

One critical need is engagement in high-success reading practice. By high-success reading practice, we mean providing struggling readers not only with texts that they can read accurately and with understanding but also with instruction tailored towards each student's individual instructional needs. Struggling readers normally do very little high-success reading, in school or out of it, even if they are participating in an intervention program. Thus, by 3rd grade, most struggling readers are at least a million words of high-success reading practice behind their on-level peers. It is those extra million words of high-success practice that produce the fluent, on-level readers that do not struggle with the texts they are assigned. Denton et al. (2003) note, "To overcome the practice deficits in relation to their non-impaired peers, students who learned to read initially in third grade would need to read for eight hours a day for a year, which would be virtually impossible" (p. 204). Of course reading for 4 hours a day for 2 years would also eliminate their reading practice deficit, as would reading 3 hours each day for 3 years.

We are not sure why struggling readers read so little, especially in their reading lessons (Allington, 1983; Collins, 1986). We have even less of a clue why pupils with disabilities rarely get either qualitatively better or more intensive reading lessons than do normally developing readers (McGill-Franzen & Allington, 1990; Vaughn, Moody, & Schumm, 1998). We have known for at least 30 years, however, that attending either remedial or intervention reading classes or special education classes does not ensure that the participants are receiving more and better reading instruction. Nor do we understand why two-thirds of classroom teachers report that it is not their responsibility to teach pupils with disabilities (Scharlach, 2008), or why they would think that the special education teacher during a 50-minute resource room session will provide all the reading instruction that pupils labeled learning disabled need. Yet every study on teaching pupils who are identified as learning disabled indicates that more and better reading is the solution to their reading achievement development (Allington, 2012).

The focus on the development of specific reading skills may also be at the root of why our instruction of struggling readers—including students with learning disabilities—pales in comparison to that provided to readers who are developing normally. When a reading diagnosis is undertaken, there is rarely any mention of the quality of classroom reading instruction the student receives or the student's current volume of daily reading. Yet we know that the quality of classroom reading lessons explains a larger portion of reading growth than any other factor (Nye, Konstantopoulos, & Hedges, 2004). Therefore, it may be that some classrooms create students who become labeled as a student with a learning disability. Consider what four senior scientists, each with a long history of research on learning disability and dyslexia, report in a recent paper on what the research indicates about dyslexia: "There is strong evidence that most early reading difficulties are caused primarily by experiential and instructional deficits, rather than basic cognitive deficits associated with neuro-developmental anomaly" (Vellutino, Fletcher, Snowling, & Scanlon, 2004, p. 28). And it is the children who arrive at school for kindergarten not already knowing all the letter names, not having been read 1,000 children's books, and not having developed a rich vocabulary that are at risk of being labeled as learning disabled.

At the same time, we have good evidence that effective reading instruction focused on high-success reading practices in kindergarten and 1st grade largely eliminates the problem of struggling readers (Mathes et al., 2005; McGill-Franzen, Allington, Yokoi, & Brooks, 1999; McGill-Franzen, Payne, & Dennis, 2010; Phillips & Smith, 2010; Scanlon, Anderson, & Sweeney, 2010). However, in the 15 years that have passed since the earliest study noted above was published, almost nothing has changed in school practice that reflects what we have learned. Consider, for instance, how few schools provide one-to-one expert tutoring to children who enter kindergarten unable to name all the letters of the alphabet or offer expert tutoring for 1st-graders struggling with learning to read. Similarly, few schools provide the one to three additional small-group expert daily reading lessons that have been used to eliminate struggling readers in the primary grades. Nor are there many examples of schools providing kindergarten and 1st-grade teachers with 30 to 60 hours of high-quality professional development plus in-classroom coaching to ensure that effective reading instruction is provided to every child (McGill-Franzen, Allington, et al., 1999; Scanlon, Gelzheiser, Vellutino, Schatschneider, & Sweeney, 2010). These are all strategies researchers have used that clearly indicate that all children could be reading on grade level by the end of 1st grade. However, instead of providing high-quality beginning reading instruction, American schools more often classify struggling readers as learning disabled or retain them in grade, or do both.

Retention, however, is an expensive proposition. It is also a disproven practice. Repeating a grade costs whatever a full year of schooling costs, approximately $10,000. However, repeating a grade proves no more effective than social promotion of low-achieving students (Jimerson & Ferguson, 2007). Members of both groups are likely to remain low-achievers over their school years. Yet several states and a number of large urban school districts now mandate retention in grade unless the student is achieving on or near grade level. This is an expensive plan that has never accelerated reading development.

SOLUTIONS FOR STRUGGLING READERS

The solution for struggling readers is not repeating a grade with more of the same, ineffective reading instruction. The solution is providing more expert, more intensive, and simply *more* reading instruction than is available in most schools. For example, rather than retaining ten 1st-graders, imagine we provided each of these 10 struggling readers with 30 minutes of high-quality, expert additional daily reading lessons for the full school year. If all of those students acquired on-level reading proficiency by the end of 1st grade, we would save the school $100,000 in costs that would have been accrued had we instead planned to simply retain the 10 struggling readers. Given average teacher salaries, in most states our total savings would be in the $30,000 to $50,000 range. Similarly, simply identifying these same struggling readers as learning disabled is another high-cost solution with disappointing outcomes. Denton et al. (2003) concluded, "Special education placements tend to stabilize reading growth of students with reading disabilities rather than accelerate it" (p. 203). In other words, current practice with students identified with disabilities rarely solves reading problems.

Special education reimbursement levels vary widely from state to state and even from community to community within a state. However, schools combining both the added state and federal funding supplied for each pupil identified with a disability would again add more than $10,000 to the annual cost of educating each pupil identified as a pupil with a disability. And, again, if expert and added tutoring for the school year resolved the reading difficulties, the savings would be immense. That is the hope the U.S. Congress has for the Response to Instruction legislation.

Members of the U.S. Congress seem to recognize that far too often federal funds intended to expand educational opportunities have not had that effect. Thus in the past decade Congress has mandated that pupils with disabilities participate in the annual state testing programs and that the results they achieve be presented to the public in the same manner and at the same time as the results for other pupils. Congress also made pupils with disabilities an "adequate yearly progress" subgroup under the No Child Left Behind Act (NCLB). Schools must now demonstrate that their efforts in educating pupils with disabilities produce more, or at least as much, academic gain as their efforts with other pupils.

Most recently, Congress created the opportunity for schools to replace their procedures for identifying pupils with learning disabilities with a process known as Response to Instruction (RtI). This change was also driven by research, research showing that a child's intelligence quotient had little relationship to reading achievement. RtI is intended to be led by members of the general education community. There is no role specified, much less mandated, that school psychologists can play in an RtI effort. Special education personnel get to work with the children only when the RtI initiative fails to accelerate reading development and move the participants closer to grade-level performance. Schools are allowed to use up to 25% of their special education budget to fund RtI initiatives, but few schools have taken advantage of this option. The thinking in Congress seems to have been that if expert early reading interventions will reduce special education enrollments, then it makes sense to allocate some of that funding to the RtI effort.

While the law authorizing Response to Instruction is fairly open on the question of just what an RtI model must contain, the intention to reduce special education placements—by as much as 70%—is quite clear (Lyon et al., 2001). Various authors of books on RtI recommend a tiered model of increasingly expert and intensive reading lessons for struggling readers, but there is no such requirement written into the federal law. Likewise, much has been written about frequent monitoring of student progress, but again the law makes no such requirement (Johnston, 2010). In addition, the research available suggests that weekly and monthly progress monitoring are no more reliable than an annual monitoring of progress (Schatschneider, Wagner, & Crawford, 2008).

While curriculum-based assessment would seem the most appropriate way to monitor progress, it seems that other one-minute measures (e.g., letter naming, phonemic segmentation, nonword reading accuracy) have gained much popularity even though their reliability as assessments of reading growth are suspect (Mathson, Solic, & Allington, 2006; Pressley, Hilden, & Shankland, 2006; Samuels, 2006). Additionally, these one-minute measures do not assess what children are being taught. These measures (DIBELS, AIMSweb, etc.) are not curriculum-based assessments because the test items are not drawn from the curriculum materials used in reading instruction. In fact, as Allington and Pearson (2011) have noted, the website for the DIBELS assessment notes that the DIBELS assessment results are not to be used to plan instruction but only to monitor progress. But if the assessment has little relationship to what children have been taught, how can the measure evaluate progress, much less inform instruction? Oral reading fluency is also frequently used as a progress indicator, but the text students read is not drawn from their curriculum but represents an attempt to provide students with standardized grade-level passages to read. However, the use of such assessments has become widespread despite their high cost and doubtful utility.

Curriculum-based assessment, on the other hand, offers an effective and lower cost means of assessing students' reading development. Ross (2004), for example, provides persuasive evidence on the utility of the running records procedure in both monitoring progress and improving the instruction provided to struggling readers. Data from running records provide both accuracy and fluency assessments on the curriculum materials students use in their reading lessons, making them both economical and reliable. Johnston's (2000) small book and audiotapes provide a cost-effective method of developing teacher expertise in the use of the running records procedure. Nonetheless, schools spend educational funds to purchase and use a commercial assessment that has so far not demonstrated it improves teaching or learning. And the process being commonly used also occupies far more instructional time than running record procedures.

Similarly, schools spend enormous sums on technology and software. Often this money is spent to purchase "reading" software purported to teach children to read better. Unfortunately, as is too often the case, the research available indicates that the software currently available is often expensive and fails to produce any substantial reading improvement. In a longitudinal study, Campuzano, Dynarski, Agodini, and Rall (2009) studied six commercial reading software products with 11,000 students in 23 low-income urban schools. There was only a single, small positive effect on reading achievement for one product at one grade level. The What Works Clearinghouse of the U.S. Department of Education identifies only one technology-based product as having "potential evidence" of its positive effects on reading comprehension—and, even then, only if implemented following the vendor's specific designs. However, "potential" evidence is not considered reliable evidence. Still, school districts continue to upgrade technology and purchase software that is supposed to teach children to read but doesn't.

Additionally, school districts and state education agencies spend hundreds of millions of dollars each year on computer-based test preparation programs—again, programs that no research has ever supported. As Glovin and Evans (2006) note, testing companies earn just 38% of their profits from testing and 62% of their profits from test preparation products. Crucially, none of the testing/test preparation companies have any evidence beyond sales figures to suggest their test preparation products actually improve test performances. Nonetheless, hundreds of millions of dollars are spent each year on such products by school systems that seem to be grasping for any simple solution to the problem struggling readers present.

In summary, it is not a lack of money that prevents schools from doing what research suggests. Instead, it is the general lack of awareness of the findings of educational research that leads school personnel to make decisions that have never been supported by research. Or a willingness to take the word of a sales representative or a company website that indicates their research supports the use of their product. However, in most cases those "studies" are not designed to provide reliable research outcomes but to convince naive buyers that this is a research-based product.

USING RESEARCH FINDINGS TO
TEACH EVERY CHILD TO READ

There are several key points that can be made from the research on interventions that produce on-level reading achievement in virtually all students who begin kindergarten in public schools. We will address each of these briefly.

Expert Teaching Matters Most

Evidence for this assertion comes from a variety of research studies. Pianta and his colleagues (2007) observed the instruction offered to almost 1,000 children in 1st-, 3rd-, and 5th-grade classrooms over 300 school districts across the United States. Based on their observations, they concluded that the distribution of reading proficiencies was strikingly related to the quality of the observed reading instruction in 1st, 3rd, and 5th grade, especially the proportion of children struggling with reading. Only 23% of the children who were struggling had had teachers rated as providing high-quality reading instruction, while 77% of the struggling readers had had teachers rated as providing low-quality reading lessons.

Nye et al. (2004) reanalyzed the data from the Tennessee STAR study, a randomized experiment focused on the effects of class-size reduction. While the original study found smaller classes generated higher reading achievement than larger classes, Nye and her colleagues found that the effect of the teacher to whom students were assigned was three times as large as the effect of class size. Some teachers with large classes produced better reading achievement than did the teachers with smaller classes. In other words, while states and school districts have been lowering class size in response to the earlier STAR study, a more powerful use of the funding for reducing class size may be to ensure the quality of the reading instruction provided in every classroom.

Taylor, Pearson, Clark, and Walpole (2000) reported that the most effective schools in their high-poverty school sample offered roughly twice as many small-group reading lessons as whole-group lessons (48 versus 25) while the less effective schools offered just the reverse, with twice as much time allocated for whole-group lessons as for small-group lessons. Teachers in more effective schools were also far more likely to ask higher order questions after reading than teachers in less effective schools and the effective teachers were far more likely to provide time for independent reading by pupils. Finally, teachers in more effective schools offered reading lessons every day that were more than a half hour longer than those offered in less effective schools. These results parallel those reported by Allington and Johnston (2002) in their study of exemplary 4th-grade teachers in five states.

Pressley and his colleagues (2003) reported on the motivational environments found in more and less effective primary grade classrooms. They found that effective primary grade teachers were from five to ten times as likely to create classroom environments that included factors found previously to foster motivation to read than were the less successful and typical teachers. Less successful teachers were, on the other hand, found to have created classrooms where factors previously noted to undermine reading motivation were far more common.

Finally, Hoffman, Roller, Maloch, Sailors, and Beretvas (2003) found that preparation in teaching reading was a compelling force in predicting both the quality of reading lessons offered by teachers and students' reading growth. Teachers with more undergraduate or graduate coursework in teaching reading were more likely to have few, if any, struggling readers. This was even true of well-prepared new teachers who typically produced reading gains in their students that exceeded those produced by more experienced teachers. As noted above, both Scanlon, Gelzheiser, et al. (2010) and McGill-Franzen and her colleagues (1999) provide powerful evidence that targeted professional development and classroom coaching foster the teacher expertise needed to become an effective teacher of reading. Yet too few schools seem to hire new teachers based on the depth of their coursework in reading and even fewer provide professional development opportunities that match the scope and intensity of the professional development provided by these researchers.

Ensuring All Students Engage in High-Success Reading

One factor that makes some teachers more effective than others is ensuring that all children have books that they can read from accurately, fluently, and with strong comprehension (Allington, 2012). There seems no better predictor of reading growth than the total number of minutes children are engaged in high-success reading activity. This is an old research finding first argued in 1949 by Betts, who concluded that, "For the instructional reading level, a child should meet a maximum of one 'new' word in 20 running words. A better average for many pupils is in the neighborhood of one 'new' word in 50 or 60 running words" (p. 274). What Betts recommended was small-group instructional materials that could be read with 95–98% accuracy. When the child was reading independently, or not in a small guided reading group, he recommended accuracy levels even higher, at or above 99% reading accuracy. Betts drew on his own research in developing these standards and later studies have largely confirmed his initial findings.

Unfortunately, Betts's research has been largely ignored in favor of one-size-fits-all reading programs, particularly in recent years. Under the federal NCLB plan, there was an emphasis on implementing one of six core reading programs and delivering reading lessons as guided by the accompanying program manuals. However, in a study of the outcomes of such a plan in one state, McGill-Franzen, Zmach, Solic, and Zeig (2006) found that roughly one-third of all 3rd-graders failed to achieve the minimal level required for promotion to the 4th grade. It mattered little which core program a district used, at least for their struggling readers. But no theory of reading suggests placing students with curriculum materials that are obviously too difficult for some readers.

All too often, we observe struggling readers attempting to read the same grade-level texts their better reading peers are assigned. In fact, our work suggests that in too many schools it is difficult to find a struggling reader who has in his desk even one text that would meet Betts's standards for appropriate level of difficulty. If we want to foster accelerated reading growth, then ensuring that struggling readers have high-success texts in their hands all day long will be a necessity.

Fostering Comprehension Development

As noted above, Taylor et al. (2000) and Allington and Johnston (2002) found that teachers in more effective high-poverty schools were more likely to focus lessons on comprehension, more likely to maintain an interactional style similar to "coaching," and less likely to subject children to low-level recall questions on trivial story content. Similarly, Nystrand (2006) reviews what we know about literate conversations in classrooms and the impact these conversations have on reading comprehension as measured by standardized tests. He notes that the evidence indicates that few teachers actually engage students in literate conversation or allow students to engage each other in such talk. When available, even if only in small proportions of lesson time (10 minutes or less), reading comprehension improves. Applebee, Langer, Nystrand, and Gamoran (2003) provide one example of how introducing literate conversation into subject matter classes influences learning. However, they also note that "lower track classes had discussions less frequently and of shorter duration (X = 3.7 min) than students in higher track classes (X = 14.7 min.). Even so, more frequent and longer discussions in lower track classes produced higher achievement. However, it is difficult to know the full impact that discussion-based lessons might have on lower achieving student performance since they were less common in lower track classrooms" (p. 685).

CONCLUSION

We have learned much about what effective reading instruction looks like. Unfortunately, most of what we know is too rarely observed in classrooms, especially classrooms serving low-income children. Instead, we see a faux version of what has been called reading instruction based upon "scientifically based reliable replicable research." This one-size-fits-all version of effective teaching has no basis in research and the recent federal evaluation of the effects of the Reading First program illustrate this point: No greater positive effects on reading achievement were observed in Reading First schools than in similar high-poverty schools which did not participate in the Reading First program (Gamse, Jacob, Horst, Boulay, & Unlu, 2009).

We have lost a decade of opportunity to teach the way we know how to teach. Struggling readers, perhaps, felt the greatest loss across this decade. Research does provide guidelines that schools might follow, but what the research actually says has been largely ignored. It is up to us to begin again and follow the guidelines that research provides, while letting the entrepreneurs and policy makers continue to talk to each other. The children are waiting.

REFERENCES

Allington R. L. (1983). The reading instruction provided readers of differing abilities. *Elementary School Journal, 83*, 548–559.

Allington, R. L. (2012). *What really matters for struggling readers: Designing research-based programs* (3rd ed.). Boston: Allyn & Bacon.

Allington R. L., & Johnston, P. H. (Eds.). (2002). *Reading to learn: Lessons from exemplary 4th grade classrooms.* New York: Guilford Press.

Allington, R. L., & Pearson, P. D. (2011). The casualties of policy on early literacy development. *Language Arts, 89*(1), 70–74.

Applebee, A. N., Langer, J. A., Nystrand, M., & Gamoran, A. (2003). Discussion-based approaches to developing understanding: Classroom instruction and student performance in middle and high school English. *American Educational Research Journal, 40*(3), 685–730.

Betts, E. A. (1949). Adjusting instruction to individual needs. In N. B. Henry (Ed.), *The forty-eighth yearbook of the National Society for the Study of Education: Part II, Reading in the elementary school* (pp. 266–283). Chicago: University of Chicago Press.

Campuzano, L., Dynarski, M., Agodini, R., & Rall, K. (2009). *Effectiveness of reading and mathematics software products: Findings from two student cohorts.* Washington, DC: National Center for Education Evaluation and Regional Assistance, Institute of Education Sciences, U.S. Department of Education.

Collins, J. (1986). Differential instruction in reading groups. In J. Cook-Gumperz (Ed.), *The social construction of literacy* (pp. 117–137). New York: Cambridge University Press.

Denton, C. A., Vaughn, S., & Fletcher, J. M. (2003). Bringing research-based practice in reading intervention to scale. *Learning Disabilities Research and Practice, 18*(3), 201–211.

Ehri, L. C., Dreyer, L. G., Flugman, B., & Gross, A. (2007). Reading Rescue: An effective tutoring intervention model for language minority students who are struggling readers in first grade. *American Educational Research Journal, 44*(2), 414–448.

Gamse, B. C., Jacob, R. T., Horst, M., Boulay, B., & Unlu, F. (2009). *Reading First impact study: Final report* (NCEE 2009-4038). Washington, DC: National Center for Education Evaluation and Regional Assistance, Institute of Education Sciences, U.S. Department of Education.

Glovin, D., & Evans, D. (2006, December). How test companies fail your kids. *Bloomberg Markets,* pp. 127–138.

Hoffman, J. V., Roller, C. M., Maloch, B., Sailors, M., & Beretvas, N. (2003). *Prepared to make a difference: Final report of the National Commission on Excellence in Elementary Teacher Preparation for Reading.* Newark, DE: International Reading Association.

Jimerson, S. R., & Ferguson, F. (2007). A longitudinal study of grade retention: Academic and behavioral outcomes of retained students through adolescence. *School Psychology Quarterly, 22*(3), 314–339.

Johnston, P. H. (2000). *Running records.* York, ME: Stenhouse.

Johnston, P. H. (2010). A framework for response to intervention in literacy. In P. H. Johnston (Ed.), *RTI in literacy: Responsive and comprehensive* (pp. 1–9). Newark, DE: International Reading Association.

Lyon, G. R., Fletcher, J. M., Shaywitz, S. E., Shaywitz, B. A., Torgeson, J. K., Wood, F. B., . . . Olson, R. (2001). Rethinking learning disabilities. In C. E. Finn, R. A. J. Rotherham, & C. R. Hokanson (Eds.), *Rethinking special education for a new century.* (pp. 259–288). Washington, DC: Progressive Policy Institute and the Thomas B. Fordham Foundation.

Mathes, P. G., Denton, C. A., Fletcher, J. M., Anthony, J. L., Francis, D. J., & Schatschneider, C. (2005). The effects of theoretically different instruction and student characteristics on the skills of struggling readers. *Reading Research Quarterly, 40*(2), 148–182.

Mathson, D., Solic, K., & Allington, R. L. (2006). Hijacking fluency and instructionally informative assessment. In T. Rasinski, C. Blachowicz, & K. Lems (Eds.), *Fluency instruction: Research-based best practice* (pp. 106–119). New York: Guilford Press.

McGill-Franzen, A., & Allington, R. L. (1990). Comprehension and coherence: Neglected elements of literacy instruction in remedial and resource room services. *Journal of Reading, Writing, and Learning Disabilities, 6*(2), 149–182.

McGill-Franzen, A., Allington, R. L., Yokoi, L., & Brooks, G. (1999). Putting books in the classroom seems necessary but not sufficient. *Journal of Educational Research, 93*(2), 67–74.

McGill-Franzen, A., Payne, R., & Dennis, D. (2010). Responsive intervention: What is the role of appropriate assessment? In P. H. Johnston (Ed.), *RTI in literacy — Responsive and comprehensive* (pp. 115–132). Newark, DE: International Reading Association.

McGill-Franzen, A., Zmach, C., Solic, K., & Zeig, J. L. (2006). The confluence of two policy mandates: Core reading programs and third-grade retention in Florida. *Elementary School Journal, 107*(1), 67– 91.

National Assessment of Educational Progress (NAEP). (2009). *The nation's report card*. Washington, DC: National Center for Educational Statistics. Retrieved from http://nces.ed.gov/nationsreportcard/

Nye, B., Konstantopoulos, S., & Hedges, L. V. (2004). How large are teacher effects? *Educational Evaluation and Policy Analysis, 26*(3), 237–257.

Nystrand, M. (2006). Research on the role of classroom discourse as it affects reading comprehension. *Research in the Teaching of English, 40*, 392–412.

O'Connor, R. E., Bell, K. M., Harty, K. R., Larkin, L. K., Sackor, S. M., & Zigmond, N. (2002). Teaching reading to poor readers in the intermediate grades: A comparison of text difficulty. *Journal of Educational Psychology, 94*(3), 474–485.

Pianta, R. C., Belsky, J., Houts, R., Morrison, F., & NICHD Early Child Care Research Network. (2007). Opportunities to learn in America's elementary classrooms. *Science, 315*(5820), 1795–1796.

Phillips, G., & Smith, P. (2010). Closing the gaps: Literacy for the hardest to teach. In P. Johnston (Ed.), *RTI in literacy: Responsive and comprehensive* (pp. 219–246). Newark, DE: International Reading Association.

Pressley, M., Dolezal, S., Raphael, L. M., Mohan, L., Roehrig, A. D., & Bogner, K. (2003). *Motivating primary grade students*. New York: Guilford Press.

Pressley, M., Hilden, K., & Shankland, R. (2006). *An evaluation of end-of-grade-3 Dynamic Indicators of Basic Early Literacy Skills (DIBELS): Speed reading without comprehension, predicting little*. East Lansing, MI: Literacy Achievement Research Center, Michigan State University.

Ross, J. A. (2004). Effects of running records assessment on early literacy achievement. *Journal of Educational Research, 97*(2), 186–195.

Samuels, S. J. (2006). Toward a model of reading fluency. In S. J. Samuels & A. E. Farstrup (Eds.), *What research has to say about fluency instruction* (pp. 24–46). Newark, DE: International Reading Association.

Scanlon, D. M., Anderson, K. L., & Sweeney, J. M. (2010). *Early intervention for reading difficulties: The interactive strategies approach*. New York: Guilford Press.

Scanlon, D. M., Gelzheiser, L. M., Vellutino, F. R. Schatschneider, C., & Sweeney, J. M. (2010). Reducing the incidence of early reading difficulties: Professional development for classroom teachers versus direct interventions for children. In P. H. Johnston (Ed.), *RTI in literacy—Responsive and comprehensive* (pp. 257–295). Newark, DE: International Reading Association.

Scanlon, D. M., Vellutino, F. R., Small, S. G., Fanuele, D. P., & Sweeney, J. M. (2005). Severe reading difficulties—Can they be prevented? A comparison of prevention and intervention approaches. *Exceptionality, 13*(4), 209–227.

Scharlach, T. D. (2008). These kids just aren't motivated to read: The influence of preservice teachers' beliefs on their expectations, instruction, and evaluation of struggling readers. *Literacy Research and Instruction, 47*(3), 158–173.

Schatschneider, C., Wagner, R. K., & Crawford, E. C. (2008). The importance of measuring growth in response to intervention models: Testing a core assumption. *Learning and Individual Differences, 18*(3), 308–315.

Taylor, B. M., Pearson, P. D., Clark, K., & Walpole, S. (2000). Effective schools and accomplished teachers: Lessons about primary grade reading instruction in low-income schools. *Elementary School Journal, 101*, 121–165.

Torgeson, J. K., Alexander, A. W., Wagner, R. K., Rashotte, C. A., Voeller, K. K., & Conway, T. (2001). Intensive remedial instruction for children with severe reading disabilities: Immediate and long-term outcomes from two instructional approaches. *Journal of Learning Disabilities, 34*(1), 33–58.

Vaughn, S., Moody, S. W., & Schumm, J. S. (1998). Broken promises: Reading instruction in the resource room. *Exceptional Children, 64*, 211–225.

Vellutino, F. R., Fletcher, J. M., Snowling, M. J., & Scanlon, D. M. (2004). Specific reading disability (dyslexia): What have we learned in the past four decades? *Journal of Child Psychology and Psychiatry 45*(1), 2–40.

Conclusion

Curt Dudley-Marling
Sarah Michaels

For all the criticism it has received, much of it justified from our point of view, the No Child Left Behind Act (NCLB) addresses a real crisis in American education. Groups of students already disadvantaged by poverty and discrimination including poor students of color overrepresented in urban schools, English Language Learners, and students with disabilities significantly underachieve in school, limiting their academic and vocational opportunities. Yet, as the Introduction to this volume by Dudley-Marling and Michaels and the chapter by Hugh Mehan show, these children frequently experience circumscribed curricular practices, justified in the name of NCLB, that virtually ensure that those students who have been "left behind" in our schools will never catch up with their peers in more affluent, high-achieving schools.

Impoverished curricular practices focusing on a narrow scope and sequence of basic skills are typically justified by pointing to research on "best practices." But too often research on best practices is underpinned by deficit thinking that situates the blame for school failure in the minds and bodies of students, their families, their language, and their communities. Collectively, the contributors to this volume vehemently reject this deficit stance that pathologizes individual students and the communities from which they come, and reject as well the limited and limiting curriculum that comes from this stance. Everyone desires to be respected and a deficit stance is fundamentally disrespectful. Children will not respond well to instruction that is based on the assumption that there is something wrong with them, their families, or their communities. Nor is it likely that any child will be able to learn how to engage in thoughtful, challenging curriculum in math, science, social studies, or language arts if they aren't routinely exposed to, and expected to participate in, rigorous reasoning practices. Moreover, as Dick Allington and Anne McGill-Franzen and Nadeen Ruiz point out in their chapters, the hyper focus on basic skills presented as best practices ignores a significant body of research evidence supporting rich, engaging curriculum for low-achieving students. For instance, Allington and McGill-Franzen cite an abundance of evidence that struggling readers need lots of opportunities to read, not just practice with skills. Similarly, Ruiz laments that 40 years of research in second language learning is being abandoned in favor of deficit-based, 1960s-era methods that fail to recognize differences between the needs of second language learners and English-dominant speakers.

The antidote to the inferior curricula that plague children who have been "left behind" is providing these students with rich engaging curricula based on the presumption of competence, the kind of curriculum commonly experienced by children in affluent schools and high-achieving classrooms. Our primary goal when putting this volume together was to provide concrete examples of a "high-expectation" curriculum for students whose competence as learners has been in doubt. In our experience, many teachers initially resist our call for a high-expectation curriculum for students presumed to be less than competent. "Show me what a high-expectation curriculum looks like with kids like mine," they tell us. Administrators are likely to add, "Show me evidence that it works." The contributors to this volume respond to these demands by offering illustrative examples of what a high-expectation curriculum looks like as well as evidence of how historically low-achieving students respond to opportunities to engage with rich, challenging curricula.

Here we highlight a few of the themes that emerge from our reading of the chapters in this volume.

WHEN STUDENTS ARE TREATED AS COMPETENT, THEY DISPLAY COMPETENCE

Deficit thinking is based on the presumption that children fail in school because there is something wrong with them, leading to instruction that is focused on remediating students' deficiencies. The problem, as we've argued above, is that this typically leads to circumscribed curricular practices that afford fewer learning opportunities compared to students exposed to a high-expectation curriculum. High-expectation curricula are underpinned by a

> philosophy of abundance . . . based on capability and competence. It presumes an optimistic explanation for human thinking, learning, and ability. This abundance perspective assumes that each person, regardless of age,

gender, economic circumstance, or geographic location, is constantly in the process of constructing meanings based on her or his own life experiences. (Miller, 1993, p. 57)

As the chapters of this volume show, when students are presumed to be competent and treated as competent, they will, more often than not, demonstrate that they are, indeed, competent, just like their peers in more affluent, high-achieving classrooms and schools. In Marty Rutherford's chapter, for example, she shows how students attending low-achieving schools can participate in the challenging work of translating great poetry and then write inspirational poems of their own, experiences these students would rarely have in school. Similarly, Debra Goodman shows how a struggling reader she calls Marco was able to engage in a wide range of rich literacy practices when he was immersed in a "richly literate community" with a high-expectation curriculum. Richard Sohmer shows how struggling and previously failing middle school students come to see themselves and their fellow "investigators" as smart, capable of understanding complex problems in physics, and teaching what they know to others.

Chapters by Sophie Haroutunian-Gordon, Suzanne Chapin and Cathy O'Connor, and Dudley-Marling and Michaels show students who attend inner-city, low-achieving schools participating in high-level discussions—making claims, citing evidence in support of their claims, and sometimes making explicit the evidentiary warrant for their claims—that resemble the kind of interactions we might expect to see in a graduate-level seminar. A rich and engaging curriculum, and a set of moves by the people who were facilitating these discussions, made it possible for children and young adults to participate in challenging math and language arts practices that they are usually denied access to because it is assumed that these tasks are beyond their ability.

Especially remarkable is the chapter by Chris Kliewer who shows LaShawn, a 4-year-old boy with severe physical disabilities and no understandable spoken language, demonstrating his knowledge of literacy by participating in various literacy activities with his peers in an inclusive classroom. We describe Kliewer's vignettes featuring LaShawn as "remarkable" because it is generally taken for granted that children like LaShawn aren't literate and, in fact, can't be literate. Kliewer's research completely upends this assumption.

The expectation of competence may lead educators to expand their sense of what counts as competent as Kliewer's study of LaShawn's inclusive classroom suggests. An expanded notion of literacy, for example, enabled Jenny Urbach and Janette Klingner to see how 1st-grade African American boys' oral stories reveal literacy knowledge that would not have been apparent in the context of more traditional, school-based literacy tasks. Still, without the presumption of competence, it would be easy to dismiss these boys' storytelling performances as evidence that they weren't literate at all.

Taken together the chapters in this volume clearly show that we should be suspicious of claims that students are less than competent—and we should reject claims of deficiencies outright. If we create the necessary conditions for learning, students will always show us how smart they really are.

HIGH-EXPECTATION CURRICULA CREATE SPACE FOR STUDENTS TO DRAW ON THEIR BACKGROUND KNOWLEDGE AND EXPERIENCE

The behavioral theory on which deficit thinking is based indicates that learning is additive and therefore learning is easiest when it can be broken down into decontextualized skills and subskills. This leads to the kind of low-level curriculum that we and other contributors to this volume have been highly critical of.

From a constructivist point of view, however, learning is a matter of integrating new knowledge with old knowledge, and therefore learning is easiest when children can draw on their language, background knowledge, and experience in support of their learning. Frank Smith (1998) puts it this way:

> The official theory of learning says that we have to learn something in order to understand it. . . . This is totally contrary to fact. We have to understand something in order to learn it. We have to make sense of it. (p. 35)

The examples of high-expectation curricula presented in this volume make space for students to draw on their language, background knowledge, and experience to make sense of new learning. Sohmer, for instance, begins with assumption that "all students come to school with well-developed theories of how the world works." Yet, "the way science is typically taught in schools . . . disparages students' already-existing knowledge" (p. 128) The Investigators Club, on the other hand, is situated in talk formats that encourage students to draw on their "already-existing knowledge" to make sense of the physical world (i.e., science). Similarly, the program Poetry Inside Out (in Rutherford's chapter) allows second language learners to draw on their first language to make sense of poetry. Chapters on discussion (Chapin & O'Connor; Dudley-Marling & Michaels; Haroutunian-Gordon; Klingner, Boardman, & Annamma) illustrate how students use language to engage with and make sense of difficult ideas. Jenny Urbach and Janette Klingner show how children's home-based language practices provide a foundation for the literacy practices most valued in school settings.

These are the sorts of opportunities routinely afforded to students presumed to be competent, students for whom high-expectation curricula are taken for granted. The chapters in this volume make a persuasive case that these same opportunities are imperative for students typically perceived to be "at risk" for educational failure.

ALL LEARNERS NEED SUPPORT AND DIRECTION

The contributors to this volume agree that high-expectation curricula are fundamental to improving the achievement of historically underachieving groups of students including students of color, poor students, second language learners, and students with disabilities. But achieving at higher levels will require more than engaging texts and challenging content. For example, Allington and McGill-Franzen assert that the solution to low reading achievement is "providing more expert, more intensive, and simply *more* reading instruction than is available in most schools" (emphasis added; p. 192). Similarly, Sohmer argues that the success of a high-expectation practice like the Investigators Club is dependent on "talk, tools, and tasks" that are interwoven in the Investigators Club science curriculum. Several chapters in this text (Chapin & O'Connor; Dudley-Marling and Michaels; Haroutunian-Gordon; Klinger, Boardman, & Annamma; Sohmer) illustrate the power of discussion as an instantiation of high-expectation curricula, but all of these contributors stress the importance of clear goals, careful scaffolding (including the strategic use of talk moves), and routine reflection in orchestrating challenging, engaging, and academically productive discussions. And what is true of discussions is true of high-expectation curricula more generally as chapters by Goodman, Ruiz, Rutherford, and others illustrate.

The value of a high-expectation curriculum may also depend on building students' cultural capital. The students at the detracked Preuss School (in Mehan's chapter), for example, are deliberately immersed in a "college-going school culture" which includes a shared purpose shown through rituals, traditions, values, symbols, artifacts, and relationships. For instance, Preuss alumni return for alumni days to give students insight in the college-going experience. Additionally, "while enrolled at Preuss, students explore different types of colleges and learn about requirements, costs, and potential sources of support" (p. 22). Similarly, the course described in Eric DeMeulenaere's chapter explicitly addresses the college application process.

THE STRUCTURES AND CULTURE OF SCHOOLS MATTER

As detailed in the Introduction and in Mehan's chapter, schools have long segregated children by ability. In secondary settings this has most often taken the form of ability tracks which have implicit links to expectations about students' academic and vocational futures. Students in honors tracks are being prepared for college and university while students in basic tracks are being prepared for work. In elementary classrooms, tracking is more likely to take the form of ability grouping for subjects like reading and math. Whatever form tracking takes, it nearly ensures that children in lower tracks will receive a form of instruction that diminishes their academic and vocational futures. Segregated schooling practices by ability will always disadvantage students perceived to have lower ability. And the degree to which poor students, second language learners, students of color, and students with disabilities are overrepresented in lower academic tracks makes tracking even more problematic. Therefore, the kind of detracking Mehan and others discuss (see, for example, Oakes, 2005) is essential to enacting the high-expectation curricula described in the chapters of this volume.

In his chapter, Eric DeMeulenaere calls for educators to confront a culture of mistrust that plagues many underfunded, low-achieving schools and classrooms overpopulated by children of color and second language learners. DeMeulenaere argues persuasively that teachers must work to establish a classroom culture of trust before high-expectation curricula can be implemented and students can achieve high levels of learning.

Arguably, all the chapters in this book, by trusting that all students are competent learners, enact a pedagogy of trust.

HIGH-EXPECTATION CURRICULA "WORK"

The chapters in this book contribute to the decades of research cited by Ruiz and Allington and McGill-Franzen indicating that all students need rich, engaging curricula to succeed in school. Some chapters, like those by Chapin and O'Connor and Dudley-Marling and Michaels, cite standardized test score and statistical evidence for the power of some high-expectation curricular practices. Chapin and O'Connor, for example, provide data showing substantial student gains on the California Achievement Test (CAT) in the context of Project Challenge. After 2 years in the project, students were scoring better than 87% of the students in the national sample. Mehan shares data indicating that the Preuss School, the detracked high school on the University of California–San Diego campus, is one of the highest performing high schools in the county with a high proportion of students attending college or university. Dudley-Marling and Michaels also provide data that students participating in Shared Inquiry at Lexington Elementary made large gains on district reading tests.

These chapters and others also offer clear qualitative evidence that students immersed in high-expectation curricular practices tend to learn those practices. Transcripts from Chapin and O'Connor's Project Challenge and the students participating in Shared Inquiry at Lexington Elementary, for example, show students making sophisticated academic arguments. In the context of Interpretive Discussion, the high school students with whom Haroutunian-Gordon worked demonstrated sophisticated textual analysis skills. The students with whom Rutherford worked learned to skillfully translate and write poetry. In the context of Collaborative Strategic Reading groups, discussed by Klingner, Boardman, and Annamma, students demonstrate they can work together to make sense of texts. Similarly, Ruiz documents the remarkable progress of Diana, a second language learner in the Optimal Learning Environments (OLE) program. Ruiz argues that this is a typical response when second language learners are immersed in an instructional context that looks like classrooms for gifted and talented programs. Chapters by Kliewer, Goodman, and Urbach and Klingner offer further evidence that high-expectation curricula *work* to promote high levels of language and literacy.

CONCLUSION

Collectively, the contributors to this volume demonstrate the power of high-expectation curricula for students who are typically denied the rich, engaging curricula common in affluent schools and high-achieving classroom. The underlying high-expectation curricula reflect a belief that all children are competent people with rich background knowledge and interesting experiences. Here's how Linda Miller (1993) puts it:

> Four major conclusions emanate from the caring ethic I have described here: (1) everyone is taken to be smart and capable of learning; (2) everyone is seen to be motivated by unique and often different things; (3) individual variation is accepted as normal, not as a disorder; (4) discovering each person's individual story is the starting point for designing meaningful and relevant instruction. (p. 75)

A high-expectation curriculum will not, by itself, overcome the crippling effects of poverty, underfunded schools, deteriorating facilities, or poor teachers that plague the education of poor students of color in this country. But these problems must not be used as an excuse for denying students the rich, engaging experience to which all of our nation's children are entitled.

REFERENCES

Miller, L. (1993). *What we call smart: A new narrative for intelligence and learning*. San Diego: Singular Publishing Group.

Oakes, J. (2005). *Keeping track: How schools structure inequality* (2nd ed.). New Haven, CT: Yale University Press. (Original work published 1985)

Smith, F. (1998). *The book of learning and forgetting*. New York: Teachers College Press.

About the Editors and the Contributors

Curt Dudley-Marling teaches courses in language and literacy in the Lynch School of Education at Boston College. He was a special education teacher for 7 years before earning his PhD from the University of Wisconsin–Madison. In the early 1990s Dudley-Marling took a leave from his professorial duties to teach 3rd grade in the Toronto Public Schools, providing the basis for the book, *Living with Uncertainty: The Messy Reality of Classroom Practice*, which received the James N. Britton Award for Inquiry in the English Language Arts. Dudley-Marling has published over 100 articles, book chapters, and books focusing on struggling readers and students with disabilities. He is a former chair of the Elementary Section of the National Council of Teachers of English (NCTE) and former coeditor of the NCTE journal *Language Arts*. His interests include the social construction of learning failures, the power of "high-expectation" curricula, classroom discussion, and disability studies.

Sarah Michaels received her PhD from the University of California, Berkeley and is professor of Education and senior research scholar at the Jacob Hiatt Center for Urban Education at Clark University. A sociolinguist by training, she has been actively involved in teaching and research in the area of language, culture, "multiliteracies," and the discourses of math and science. She works to bring together teacher education, practitioner research, university-based research on classroom discourse, and district-based efforts at educational reform. She is currently involved in a variety of research projects that focus on academically productive talk in math, science, and English language arts, from prekindergarten through 12th grade. She recently coauthored a book, sponsored by the National Research Council, called *Ready, Set, Science!: Putting Research to Work in the K–8 Science Classroom.* Sarah has published widely in the area of classroom discourse analysis and has received numerous awards for both teaching and scholarship.

Richard L. Allington is professor of Literacy Studies at the University of Tennessee and a past president of the International Reading Association and the Literacy Research Association. He was awarded the William S. Gray Citation of merit for his contributions to the profession and was corecipient of the Albert J. Harris Award for his contributions to the understanding of reading and learning disabilities. He has also been named to the Reading Hall of Fame. Dick is author of over 150 research articles and several books, including *What Really Matters for Struggling Readers* and the *Handbook of Reading Disabilities Research,* coedited with Anne McGill-Franzen.

Subini Annamma is currently a doctoral candidate at the University of Colorado at Boulder. Previously, she had been a special education teacher working with culturally and linguistically diverse students with emotional, behavioral, and learning disabilities in a variety of settings. Subini's research interests include educational equity, racial identity development, transnational and transracial adoption, and the disproportionate representation of culturally and linguistically diverse students in special education.

Alison Boardman is an assistant research professor in the School of Education at the University of Colorado at Boulder where she conducts reading intervention research and teaches graduate and undergraduate courses. Alison has published numerous articles and coauthored two books on reading comprehension. She has extensive experience providing professional development to teachers across the nation to successfully teach comprehension strategies in their classrooms. Alison has years of experience as a special education teacher in elementary and middle school.

Suzanne H. Chapin is professor of Mathematics Education at Boston University, where she teaches graduate-level courses and conducts research. Her work covers the areas of gifted education, curriculum design, teacher professional development in mathematics, and teacher and student discourse in mathematics. Suzanne is the principal investigator of two Robert Noyce Scholars programs that recruit and prepare mathematics students for teaching careers in urban school districts. She is coauthor of *Math Matters: Understanding the Math You Teach, Grades K–8* (2006); *Classroom Discussions: Using Math Talk To Help Students Learn* (2009); and *Math Innovations.* Suzanne is a frequent speaker at national meetings of mathematicians, mathematics educators, researchers, and policy makers.

Eric DeMeulenaere is an assistant professor of Urban Schooling in Clark University's Education Department. Prior to joining Clark University's faculty, he taught middle and high school social studies and English in Oakland and San Francisco. More recently, Eric cofounded and directed an innovative small public school in East Oakland that focused on social justice and increased academic outcomes for youth of color. Before opening the school, he earned his PhD in the Social and Cultural Studies Program at the University of California, Berkeley Graduate School of Education.

Debra Goodman is an associate professor of Literacy Studies at Hofstra University. She is author of the book *The Reading Detective Club*. She received her PhD from Michigan State University where she explored the social nature of literacy learning in whole language classrooms in inner-city Detroit. Debi was a teacher in Detroit Public Schools for 15 years and has worked with teachers and teacher educators across the country and in Taiwan, Guatemala, and Mexico. Her professional writing and research focuses on early literacy, writing evaluation, language learning, language and culture, urban teaching, and revaluing struggling readers and writers.

Sophie Haroutunian-Gordon is a professor and the director of the Master of Science in Education Program at Northwestern University. She earned a PhD from the University of Chicago. She is a past president of the Philosophy of Education Society (2003). Her books include *Learning to Teach Through Discussion: The Art of Turning the Soul* (Yale, 2009) and *Turning the Soul: Teaching Through Conversation in the High School* (Chicago, 1991) which received a Critics Choice Award from the American Educational Studies Association. Sophie has coedited special issues of the *Teachers College Record* and *Educational Theory* on "listening" and is completing a new book on interpretive discussion for Harvard Education Press.

Chris Kliewer received his PhD from Syracuse University and currently is an associate professor in Special Education at the University of Northern Iowa where he codirects the UNI Center for Disability Studies in Literacy, Language, and Learning. His scholarly interests include the literacy development of young children with and without disabilities, early childhood inclusive education, and family advocacy. Kliewer is author of *Seeing All Kids as Readers: A New Vision for Literacy in the Inclusive Early Childhood Classroom* (Paul Brookes, 2008) and is currently codirector of a grant focusing on professional development in the area of literacy and communication to Iowa's teachers of students with low-incidence disabilities.

Janette Klingner is professor of education at the University of Colorado at Boulder. She was a bilingual special education teacher for 10 years before earning a PhD in Reading and Learning Disabilities. To date, she has authored or coauthored more than 100 articles, books, and book chapters. Her principal areas of research focus on reading comprehension strategy instruction for culturally and linguistically diverse students and Response to Intervention for English Language Learners. Currently, she is the principal investigator or coprincipal investigator on three U.S. Department of Education grants. In 2004 she won American Educational Research Association's Early Career Award.

Anne McGill-Franzen is a professor of education and the director of the Reading Center at the University of Tennessee. She is a member of the International Reading Association's Reading Hall of Fame, past member of the LRA/NRC board, recipient of both the IRA Nila Banton Smith and the Dina Feitelson awards for empirical work in early literacy, and corecipient of the Albert J. Harris Award for research in reading disabilities. She is published widely in literacy journals, recently coedited the *Handbook of Reading Disability Research* (2011), and was the codirector (with R. Allington) of a summer books intervention with high-poverty children that earned the Congressional "Top Tier" Evidence of Effectiveness identification.

Hugh Mehan is professor emeritus of sociology and founding director of The Center for Research on Educational Equity, Access, and Teaching Excellence at University of California, San Diego. He has authored and edited numerous books including *The Reality of Ethnomethodology, Learning Lessons, Handicapping the Handicapped,* and *Constructing School Success.* He was elected to the National Academy of Education in 1997, and has received the following awards: the George and Louise Spindler Award for outstanding contributions to anthropology and education by the American Anthropological Association, the Elizabeth Cohen Award for outstanding contributions to applied Sociology by the Sociology of Education SIG of the American Educational Research Association (AERA) in April 2007, and a Lifetime Achievement Award by AERA.

Catherine O'Connor, a professor at Boston University, is chair of the Department of Educational Foundations, Leadership, and Counseling, and irector of the Program in Applied Linguistics. She received her PhD in Linguistics at the University of California, Berkeley. Her work within applied linguistics centers on language use in school settings, including classroom discourse and its role in mathematics learning. Among her recent publications is *Classroom Discussions: Using Math Talk to Help Students Learn,* and the 2012 AEP award-winning book, facilitator's guide, and 5 hours of mathematics classroom video, *Classroom Discussions: Seeing Math Discourse in Action, K–6* (Anderson, Chapin, & O'Connor, 2011, Math Solutions).

Nadeen T. Ruiz is professor emerita at Sacramento State University. Recipient of multiple education grants, Ruiz is currently director of the *California*

Bi-National Teacher Education Project, a U.S.-Mexico transnational teacher education program. She holds a PhD from Stanford University, and has worked as a teacher educator and administrator at both Sacramento State and Stanford, winning 3 awards for outstanding teaching. Ruiz received the California Association of Bilingual Education Teacher Educator Award and the Outstanding Alumna Award from the University of California, Davis School of Education. She is an active scholar, writing multiple books and articles on the development of English Learners' bilingualism and biliteracy in both general and special education settings, many grounded in her work with the Optimal Learning Environment (OLE) Project. Ruiz regularly presents on these topics in the United States and Mexico.

Marty Rutherford completed her doctorate in language and literacy at the University of California, Berkeley after having worked for several years as a bilingual teacher in Oakland Unified School District. Since that time she has worked on disseminating culturally relevant, high-expectation literacy programs that offer the promise of transforming high-poverty schools into vibrant learning communities. Currently, she is director of research and dissemination for the Center for the Art of Translation's Poetry Inside Out program.

Richard Sohmer received his PhD from Clark University and now works as a researcher, curriculum developer, and educator focusing on science education. He has developed innovative science curriculum for pre-K through grade 8, successful ways of teaching and learning science in urban schools, and demonstration after-school programs. He is the founder and codesigner of the Investigators' Club, an after-school science program for inner-city middle school students, which grew out of a Spencer Foundation major grant, "Socializing Motivation and Academic Efficacy: The Power of a Practice." He is interested in the architecture of intersubjectivity via apprenticeship structures. His current research focuses on the principles and practices that facilitate intersubjectivity and successful science learning in the Investigators' Club and with prekindergarten children, as well as the apprenticeship of teachers new to these teaching and learning practices.

Jennifer Urbach is an assistant professor in the School of Special Education at the University of Northern Colorado. She received her PhD from the University of Colorado at Boulder in Instruction and Curriculum in the Content Areas with a concentration in literacy. Her primary research interests are in the areas of literacy, culturally responsive pedagogy, and teacher development.

Index

An *f* or *t* following a page number denotes a figure or table, respectively.